Th
Advisory Effort
in Vietnam

The U.S. Naval Advisory Effort in Vietnam

An Inside Perspective

CDR R.W. Kirtley, USN (Ret.)

McFarland & Company, Inc., Publishers
Jefferson, North Carolina

Front cover patch translation:
South Vietnamese Navy Mobile Riverine Forces
Official Unit Patch
GDNC 40
Giang Doan Ngan Chan
(*Riverine Stopping/Disrupting Force*)
Unit 40
Thang Khong Kieu (*Not becoming complacent in victory*)
Bai Khong Nan (*Not becoming distressed/despairing in defeat*)

ISBN (print) 978-1-4766-8695-0
ISBN (ebook) 978-1-4766-4469-1

Library of Congress and British Library
cataloguing data are available

Library of Congress Control Number 2021051192

On the cover: Armored Troop Carriers (ATCs), referred to as Tango boats, were the workhorse of the Mobile Riverine Force (MRF). Heavily armored for protection against rocket and small arms attack, and bristling with weapons, it could carry the fight to the NVA/VC in the form of ARVN troops in the well deck. The ATC, like most of the MRF craft, were converted WWII landing craft; The author, age 26, served a voluntary one year tour in Vietnam as Senior Advisor to Vietnamese River Interdiction Division (RID) 40, April '70–April '71. In his words: "It seemed like a good idea at the time"; South Vietnamese Navy Mobile Riverine Forces Official Unit Patch

Printed in the United States of America

McFarland & Company, Inc., Publishers
Box 611, Jefferson, North Carolina 28640
www.mcfarlandpub.com

To all Veterans; thank you for your service.

To all Vietnam Veterans; welcome home!

To the advisors to South Vietnamese Navy
River Interdiction Division (RID) 40;
to "Rat," who waits at the Rainbow Bridge;
and to my amazing wife, Debbie,
who fortunately did not know me then,
long ago in a galaxy far far away:
Thanks for your support and patience,
and for rescuing me from myself!

The author, early in his one year voluntary tour of duty as an advisor in Vietnam, when he still naively believed that the U.S. was in it to win it and that victory was in the offing.

Table of Contents

Table of Contents

Preface

I am a patriot; I love America, its foundation and its unique offer of freedom to so many for so long. I am proud of my twenty years of active duty service as a naval officer, and my subsequent eighteen years as an executive with a major Defense Department contractor, manufacturing electronic warfare systems that protect our war fighters. I stand with my hand over my heart for the playing of our National Anthem. I have spoken openly about this love of country at many Memorial Day and Independence Day celebrations over the years. I feel the need to express these feelings very strongly here, up front, because I don't want my personal opinions of the Vietnam War, in particular my disillusionment, expressed herein, to bring into question my overall love of country or pride in our military services.

The Vietnam War crept into my life slowly during my four years at the Naval Academy (1963–1967), then pulled me all in by my patriotic coat tails after graduation in 1967, consumed me through my last official visit to Saigon in 1972, antagonized me thereafter, and finally spit me out, exhausted, with the fall of Saigon in 1975. In hindsight, my role in the entire debacle exemplifies, on a small scale, the ultimate failure of the country's war effort, our attempt to turn over the fight to the South Vietnamese military, called "Vietnamization," and, in particular, the Navy's program in support of Vietnamization called ACTOV—Accelerated Turnover to the Vietnamese, with unfortunate emphasis on "Accelerated."

To put things into perspective, in 1968, when Lyndon Johnson decided not to seek another term as president, Richard Nixon ran and won on a platform built around ending our role in Vietnam through "peace with honor." American personnel strength had reached over half a million, and Nixon's stated objective was to complete a gradual withdrawal of all U.S. troops by the end of 1972.[1] Nixon really believed that objective could be met, and that at the same time the U.S. could prepare the South Vietnamese military to continue the fight against the NVA and VC. That was a severe miscalculation that I believe was well understood at all levels of leadership below the president.

The actual situation at the time was perhaps best summarized in "The Politically Incorrect Guide to the Vietnam War," by Phillip Jennings, as follows:

> By the end of 1969, peace negotiations were deadlocked. The Communists so frustrated Ambassador Lodge, America's chief negotiator at the Paris Peace talks, that he resigned. Hanoi saw the withdrawals of American troops, snickered at the notion that the ARVN could ever withstand the NVA, noted the anti-war mood of the Democrat Congress, and cheered the demonstrations of so-called peace activists. They saw no reason to negotiate. Victory was in the offing.[2]

Please consider that last sentence as you continue reading; in 1969, six years before the fall of Saigon, as far as the North Vietnamese were concerned, victory was already in the offing.

Meanwhile, feeling my patriotic duty, and still believing that we, the United States of America, the most powerful country on Earth, never having lost a war, would stand by South Vietnam at all costs, I had just volunteered for duty in Vietnam. I asked to be assigned to the U.S. "brown water" riverboat Navy, operating in the vast Mekong Delta of South Vietnam since the mid–'60s. However, before I even arrived at my training assignment en route to Vietnam, the Navy had initiated ACTOV in support of Nixon's "Vietnamization" of the war. At the direction of Rear Admiral Elmo Zumwalt, the Commander of Naval Forces in Vietnam, the Navy planned to transfer all "brown water" (river) craft to the South Vietnamese Navy by the end of 1970.[3] Therefore, much to my dismay, in early 1970, after a severely truncated training period, I was off to serve ACTOV, a program, like its larger parent, Vietnamization, that I believe most senior leaders knew was doomed to fail. Failure would be driven for the most part by lack of sufficient implementation time. The Navy's expectations of me at the time, however, were clear, regardless of my lack of preparation:

> The hallmark of a successful advisor is professionalism. The US advisors with the Vietnamese Navy have more than their share, having been specially selected for their assignments. Although many assigned duties are well outside the normal range of US Navy experience, for instance, laying a night ambush or operating armed junks from outposts located in VC controlled

territory, the advisors' enthusiasm, their ability to adapt and their pride in service are ensuring top performance.[4]

Because of the uniqueness of the river warfare assignments, a lot of the experience required for this type of advisory duty was expected to be gained on the job. I believed my biggest shortcoming to be my lack of any basic Vietnamese language training. However, I was completely unaware at the time of my arrival in-country in April 1970 that the NVA and, for that matter, most senior American military leaders, considered that NVA victory was in the offing, that the U.S. Army's primary mission had apparently become evacuation with the least cost of lives, that Vietnamization and ACTOV were terms created, perhaps inadvertently, to cover our ultimate abandonment of our friends, and that, worst of all, the undeniable signs of the certain failure of ACTOV were already apparent at all levels of our government and military services.

Keep in mind as you read this book that it is a *personal assessment*, based on personal experience gained in the middle of the turnover of the war effort to facilitate Nixon's pledged "peace with honor" solution, and also on original notes written over 45 years ago. Additional research cited throughout was mainly used to maintain historical accuracy as to the timeline. However, in my final chapter, "Reflection and Takeaways," I use facts and opinions from two individuals who were in positions either higher up in the chain of command than me, or in Vietnam after me, during the final years before the fall to the North in 1975, to validate my personal assessment of the situation when I left Vietnam, and my predictions regarding the ultimate outcome. Their accounts, also written many years after the war, support the fact that my personal experience at the single unit level, and my conclusions and predictions, are representative of the totality of the disastrous results of our failed "peace with honor" Vietnamization plan.

Introduction

I still often think about Vietnam. No, I don't have PTSD, no night terrors; nothing like that. However, including my time on a Navy destroyer in the Gulf of Tonkin, my pre–Vietnam training, my time in-country Vietnam as a Naval Advisor (to the Vietnamese), and my follow-on assignment in the Bureau of Naval Personnel, reassigning Navy personnel coming out of Vietnam, more than six years from the prime of my life was consumed by the war-that-wasn't-a-war. At the time of this writing, I'm one of a dying breed—Vietnam Veterans, and more specifically, an even smaller group of U.S. Navy Vietnam Veterans who served on river boats in the Mekong Delta, and smaller still, those of us who served as advisors to the Vietnamese Navy on the river boats after their turnover from the U.S. Navy. That remaining group, i.e., members of the Naval Advisory Group Vietnam, who rode on river boats manned by young, untrained Vietnamese sailors... But I digress.

More than forty-five years since the war ended with the fall of Saigon, we (all Vietnam Vets) still pass each other, take note of the beat up old "Vietnam Vet" ball cap with its embroidered service ribbons, and with a nod or a fist bump, mumble the three words that forever bond us, "Welcome home, Brother!" If we find ourselves waiting in line together somewhere, we start with the inevitable "when, where, what" questions, and end up trading embellished war stories. We are more and more irritated by the pretenders and their "stolen valor." We easily pick them out, wearing their piecemeal mismatched, camouflaged, Army surplus shirt and their ball cap laden with an impossible multi-service mix of fake service ribbons. Yet we don't challenge them, on the small chance that they are actually Vietnam Vets, but just a bit confused. It's hardest not to challenge the imposters when their war stories, delivered with too much bluster, become obvious BS, lifted from too many war movies. They go something like this: "I was a SEAL with the Army's First Air Cav, operating out of Kung Fu. I was in the same PLATOON as Charlie Sheen. We was on patrol in the Ah Choo Valley, along the U Kum Yet River, when the Victor Charlie hit us from all sides! I yelled to Sheen, 'We in a real APOCALYPSE NOW! Good thing we got our FULL METAL JACKETS!' Next thing I know, I'm being dragged to safety by my buddy FOREST GUMP." What is our response to all of this nonsense? Yup; a smile, a fist bump and "Welcome home, Brother." Let it go; it just ain't worth it.

A few years after Saigon fell, I decided to write a book about the Navy's advisory effort in Vietnam from my personal perspective. My views about the war were changing, and I had to come to grips with those evolving beliefs. This book represents the end of that 45 year struggle. On my first try, I got as far as completing a synopsis and an outline, even four or five sample chapters. I submitted the idea to a publisher, and surprisingly got a sincere and detailed reply. My book would be considered if I made it more than just a chronological documentation of my experience, and went deeper into my conclusions about the ultimate futility of the conflict. That's where it ended; life interfered. All of my notes, reference material and a completed rough draft went into a box. Over the years I threatened to pull it all out and revive the effort, but it never quite reached the top of my to do list.

During those years, as my potential best seller languished in the dark recesses of my closet, I had numerous Vietnam related opportunities for a restart. I spent an hour with my oldest daughter's high school history class discussing the answer to their question, "How do you cope when you are in the middle of a wartime situation?" I tried to keep my responses broad and generic, but found myself drifting into personal memories and fighting to hold back the tears.

In the late '90s, my son's eighth grade history teacher asked if any of his students could bring in a relic of the Vietnam war. Naturally my son brought me! The eighth graders were in the last day of a weeklong look at the 1960s, and the impact of the changing politics, moral values, music, dress, foreign relations, etc., all against the backdrop of the Vietnam war. By the end of that day, I had done seminars with over 250 eighth graders in groups of 50. It was easy to connect with those kids since my son was in the class, and I had coached many of them in recreational soccer and basketball. Working with their boring historical timeline, I took them back in time and made the war relevant. Calling on my skills as a veteran, actor, motivational speaker and stand-up comic, I had them laughing and crying, but, above all, listening!

After that day, I was asked to come back every year for the next 14 years. My time was expanded to two hours, with two sessions for one half of the class in each. By the third year, all of the teachers sat in on the sessions, and by the next year, many parents asked to attend. The response was overwhelming. All the kids, and their parents and teachers, wanted was an honest, human, discussion about the basic facts, and what was it really like to be there? When the sponsoring teacher retired and I relocated to Florida in 2006, that incredible annual experience became logistically unsupportable and finally ended. I had withdrawal as bad as any chain smoker trying to quit cold turkey. Once again, I determined to get back to my book. But now I had another dilemma: did I stay with my original goal, or did I regroup and put together some sort of Vietnam War primer for students? Too confusing, and again life took over. It was 2006, and once again the book project was shelved.

Shortly after my move to Florida, I discovered through my Naval Academy Class of 1967 Facebook page that there was a Class of '67 email chat group, which I immediately joined. There were loose rules for behavior, but otherwise the discussion chains could go anywhere. Chatter was dominated by politics and physical ailments, but other topics came and went. Because all of the members of the group were Vietnam veterans, we had Vietnam topics constantly in the background, and occasionally taking center stage. During one such center stage discussion it hit me that we had chat members from every possible Navy career path, including Naval Aviation (fixed wing and helicopters), Surface Ships, inland "brown water" Navy (Swift Boats, PBRs and Heavy Assault Craft), Naval Advisors, SEALS, Marine Corps (Infantry and Aviation), and other specialties. Eureka! Another book possibility; I even had a working title, "Choosing the War Path." What kind of upbringing brought 1250 young men from all walks of life together in 1963? Why did they choose the Naval Academy?

I planned to enlist the help of one classmate from each career path who had completed at least twenty years of service and had served at least one year in-country. I would tell their personal stories, from their decision to compete for an appointment to the Naval Academy, through their experiences in Vietnam, to their retirement, and into their twilight years. Each would be an integral part of the book development, including their thoughts about Vietnam in retrospect. From the start it was a coordination disaster! The prospective book went back in the box.

What, one might ask, finally drew me back to yet another attempt?

Introduction

Well, it started as my Class of '67 began planning our 50th Reunio 2017. As I prepared my personal input for the commemorative book, came across some material on the Vietnam Memorial, "The Wall." I was struck by the thought of our nine classmates whose names are on that wall. I got up and stood for a few moments in front of my favorite Wall picture, "Reflections," hanging in my condo. I couldn't stop thinking about my classmates and their ultimate sacrifice. So, I decided to compose a letter from those nine to their classmates at the reunion. I was so pleased when the letter was published anonymously, as if from those nine, in the Naval Academy Alumni magazine *Shipmate*; the response was heartwarming. The letter is included herein as Appendix 1. Funny how different events or moments in our lives stimulate us and move us to act. For me it was that simple re-focus on the specific names of my classmates on the Vietnam Memorial. It all came rushing back, and I had to get it out.

This is not another history book; the story of U.S. involvement in the Vietnam War has been told many times. That timeline and the basic facts never change; I have included enough historical facts and dates throughout to refresh your memory. However, this timeline is very simple—my assignment in Vietnam from April 1970 to April 1971, followed by two years in the Bureau of Naval Personnel, Washington, D.C., in charge of the reassignment of enlisted personnel coming out of Vietnam. I do spend some time in the beginning of the book running a simple parallel history with my pre–Naval Academy years, and the concurrent developments in Vietnam. (I used that technique with the middle school kids for years in "Vietnam and the 60s" to show them that the news of today is what is creating the world they will face as young adults.)

I have also chosen not to introduce a large cast of characters by name, including the fourteen Navy Advisors under my direct command, partly because I could not do justice to the sacrifices and contributions of each man individually, and, since the events herein took place fifty years before I wrote this book, I would most certainly have forgotten some names. When I do use names necessary for the furtherance of the story, I use fictitious names, with the exception of those considered senior enough to be public figures.

In a way this is an expose and a confession of sorts by a young, naive Navy lieutenant, thrust into a relatively brief (one year), sometimes dangerous, and often confusing assignment. In hindsight, I was actually an n, in a game beyond my comprehension at the time. was a pivotal year in the war, with historical ramifica- too far down on the international org chart, the food about anything but survival for me and my men. Mean- le levels, far above me in the pecking order, South Vietnam's fate was being decided based on many factors, not the least of which was public opinion.

I have also included throughout a number of seemingly unrelated stories, or vignettes, in order to portray the uniqueness of the advisory position. Most Americans assigned to duty in Vietnam with American units, associated almost exclusively only with other Americans, and rarely, if ever, got a look at the lives of those we were there to defend.

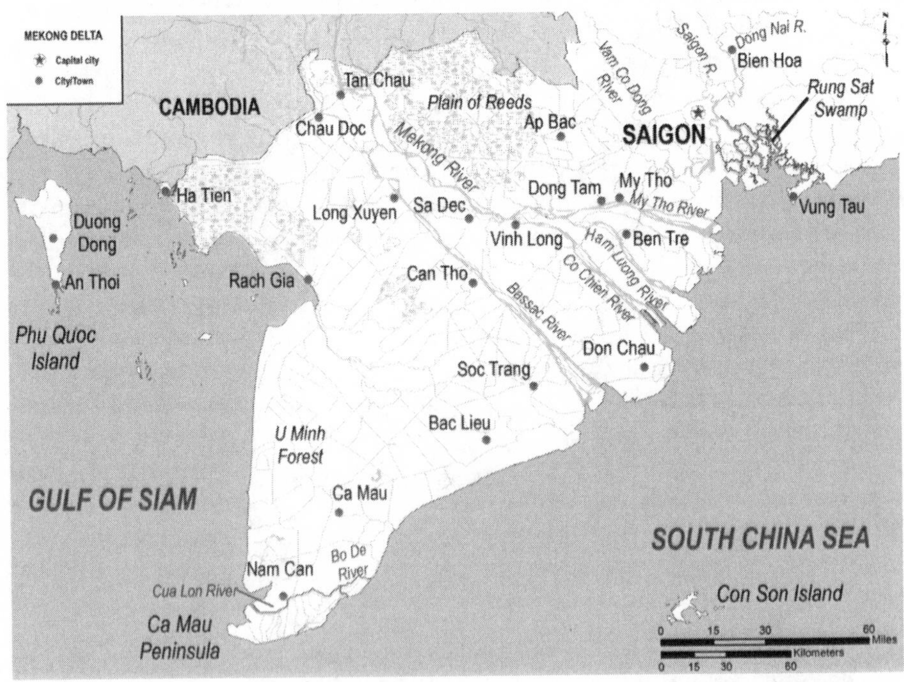

Map of the Mekong Delta region of South Vietnam circa 1968–1971. Vietnamese River Interdiction Division 40, with the author assigned as Senior Advisor, patrolled the Vam Co Dong River from Go Dau Ha until October 1970, and then traveled to Dong Tam, My Tho, Vinh Long, Long Xuyen, Can Tho, Ca Mau, Rach Gia, and Kien An. (Go Dau Ha is located west of Saigon on the Vam Co Dong River, and Kien An is located just south of Rach Gia at the north tip of the U Minh Forest.)

Introduction

There was a personal side to the war that only an advisor, living and working with the Vietnamese, could understand. While we all took the war and our role in it seriously, the very nature of the situation, in which two extremely different cultures collided at the individual advisor and small unit level, lent itself to frequent humorous and/or personal situations, some of which brought us perhaps too close. However, the underlying story reflects *frustration* and *futility*. The Vietnamese people put their faith and trust in us, and in the end we abandoned them. So don't be deceived into thinking that I thought there was anything funny about the war or the lives lost. I sat safely, with several awards, and my "ticket punched" for my next promotion, praying for the Vietnamese friends we had abandoned, and I watched with the rest of the world the frantic evacuation of the U.S. Embassy and the fall of Saigon. I cried.

During our tours in-country, we all counted the days on short timers' calendars 'til our departure, rarely stopping to think that our Vietnamese counterparts were counting the years on open ended calendars. As advisors we took them from farmers, to sailors, to ... what? Was it good advice? I'll tell my story and let you decide.

1

The Early Years

I'm not a hero; let's get that straight up front. In fact, when the first Viet Cong B-40 rocket exploded against our lead river assault boat, mild panic (okay ... severe PANIC) set in. I yelled into my radio, "This is Remittance! We're taking shit out here ... where the hell is our air cover?" In my mind I was yelling, "What the fuck am I doing here?" Well, Toto, this wasn't Kansas; it was the Republic of Vietnam. The Wicked Witch was very much alive, and her flying monkeys were firing rockets and small arms at us from the encroaching jungle. Clicking my heels wasn't gonna get me back home! To be exact, home was 9,000 miles away, and I was on one of 13 river assault boats, trundling ponderously along a canal in the middle of the U Minh Forest, at the southern end of South Vietnam. My life was in the hands of my counterpart, a young Vietnamese Navy lieutenant, a converted Army officer, and a completely inexperienced Vietnamese crew, most of whom had been rice farmers less than one year before.

Up until that time these boats had been operated by highly trained sailors of the United States Navy. However, the year was now 1970, and President Nixon was attempting to negotiate "peace with honor" with the North Vietnamese, while concurrently withdrawing U.S. troops from South Vietnam. The heart of this plan involved having U.S. military personnel, who were previously fighting the war directly, suddenly relegated to "advisors," tasked with training the aforementioned rice farmers to be a self-sustaining fighting force. Therefore, though I had volunteered for the U.S. Navy's elite riverine warfare group, nicknamed the "Brown Water Navy," upon arrival I was assigned as Assistant Senior Advisor to a recently formed and staffed South Vietnamese River Interdiction Division. Within weeks I was the Senior Advisor. Six months later, here I was receiving enemy fire, trying desperately to call in U.S. close air support, and watching guns of all shapes and sizes being fired in all directions by our converted farmers!

"There's no place like home! There's no place like home!" What was a good looking, happy-go-lucky, twenty-six-year-old Southern boy doing riding a heavy assault river boat on a canal in the middle of the U Minh Forest? Well, in order for you to understand that situation and my somewhat skewed perspective of a war that wasn't a war, you should understand a little about how I became involved.

I was certainly not a student of Southeast Asia. Vietnam's history of pain and suffering under Chinese, French, and Japanese occupation was of little interest to me. However, the native resistance movement, sparked by the Japanese occupation, would have a lasting effect on my life. As I grew and matured through elementary and high school, so grew the resistance of the Viet Minh. Through the fall of the French and the division of Vietnam along the 18th parallel in 1954, I enjoyed Little League and Cub Scouts. As I stumbled into my teenage years with youthful exuberance, so did the U.S. naively stumble into Vietnam. As my excitement grew over making the junior varsity football and basketball teams, American advisors helped the South Vietnamese Army (ARVN) develop, and the Viet Cong campaign began in South Vietnam. By the time I moved to the new high school and played basketball against my older brother in 1960, the U.S. had 900 military advisors in Vietnam, and there were already traffic jams on the "Ho Chi Minh Trail,"[1] moving men and materiel to the North Vietnamese Army and Viet Cong fighting in South Vietnam.

In 1961 and 1962, as I became committed to earning an appointment to the U.S. Naval Academy, President Kennedy became convinced that political and economic reform, along with U.S. support, could win in Vietnam. At the same time, after stiff competition, I already had an appointment to the Air Force Academy in my back pocket, when my congressman decided that I was his best choice for the Naval Academy. I agreed with him, so while my Academy class of 1,250 "Plebes" endured that first hellish Annapolis summer in 1963, there were 16,000 Americans enduring Vietnam. As we strived to pass exams and beat Army that year, both South Vietnam and the U.S. saw their presidents assassinated. I struggled with the Theory of Relativity; Lyndon Johnson struggled with the "Domino Theory."

In August 1964, I enjoyed Europe on my summer training cruise, while two Navy destroyers, the USS *Maddox* and the USS *Turner Joy*, cruised the Gulf of Tonkin. Following the Gulf of Tonkin "incident"—an abortive attack on those destroyers by North Vietnamese torpedo boats—the U.S. entered the war in earnest under the Tonkin Gulf Resolution.

From 1964 until my graduation in 1967, I watched the void increase between the U.S. government's commitment of assets to the war and the U.S. citizens' lack of commitment to support of the war. The year of 1964 saw the first Berkeley campus demonstration as Lyndon Johnson branded Goldwater a warmonger and promised a "Great Society." In December a VC car bomb exploded outside of the Brinks Hotel in Saigon housing senior American military officers.[2]

Early in 1965 my brother, a West Point cadet, stayed with me on his exchange week at the Naval Academy. While I arranged various practical jokes on brother Bill, General William Westmoreland, Commander of U.S. Forces in Vietnam, requested that U.S. Marines be sent to South Vietnam in order to establish a defensive perimeter at Da Nang. South Vietnam controlled only about 40 percent of its own country, and three U.S. aircraft carriers in the Gulf of Tonkin had begun retaliatory air strikes against North Vietnam for VC strikes on American support facilities. In 1965, there were 1,350 U.S. servicemen and 11,000 ARVN soldiers killed in action.[3]

I suffered through a statistics course, and statistics became the measure of success in Vietnam. The term "body count" came into vogue; "count the pieces and add 10%"; highest body count wins. The one year tour rotation policy became effective, leading some to say later, in hindsight, that cohesion for American forces in Vietnam was impossible; we fought a one year war ten times!

In the summer of 1966 my brother Bill, having graduated from West Point, married his high school sweetheart. I enjoyed my 1st Class, or Senior, cruise (not exactly 1st class accommodations) on a guided missile destroyer in the North Atlantic. I was having such fun in Copenhagen, Denmark, that I "forgot" to go back to the ship for three days ... an act commonly referred to as AWOL (Absent Without Leave). The only thing that saved me was a commanding officer who understood youthful indiscretion, and couldn't bear to see my Navy career end before it began. Besides, my short AWOL paled in comparison to the 90,000 ARVN's who deserted the South Vietnamese Army the year before.[4]

By the time I returned to Norfolk that summer, the U.S. had over 300,000 personnel in Vietnam, and they had been joined by troops from South Korea, Australia, and New Zealand. Meanwhile, the seagoing Navy, with which I was on a collision course, had greatly expanded its mission. "Operation Sea Dragon" provided Naval interdiction of North Vietnam coastal supply lines to its troops and VC in the South; "Operation Market Time" was established to interdict supplies entering the South along its coast; and "Operation Game Warden" was underway in the MeKong Delta waterways, the culmination of the 2,500 mile long MeKong River in a huge delta dominating the Southern portion of Vietnam.

My 1st class year at the Naval Academy was exciting. I could now legally keep and drive my MGB (as opposed to "stashing" it the year before at the Episcopal minister's house in Annapolis). I was president of the Brigade Activities Committee, in charge of shenanigans at pep rallies and football games. I dated the superintendent's daughter, escorted astronaut Wally Schirra to a pep rally, and was reduced to the privileges of a junior for being caught in another indiscretion. My parents wondered when they could uncross their fingers. They breathed easier after brother Bill's graduation (barely surviving a "Beat Navy" panties sales scandal at West Point), and now they anxiously awaited my June graduation.

While my folks' confidence in me was shaky, at least one half of the U.S. population had lost confidence in the war effort. In October '67, 50,000 people demonstrated against the war at the Pentagon. The U.S. personnel in Vietnam numbered nearly 400,000, double the ARVN's 200,000, and it was estimated that the NVA/VC had at least 250,000 troops in South Vietnam.[5] More than 11,000 U.S. personnel had died in Vietnam before I graduated from the Naval Academy and was commissioned an Ensign in the U.S. Navy in June 1967.

2

Vietnam from the Gulf

As graduation from the Academy raced my way, I had to choose a career path—aviation, surface ships, or submarines. I omitted the Marine Corps option since I was not committed to the Corps like those few Academy grads who chose the Corps. For me it was a simple process of elimination: if there was trouble in an airplane, it was a long way down; trouble in a submarine, it was a long way up; so I chose the surface Navy. Besides, my eyes had gone from 20/20 to about 20/100, which would have relegated me to non-pilot, "backseat" flying status had I chosen Naval Aviation. If I was going to be in a Navy fighter aircraft, especially in combat, I would want my hands in control of my own stick, so to speak. As for submariners, they sold their souls to Admiral Rickover, father of our nuclear Navy ... no thanks! Actually, the guys chosen for the nuclear program were the pick of the litter; God bless them!

And so it was that in June 1967, after tossing my cap in the air, I loaded all of my belongings into my MGB and drove west, in the general direction of Yokosuka, Japan, to rendezvous with the USS *De Haven* (DD 727). I won't digress to the adventures of life in Japan—sleeping on mat floors and dueling Japanese taxi drivers in Tokyo. Suffice it to say that kamikaze pilots who never "got the call" drove taxis in Tokyo! I will also leave it to the recruiting commercials to generally describe the Navy on deployment—"not just a job, but an adventure." Ports of Call—Taiwan, Subic Bay, Singapore, Hong Kong, etc. Between those exotic ports, I was introduced to the war in Vietnam from a spectator vantage point in the Gulf of Tonkin.

Destroyers in the Gulf of Tonkin served numerous functions, all in support of the U.S. effort in Vietnam: gunfire support to troops ashore in the South; "Operation Sea Dragon" raids on the North Vietnamese coast; search and rescue (SAR) off the northern coast in case of "ditched" aircraft returning from missions over North Vietnam;

The Navy destroyer USS *De Haven* DD-727, the author's first duty assignment following his 1967 graduation from the Naval Academy. Operating out of Yokosuka, Japan, *De Haven* gave the author his first taste of the war from the Gulf of Tonkin in 1967–68.

protective screening of aircraft carriers; and the "plane guard" position 2,000 yards behind the carrier during flight operations.

Typically, we would leave our home port in Yokosuka, stop for a port visit in Taiwan or Hong Kong, top off the supplies in Subic Bay, Philippines, and head for the Gulf of Tonkin. There we would alternately support the various missions mentioned above.

By far the most boring (much to the delight of the carrier pilots) was SAR. We would sit several miles off of the North Vietnamese coast and wait ... and wait ... and wait! Our Combat Information Center (CIC) would monitor the air sorties in and out while the rest of the crew went about its duties—planned maintenance and training by day, and books, movies, or watch standing by night ... boring! Occasionally the monotony was broken by "small arms firing off the fantail." That entailed shooting at the Gulf of Tonkin with a .45 caliber pistol ... the only target most people could hit with a .45! The highlight of any daytime watch on the bridge, for me as an OOD (Officer of the Deck), was the random opportunity to annihilate a sea snake. The CO allowed us to keep an M1 rifle and ammo clip on the bridge for such an exhilarating opportunity. The cry "sea snake" from the lookout brought excitement to the lucky OOD, and envy from the rest of the bridge watch members. Such were my first Tonkin Gulf incidents. The news release would have read, "Today the USS *De Haven*, while on search and rescue station in the Gulf of Tonkin, successfully repelled an attack by two North Vietnamese sea snakes. There were no American casualties, and, while no bodies were recovered, enemy dead was estimated at two." Luckily we never did have to actually search for or rescue any ditched pilots.

After a week or so of SAR, it would be our turn to join a carrier task force operating at "Yankee Station"—the code name for a mystical location in the Tonkin Gulf from which the 7th Fleet aircraft carriers launched their strikes against the North. Here it was a strangely mixed atmosphere on the destroyers; the tedium of planned maintenance, training, movies, reading, etc., continued for all but those on watch on the bridge or in the Combat Information Center (CIC)—the nerve center of a Navy combatant. It sounds simple—maintain the ship's position in a protective "screen" around the aircraft carrier, at ranges of 6,000 to 10,000 yards, as the carrier alternately meandered leisurely, and then turned suddenly to race into the wind at top speed to launch and recover its airplanes. On a nice sunny day such maneuvering was stimulating and excellent training for young Naval officers learning the intricacies of "station keeping," while giving commands from the pilot house, or out on the external wing of the bridge. You've seen it in the movies.... "Right full rudder ... come to course 270 ... all engines ahead full!"

"Range to the carrier?"

"Six thousand yards, sir!"

"Sir, CIC holds the carrier on course 260!"

"Steady up on 260!"

"260; aye, aye, Sir!"

The teamwork was impressive and thrilling. Lookouts, helmsman, radiomen, signalmen, radarmen, etc., working in concert to recognize and adjust to a constantly shifting set of circumstances, not only on *De Haven*, but on the bridges and in the CICs of the carriers, and the other five to seven ships of the screen.

The scene could quickly become one of stark terror, however, when you added the inky blackness of a stormy night, howling winds, blinding rain, and heavy seas. The only hint of the other ships was either the small green "blips" on the radar or the barely visible red and green "running lights" on the port (left) and starboard (right) of each accompanying ship. Screening ships would take orders concerning their locations and movements from the carrier.

Under normal conditions (those taught in Academy navigation classes and on their small Yard Patrol/YP craft in the Chesapeake Bay), the carrier would notify the screening ships of an impending change through a coded transmission, for instance (translated): "Stand by to execute a turn to starboard to a new course of 320." The bridge watch and the CIC watch would separately plot the maneuver, figure out the necessary course and speed for realignment of the formation, and compare and agree on the solution. After several minutes the command to "execute" would be received, and a beautiful Naval ballet would be performed, resulting in a reoriented screen going in the right direction at the right speed.

Occasionally, however, the carrier might overlook the standby message, and pass an "immediate execute," in which case the skills of the OOD would generate initial turn/speed orders, followed quickly by the calculated solution. In the worst of all situations, without warning a subtle change might be noticed in the alignment of the carrier's running lights, and the CIC would call the bridge with something like "we hold the carrier in a starboard turn"! By then, only instinct, instant reaction, and experience could generate the maneuver necessary to get to the right place, or, in some cases, just get out of the way of the 40,000 to 90,000 tons of high speed metal that could be coming your way! Just such a set of circumstances led to the slicing in two of one destroyer by a carrier at Yankee Station, with tremendous loss of life. A four hour bridge watch under those conditions would test the nerves and skill of any man.

There were two "fun" times to be the OOD of a destroyer with the carrier group—"plane guarding" at 2,000 yards behind the carrier, or pulling up alongside for replenishment from a supply ship. Both situations allowed the young officer to literally handle the destroyer like a sleek sports car. It was at times such as those that the destroyer lived up to its reputation as "greyhound of the fleet"! Under the tutelage of a master "salt"—LT Tom Wyatt, *De Haven*'s crusty Engineering Officer, with 20 years of service, both enlisted and officer—I learned to feel the subtle changes of the destroyer, as I called "steer left one degree," or "add 10 turns" to change the number of revolutions of the ship's massive brass propellers, or "screws." Those are by far my fondest memories of destroyer life at sea. Under Tom's watchful eye I became the first ensign on *De Haven* to qualify as an Officer of the Deck (OOD), and wear the gold pin with crossed swords and destroyer bow signifying that achievement.

There were two missions in the Gulf during which we destroyer men directly participated in the war, both of which allowed us to exercise our six 5-inch guns—the heart of our armament. The least hectic of the two missions was that of providing gunfire support to U.S. and South Vietnamese troops ashore in the South. We would loiter off the coast and await the call of either a small spotter plane or a forward observer on the ground. We would receive the map coordinates of a target (suspected VC forces), and fire a "spotting round." After adjustment directions from the observer or spotter, we would fire another round in hopes of bracketing the target—landing on the opposite side from the first shot. Based on the result, we would adjust once more and "fire for effect"—disperse a certain number of rounds in the vicinity of the target. For spotting, we fired "Willy Peter," or white phosphorous, for obvious easy observation. For the effect we would fire H.E. (high explosive), or FRAG (fragmentation), depending on the target. At night we would also fire illumination rounds from one set of guns, and spotting/effect rounds from the others. This was all particularly exciting for me, since besides being the DASH officer and first lieutenant—a funny title for an ensign in charge of the Deck Division Boatswains Mates (Bos'n's), I was also being trained as the ship's future Gunnery Officer.

The second type of gun fire mission was the real-war scenario—the battle stations, John Wayne action-movie Navy! Code named "Operation Sea Dragon," this was the destroyer's chance to join the larger cruisers, and actually attack the North! Whether firing on WBLC's (Waterborne Logistics Craft) or truck convoys on the coastal highways, this was the highlight of surface Navy duty in the Tonkin Gulf.

"Wiblicks," as we called the unfortunate boats, were anything of sufficient size to make a blip on the radar, and to be moving in a southerly direction along the North Vietnamese coast. It was not unusual to read a press release in the radio message traffic from an accompanying cruiser such as: "Today the USS *Boston* destroyed or damaged 57

WBLC's off the coast of North Vietnam." Unfortunately, we never really saw those WIBLICKS, and therefore weren't actually sure they weren't unfortunate fisherman just trying to make a buck. You can imagine that the first rule of any North Vietnamese fisherman was "for God's sake, don't head south"!

The best action came during actual firing runs on the coastal highways. Large North Vietnamese truck convoys would move war supplies at night towards the Demilitarized Zone (DMZ), the boundary between North and South Vietnam. There were points at which coastal mountains forced the highway to the water's edge—much like California's Highway 101 from Big Sur to Santa Barbara. It was these "choke points" that we would attack. In the early evening the cruiser and perhaps two destroyers would make a high speed, zigzag run towards the coast to come within range of the 5- and 8-inch guns. The cruisers' 8-inch guns would pound the highway at the choke point, hoping to wreak enough damage to halt any truck convoy later that night. The plan was to return at first light and turkey-shoot the trucks awaiting highway repair. A spotter plane would assist in this endeavor. The only drawback to this plan was that once we were within range for our guns, we were also in range of the North Vietnamese shore guns or batteries—fortified artillery capable of firing armor piercing shells at enticing U.S. Navy targets. It was the destroyers' job to target predetermined shore batteries and then react to suppress "targets of opportunity"—any active shore batteries that dared shoot back.

I never thought until much later the fallacy of the destroyer role in this action. Remember the shore bombardment in the South? We fired leisurely, with plenty of time to accurately plot our own position, and then used spotting rounds to zero in on our target. Well, here we were, racing in towards the coast, zigzagging to confuse the enemy gunners, and firing at predetermined target locations on a map! How close did we possibly think we were hitting?

It was during my first "Sea Dragon" mission on *De Haven* that I experienced what I call my initial "combat personal vulnerability realization." The preparation was all Hollywood; the Task Force Commander from the cruiser flew by helo to *De Haven*, and we officers were assembled in the wardroom for a briefing. The briefing captain could not have been cast better—graying temples, hat at a jaunty angle, stub of a cigar in the corner of his mouth, and a Cagney-esque bravado. His minions produced a large chart of the North Vietnamese coast and moved little ship silhouettes as the captain outlined the plan. "We'll meander northwest along the coast, about 12,000 yards off of Hon Mat Island ... there's guns there; Orleck will lead, then Boston, then DeHaven." (Puffs of cigar smoke for effect.) "When we're abreast of Phu Diem ... here (pointer) ... we'll all turn to port and head in a line abreast at flank (max) speed directly toward the beach. At 10,000 yards, we'll turn south, in a column, slow to 16 knots, and commence fire. Boston's target is the highway choke point at Xuam Loi. There are known shore batteries here, here, here, and here (pointer). These are Orleck's; these are DeHaven's. Any others that fire on us are also your targets." (More smoke ... pause for effect) "Any questions?" By now, I wanted to know who the leading lady would be in the movie version and how she would be worked into the plot ... perhaps a nurse, afloat in a life raft, or a beautiful Vietnamese teacher fleeing the North. This couldn't be real ... someone please yell "cut"!

Because I had just joined the ship, I didn't yet have a meaningful battle station assignment, so I was sent to stay with the DASH crew in the DASH hanger. (DASH stands for Drone Anti-Submarine Helicopter, an infamous remote controlled beast, which would later play a direct role in my inevitable journey towards an assignment in Vietnam.) As we meandered North, I outlined the plot to the four enlisted members of the DASH crew, and we popped some popcorn and set up some chairs on the small flight deck to watch the war. Suddenly, the whole aft (back) part of the ship began to shudder as the engines were brought to flank speed; we commenced a sharp left turn, and the cruiser *Boston* came barely into view off to our starboard, as we shifted our chairs in the fading light. The ship rolled sharply to port and starboard with each turn as we zigzagged toward the shore. And then, just as suddenly, we turned sharply to port and the engines slowed. Now the *Boston* and her running lights were directly astern and the coast of North Vietnam was to our right ... North Vietnam!

"Egad! Here I am, Mom!"

My Avionics Technician pointed toward the shore and some faint flashes in the half darkness. Those would be the impacts of the fierce bombardment from the *Boston*'s 8-inch guns. Wrong! None of the good guys had fired a shot. As a sense of foreboding crept in, so did the whining of incoming shells. The night exploded in blinding flashes well behind us and off to the side of the *Boston*. At least the bad guys had picked the biggest of the three targets. Almost simultaneously, the

8-inch guns of *Boston* commenced firing. As if perfectly choreographed, five very stupid figures rose, spilling popcorn and soda, and raced for the DASH hanger! In that instant, *De Haven*'s own guns opened up ... two of which were directly aft of the flight deck! As the hanger's overhead door slowly closed, my only thought was that this must be what the Apocalypse would be like! As I lay on the darkened floor of the hanger, I was thankful that I was not a ship's laundry man, because there would be five pairs of heavily soiled skivvy shorts the next day!

For the next "Sea Dragon" raid I was stationed on the bridge, fully laden with flak jacket and helmet, to observe the Junior Officer of the Deck (JOOD) in action. I was extremely impressed throughout this particular exercise, similar to the one previously described. First, I'll describe what I saw, and then, in quick hindsight, what actually happened.

In the same scenario described in the previous raid, we had turned south and slowed; the cruiser had fired, and the word came from the lookouts "stand by for incoming"! I was on the left wing of the bridge with the JOOD; the OOD and our Commanding Officer were on the starboard wing facing the beach. The OOD yelled "left full rudder" to bring us to a course away from the shore and "All engines ahead flank!" About halfway through the turn as we leaned sharply to the right, there was a tremendous explosion and flash just in front of the starboard bridge wing! Glass from two bridge windows was blown in, and the OOD, who was just coming into the pilot house, was literally blown to the pilot house floor! For an instant, I could not see or hear; I could, however, smell a heavy gunpowder odor. The OOD jumped up, yelled "steady on course 090," and called for a damage report! I feared the worst.

Now, let's run that back in slow motion. The *De Haven* had two gun mounts forward of the bridge, each with two 5-inch guns. One sat on the main deck and one was immediately forward of, and one deck below, the bridge. Without some sort of checking action, that particular gun mount, if turned aft, would blow off the bridge wing on the side to which it turned. So, Naval ship designers created what we call "stops" ... that point at which the gun turret automatically stops turning and will go no further. The stops for the number 2 gun mount, immediately forward of the bridge, allowed the closest barrel within a couple of feet of the wing of the bridge.

As we began to execute the sharp turn to port, the gunnery officer, high above the bridge in the gun director, had taken manual control of the guns in order to direct our return gunfire at the active shore batteries. Therefore, all mounts continued swinging to the starboard side towards the aft "stops" in an effort to stay trained on the beach. Just as Mount 2 reached its stops, next to the starboard wing, both guns fired. The flash and concussion smashed the two windows (which should have been hanging loose under battle conditions to absorb any blast), and blew the OOD to the deck. The C.O. fortunately had preceded the OOD into the pilot house, and narrowly missed the concussion effect. As word spread on the bridge that, indeed, it was just the concussion of our own guns, hearing slowly returned and anxiety levels lowered. Within minutes we were out of range, our fantail (rear) guns had ceased fire, and nerves began to return to normal.

Aside from some knowing looks and raised eyebrows by those few who were present, there was nary a mention of what we saw that night. No one would know that the bridge crew, from the captain down to the petty officers, thinking we had been hit, would probably again tax the talents of the ship's laundry! And although at the time I was shaken and shocked, I didn't realize that four years from that moment, about six hundred miles southwest, I would face a personal panic situation which I would gladly have traded for that night on the bridge.

3

"DASH" to Vietnam

Stateside Navy—what a bitch! December 1968, our home port time in Japan completed, *De Haven* headed back to our new home port in Long Beach, California. Bummer! That was like playing in the World Series one year and then being sent down to the minor leagues. Fresh from the excitement of the Tonkin Gulf, life in Japan, and exotic port visits, including stops on the way to California in Manus, Pago Pago, Australia, New Zealand and Hawaii, *De Haven* reached its new home port of Long Beach, California. Hell, we'd even had our last mission in the Gulf punctuated with a firepower display by the battleship USS *New Jersey*, re-activated from "moth balls" in order to bring her 16-inch guns to bear on the North Vietnamese. She could lob 1,900 lb. shells over 18 miles! Awesome! Yes sir, we were big bad muthas from West Pac!

Welcome to the real world! "Sailors and dogs keep off the grass" was the attitude of most civilian communities at the time. As for the stateside Navy routine—the pits! Spit and polish; drills without action; inspections by every organization imaginable; shipyard repair, where the ship was stripped naked—dirt, grime; and crew turnover. The well-oiled machine was slowly dismantled. And we certainly were not contributing to the war effort.

Meanwhile, the year 1968 had been perhaps the most volatile of the long war—politically and militarily. Robert McNamara had quit as Secretary of Defense. President Johnson had announced he would not seek reelection, there were riots in the cities, and then Nixon won election on a "peace with honor" platform. In early 1968, the North Vietnamese and Viet Cong had launched the TET offensive—a simultaneous, country-wide assault. Amazingly, though TET was a disaster militarily for the communist, especially the Viet Cong, American public opinion made it a psychological victory for the enemy. That fact, the loss of the USS *Pueblo* to North Korea, and then the My Lai massacre, was all too much for the country to bear. The future became U.S. withdrawal. Nixon took office and mandated "Vietnamization" of the war—turnover of responsibilities to the South Vietnamese forces, and expedited withdrawal of U.S. forces. When you think about it, the first piece of the original feared "Domino Theory" was essentially assured; it would just take seven more years to fall.

The crew of *De Haven* had its own problem—a new Executive Officer (XO), the number two in command. Suffice it to say that if he'd had a palm tree, I'd have ripped it out and thrown it overboard! "And what's all this crap about no movie tonight"! I quickly had enough of this guy and the stateside Navy; I needed an out, and that's where the DASH drone helicopter came in.

Back in 1967, shortly after arriving in Japan on the *De Haven*, I had been sent back to San Diego, California, for a month of DASH training. Students stayed in the Bachelor Officers' Quarters at the Coronado Naval Air Station, and had the run of beautiful San Diego from Thursday evening through Monday noon. I learned about Saturday night "trolling" at the Marine Corps Recruiting Depot (MCRD) Officers' Club, commonly referred to as "McCrud." I also waded through beer an inch deep on the cement floor of the "Downwinds"—the O'Club annex on Coronado every Sunday afternoon. I was actually bitten on the ass by a female "assailant" while dancing (or treading beer)! On Monday afternoons we were flown out to San Clemente Island, almost within sight of Santa Catalina, but light years away in atmosphere. To most surface ship Navy men, San Clemente Island was known for goats and shore bombardment practice—one end of the island was used as a Naval gunfire practice range; the rest of the Island was overrun by wild goats. Much to my surprise, the other end of San Clemente was home to the Navy's training facility for its Drone Anti-Submarine Helicopter (DASH).

This strange beast was a remote controlled helicopter which looked like a very large, alien insect. It was all engine and gas tank on skids, with a pair of counter-rotating blades on a center mast. It was designed to be launched from the deck of a destroyer, carrying two Mark 48 anti-submarine homing torpedoes, fly to the approximate location of a hostile submarine, and deposit its load on the unsuspecting enemy. The drone was hated and ridiculed by Naval aviators, who wanted a small manned helo for destroyers. That, and the fact that the DASH was never sufficiently qualified, and no flight capability data developed, was the eventual downfall (often literally) of the unmanned craft.

The Drone Anti-Submarine Helicopter (DASH), flown from the deck of destroyers like *De Haven*. As a qualified DASH operator, the author volunteered and was chosen to lead a special development program for Vietnam utilizing a modified DASH for naval gunfire support.

Flying the DASH was much like rubbing your belly and patting your head; a dial at your left hand controlled altitude and a joystick in your right controlled direction. After graduation I returned to the *De Haven* armed with yet another useful trade.

There are some famous DASH stories in Naval lore, including an admiral-directed fly-by of an aircraft carrier, in which the drone flew into, rather than around, the carrier bridge! I can personally attest to the facts in one equally famous DASH-*crash* yarn. The *De Haven* was pier-side at the busy destroyer berths in Yokosuka. Numerous ships were tied side-by-side along the pier, and the pier itself was usually as busy as a city street. On this glorious day in late 1967, my predecessor as DASH Officer was demonstrating for me a maintenance activity known as "Torque Neutralization." The drone was secured to the flight deck by a single steel cable under its belly. Two large umbilicals provided power from the ship. During actual operation, these umbilicals would be jettisoned just prior to lift off. The purpose of this drill was to ensure that there was equal torque generated by each set of counter rotating blades. There was just enough slack in the tie down cable to allow the drone to lift approximately two inches off the deck. With the blades straining for freedom, the crew would verify that the body of the drone did not rotate in either direction. This was the only drill allowed with the DASH in port because of the safety insured by the steel tie down ... when properly secured. Just prior to any startup of the drone, the DASH Officer performed a safety check. For Torque Neutralization, this check included the tie down cable ... except on this day.

There was a keen interest in the potential use of the drone for aerial observation. A technical team was to ride *De Haven* on our next Tonkin Gulf trip, to experiment with a drone-mounted camera and transmitter, and a receiver and video monitor in CIC. As my predecessor gradually increased the lift, the drone began a slight tap dance at the end of the taunt cable, just as the admiral sponsoring the observation experiment arrived on the pier in his shiny black Navy sedan. The admiral had just walked up the gangway from the pier to the ship and had turned towards the fantail to salute the colors prior to coming aboard, when the cable released and the drone popped straight up! In a split second the two umbilicals tilted the drone towards the pier and then they released. The helicopter dove over the side of the flight deck and slammed full speed into the rear of the admiral's sedan! The admiral's jaw dropped, as did every sailor on the pier. Blades and windshield disintegrated; shrapnel flew in all directions. It was truly a miracle that no one was injured ... except my predecessor ... and his injuries were psychological. As the drone was completing its death throes on the pier—flopping around on its side like a mortally wounded bird—he began to mutter, "Holy shit ... holy shit ... holy...." I reached over and turned the console power off and joined my predecessor at the edge of the flight deck. I thought he might keep on walking! That was the last time he ever flew the DASH drone.

We went on to complete a very successful demonstration of the drone as an observation platform, and actually spotted for some gunfire support missions over South Vietnam. Back in Yokosuka, the technical team packed up for the States, and we went back to war. I had no idea at that time that my DASH experience would be my ticket to freedom and my catalyst into Vietnam.

Back in Long Beach, just when I thought I could not stand another inspection or XO-encounter, one of those change-your-life flukes occurred. A friend mentioned that the Navy was looking for a DASH trained officer to go on temporary duty for several months to Patuxent River Naval Air Station in Maryland to test fly the drone. Without further question I volunteered, and in view of my Tonkin Gulf experience, was accepted. I received immediate temporary orders, and much to the envy of my wardroom mates, and the ire of the XO, my ass was temporarily my own again! I was off to Maryland!

It did not take me long to recognize a good deal. There were only four things on the Chesapeake Bay side of the Pax River NAS—a radar site, the DASH test facility, the Officers Club, and a golf course! The DASH facility was maintained by employees of Gyrodyne—the manufacturer of the drones. The arrangement was simple: their civilian pilot flew the Gyrodyne-owned drones, and I flew those owned by the Navy. Actually, the Defense Department's Advanced Research Projects Agency (ARPA) had bought the drone project from the Navy; manned helo enthusiasts had prevailed and I was to fly for ARPA. At first the plan was to further test the drone's gunfire spotting/observation potential, but that quickly expanded to include the development of a Navy team and a jeep-mounted control station. The ultimate vision was for ships in the Gulf of Tonkin to launch observation drone helicopters, fly them in over land at 3,000 feet, and transfer control to the team on the ground in Vietnam. Now that might not sound like your normal wet-your-whistle opportunity, but for me it was a permanent ticket west from XO-Land! I flew back to Long Beach, enjoyed the XO's "what the fuck's this" reaction when my permanent transfer orders arrived, and headed for a one year tour in Maryland.

Let me describe that dream assignment for a young Navy lieutenant in 1969. I rented what had been servants' quarters on the extensive grounds of a mini-estate in Ridge, Maryland. The land was on a small inlet off of a tributary where it met the Potomac River, as it in turn met the Chesapeake Bay. Immediately out of my back door was a sea wall and a pier, to which was moored the owner's fishing boat, a rowboat, a canoe and also a ski boat, owned and operated by the four Naval Aviators who rented the main house. The cove by the pier was a plentiful, private oyster bed—mine for the "tonging" from the rowboat. Within minutes I could dredge a bushel of succulent oysters; shuck them; eat them raw; steam them; fry them; you name it. Chesapeake Bay blue crabs ran and mated in the inlet; I reestablished my boyhood expertise in crabbing. On nice weekends I split my time between fishing excursions on the bay or water-skiing with the pilots. An occasional beer was consumed, and the line "it don't get no better than this" might also have been uttered a time or two!

Professionally things were also excellent. Though my program was owned by ARPA, my boss was a Navy commander with the Naval Air Systems' Command in Washington, D.C. I spoke to him a couple of times a week and saw him about every month. Until the first two members of the planned Navy crew joined me after several months, I was the only active duty person in the facility. If there was a day with no Navy/ARPA mission planned, I would lie on the beach or play a round of golf. I'd watch and learn from the Gyrodyne pilot, and when neither of us were flying, we ran the company minibikes over the sand dunes around the facility! When my boss would visit, I'd give him status reports over a table full of steamed crabs or a couple of dozen oysters, depending on the season!

We did some really neat stuff with that drone. We had a camera with 10-to-1 zoom and 2× multiplier; we could hover undetected at 3,000 feet and watch a couple of teens make out on a deserted beach. We fired mini-guns and dropped bombs on water targets, and added a laser range finder. We successfully transferred control to a jeep mounted station. Oh yeah, for all of you ex-DASH pilots who watched a drone disappear over the horizon, dive into the ocean, or disappear over the side shortly after launch, we ran a complete flight envelope on the drone. Guess what? We discovered that there should have been restrictions on certain maneuvers. For instance, at temperatures over 90 (frequent in the Gulf of Tonkin), the drone could not hover with two torpedoes once it cleared the lift effect of the flight deck ... surprise! Also at a certain forward speed a sudden full turn would send the drone into an uncontrolled spin and dive. With just those two restrictions, imagine the number of drones and egos that could have been saved. For all of you who shrugged and wrote "gyro failure" on your accident reports, we found the gyro to be the most reliable piece of equipment on the drone.

April 1969 marked the high point in the number of U.S. personnel in Vietnam, 543,000, and in June, Nixon began the first real withdrawals. As a result, the role of our troops became more of support pending withdrawal, and a new reluctance to participate; no one wanted to be the last one killed in Vietnam.[1] Reports surfaced of troops actually refusing to go on patrol.

It was also becoming evident that enthusiasm for my DASH project was dwindling. My boss, the last supporter in NAVAIR, was being transferred. Navy funding for the DARPA project was cut, and I was being pressured to get "back in line," i.e., go to Destroyer School in Newport, Rhode Island, and get back to "haze grey and underway!" I wasn't sure what I wanted to do for the rest of my life, but I knew what I didn't want to do—ride ships for 80 percent of my prime years. I had to buy time and not lose favor should I decide to stay in for a career; I still had two years left of my four year commitment. The only way to avoid sea duty and yet get the right promotion assignments was to volunteer for Vietnam. Besides, somewhere deep down was this nagging feeling that I had some moral obligation to repay someone for my free four year Academy education. My brother was already paying his dues with Army artillery in Vietnam. So it was in November 1969, with mixed emotions and motives, I made the call and requested an assignment with the Navy's "Brown Water" river forces in the Mekong Delta canals of South Vietnam.

What I didn't realize at the time was that 1969's "Vietnamization" included the turnover of the Brown Water Navy's River Patrol and Riverine Forces' river assault craft to the Vietnamese. The fastest set of orders I ever received directed me to report to the Navy Inshore Operations Training Center (NIOTC) in Vallejo, California, for six weeks of "Riverine Warfare" training, to be followed by assignment to the U.S. Naval Advisory Group in Vietnam as "Assistant Senior Raid Advisor" ... whatever the hell that meant!

4

Riverine Training

Prior to 21 February 1970 I had very little, if any, knowledge of the Navy's "Mobile Riverine Force." I knew that PBR's were small, fast, fiberglass River Patrol Boats ("Patrol Boat, River" to be exact). I had never heard of a RAID until my Vietnam orders said I was to be a "RAID Advisor." For all I knew I was destined to rid Southeast Asia of its insect problem. "RAID's HERE!" I certainly could not have identified a Monitor, an ASPB, an ATC or a CCB. However, on that date I arrived for six weeks of "instruction in small riverine craft operations" at the Naval Inshore Operations Training Center, Vallejo, California.

In that short six weeks (excluding weekends, which were reserved for touring the wineries of Napa Valley), I was going to master the craft and tactics associated with mobile riverine operations well enough to advise the South Vietnamese in the creation and sustenance of such a force.

Strike that; after one week of "Counterinsurgency Orientation," one week of "Survival, Evasion, Resistance, and Escape (SERE) training," and one week of "Heavy Weapons training," I would get *three* weeks (excluding weekends) to master small riverine craft operations. Possessing a can-do spirit, and having volunteered, I began my transition to Naval Advisor. I did find out later that normally officers destined for Naval Advisory duty attended a longer, more structured course, as well as a Vietnamese language course at the Army's language school. Because I was needed in a hurry (which should have bothered me), I was handled as a "special case." As I would find out later, where I was going, OJT was not the optimum learning method.

I really don't remember a lot about the counterinsurgency course. The dictionary defines "counterinsurgency" as "political and military action taken to counter insurgency." It further defines "insurgency" as "the quality or circumstance of being insurgent." Finally,

"Insurgent"—"rising in revolt against civil authority or a government in power." Aha! The Viet Cong! The week was spent in class learning a little about the history of Southeast Asia and the rise of those nasty little guys in black pajamas and rubber tire sandals. They were the insurgents. It was then explained how the U.S. and South Vietnam were countering their rise, and the U.S. Navy's role to date (the role for which I had volunteered) in attempting to control the inland waterways in the Mekong Delta, and stem the flow of supplies to the Viet Cong. The Mekong Delta is composed of 10,000 square miles of marshland, swamps and forested areas. The region is interlaced by rivers and canal ways. Controlled by the Viet Cong, the interior waterways of the Mekong Delta were used to transport Viet Cong supplies and weapons. Responsibility for control of those inland waterways was quickly being turned over to the fledgling Vietnamese Navy; hence the creation of the U.S. Naval Advisory Group. Further, I learned that a "RAID" was a River Assault and Interdiction Division.

In fairness to the over-the-counter insurgency instructors, the remaining five weeks, in terms of physical and psychological impact, simply overwhelmed that first week. The Navy had a little gem of a semi-secret training course, taught at several remote locations, called "SERE" (Survival, Evasion, Resistance, and Escape). Originally designed for Naval Aviators, and based on the experiences of downed pilots and POW's, the training had been expanded to include all Naval personnel destined for duty in-country (Vietnam).

So, off we flew to Whidbey Island Naval Air Station, Washington State. We arrived on a Sunday, and were advised to have dinner, relax and get a good night's sleep; we'd need it. Yea? How tough could it be? I could stand on my head in a bucket of shit for a week, knowing I'd be back in wine country thereafter. So, along with a couple of other independents, I went bowling and drank beer, followed by dinner and drinks at the Officers Club ... many drinks! Lord only knows what time we crashed ... only to learn all too quickly just how tough it could be!

Way too early the next morning we were rousted out of bed and bused to the remotest corner of Whidbey Island. We could wear only our green, new issue, fatigues and boots. We were issued pilot survival kits—an ominous sign; oh yes, and a nylon parachute! I could tell by now that whatever I learned to do with that parachute would rank right up there with my DASH training as a valuable trade.

After an introduction in a simple wooden building/classroom, we were led into a pine forest, in which, we quickly learned, we would practice the survival portion of SERE. The fallacy of our situation hit some sooner than others. For the first couple of days, we would get lectures in the simple classroom on survival in the hot, humid, jungle environment of Southeast Asia, and then go out to practice those techniques in a frigid pine forest in the remotest part of Washington State in the middle of February! Needless to say, we all starved and froze our tits off! After films on the various edible vegetation and abundant animal life in the jungle, we returned to the pine grove and the few strips of raw beef we'd been provided the first day to make beef jerky. On the second afternoon someone successfully trapped a squirrel, which we threw in a boiling kettle of water in a vain attempt to make soup for 40 guys!

After proving to myself that the theory of body warmth being contained within nylon parachute on a bed of pine needles was bullshit. I spent the next two frigid evenings as close to the campfire as I could without actually suffering serious burns. God did I already envy those who had followed orders that first night. The alcohol consumed that night provided no warmth now ... and I was one tired son of a bitch! But things would get worse.

By Tuesday afternoon we were practicing the "E"—evasion. Wandering through some incredibly harsh terrain, in groups of two or three, we pretended to use our compass, but actually just looked for the path worn by the hundreds trained before us. I think that was also the day we repelled down some beach-side cliffs. I did a quick look for crabs, muscles, or even dead but-not-yet-rotting fish, to no avail; sand and rocks as far as the eye could see. I was dying, and we hadn't even gotten to the "R" and "E"!

On Wednesday (I think; I had already lost track of time) we were to transition from evasion to resistance. We were taken to a spot in the woods and told that we were behind enemy lines. We were given the direction of friendly lines and told that the terrain between us and the friendlies was heavily patrolled by the enemy. If we could successfully evade the enemy and arrive at the friendly camp we would earn a two hour break, and a snack—a sandwich, an apple, and a cup of coffee! I was determined to get that prize.

As the groups dispersed, I waited; I mentally plotted a zigzag course of various approximated distances and directions, the sum of which would carry me safely through the enemy lines and into that big snack bar in the woods! So, for about two hours I sneaked, ran, crawled and hid, while heading generally towards the pie in the sky. I watched and heard others being captured; I hid in brambles and briars as enemy soldiers passed within spitting distance... God, I was good! Warm up the coffee and polish the apple! Finally, exhausted, scratched and bruised, I crawled over a small rise and couldn't believe my eyes. There about 10 to 15 yards through the underbrush was the big tent that could only house two hours of heaven! I'd made it! I stood up and ambled around to the front of the tent, and froze!

Something was very wrong with this scene; there were several guys in outfits like mine on their knees with cloth bags over their heads and their hands tied behind their backs. I heard yelling from inside the large tent to my left, such things as "Yankee Dog" and "war criminal" etc. And it hit me! I had worked so long and so hard to simply stand up and stroll into an enemy holding camp! I wanted to crawl into a hole. Unfortunately, two enemy soldiers got over the shock of my stupidity quicker than I did, and reacted swiftly. Both yelling, one held a rifle pointed at me, and the other ran up, grabbed me by the hair and forced me to my knees. A third joined them, and placed a cloth bag over my head; my hands were tied behind my back. All I could think was "dumb shit ... dumb shit ... dumb shit."

After an eternity (probably about an hour) I was roughly dragged to my feet. My hands were freed, but a rope was tied around my waist. I could tell that we were now in a single file line much like preschoolers on a field trip to the zoo. We marched and stumbled in what seemed like endless circles. When we stopped we were told to take off the bags. We stood in a small clearing outside of what looked like the prison in *Cool Hand Luke*. My entire class was there; I wondered how many had evaded to the degree I had, and how many had just said "Fuck it," and walked straight until captured.

Next we were introduced to the camp commandant, who told us we were not prisoners of war, but war criminals with no rights. He walked slowly down our ranks and selectively asked questions about our assignments, etc. Each time someone gave the name, rank, serial number speech they were berated or smacked by a guard. We were reminded that there was no rank among war criminals. That mind game was significant throughout our stay in the prison—we strove to maintain a military structure, and they strove to break us into individuals.

Two places down from me in line was an aviator (they stood out in their flight suits). The Commandant chastised him for napalming women and children, etc., and the pilot responded with a very Tom Cruise "Maverick"–like line, "Why don't you go fuck yourself!" Now I dare say that if this young aviator had it all to do over again, he might say something a little less condescending. He was yanked out and targeted from then on for some pretty severe treatment.

All we knew about this phase of SERE—Resistance and Escape—was that it was "open ended"; i.e., depending on how well or how poorly we were doing as a class, we could complete the course on Friday, Saturday, or Sunday. God, what day was it? The rules were apparently simple; we could not suffer any lasting physical damage; anything else was O.K. We were to resist until unable to resist further, and then re-group and resist some more. We were at all times to look for potential escape. If an escape was successful, we were to proceed away from the camp and would find a field telephone, from which we would call and simply report our escape, and wait.

In hindsight this was an amazingly well organized training exercise. We prisoners were already fatigued and starving, and for the next few days were put in every conceivable prison situation possible in a textbook scenario, short of actual debilitating torture. We received "repatriation" lectures, at which occasional punishment was given for failure to show the proper attitude. At one such session, after I continued to insist on being addressed by my rank, I was thrown to the ground on my back and held by two guards while a third pulled my tee shirt tightly over my face and poured water over it when my answers were politically incorrect. Maybe those guys knew when to stop, but there was a time I thought I would drown! Finally, a politically correct enough response brought relief, and I was up to resist again. I now had firsthand knowledge of the term "waterboarding" when it made the news years later. I would have told them anything they wanted. At risk of alienating myself to some, I will state that I absolutely support waterboarding as an interrogation method on high value prisoners if the information gathered saves American lives.

In interrogation rooms we were subjected to good cop/bad cop routines—offers of cigarettes or water, versus slaps to the face and slams against the walls. Again, resist until unable and then fall back to resist again.

We spent unknown lengths of time locked in a crouch inside small wooden boxes in which any attempt to move caused agony in several muscle groups. If we were lucky enough to doze, a rifle butt without warning to the side of the box would bring us back in a hurry.

Throughout our prison stay, each officer, at some time, found himself the senior person in a group, faced with a situation challenging his authority. We reacted, never knowing if our actions shortened or lengthened our prison stay.

There were a couple of foiled escape plans over the first couple of days. My escape on the third day was almost an afterthought. About ten of us were in a holding pen adjacent to the main "yard." There was a sandbag bunker in the center and a guard tower at the one end. The guard could see into our area and the main yard. We could not sit, nor could we talk; we could only walk in endless circles. Periodically, for further harassment, there would be an air-raid drill. The incessant Oriental music, which played night and day over the camp speakers, would be interrupted by air-raid sirens. We would have to run and crowd into the small bunker. The drill would last only minutes and we would be called back outside to resume our wandering.

On one such drill, while huddled on pallets on the dirt floor of the bunker, I noticed a drain at the end of the bunker away from the guard tower. One of the other guys helped me lift one of the wood pallets to reveal a drainpipe about 18 inches in diameter; it was dark, muddy and ominous, but I started to think that it might be there as a test. After we were called out, I wandered along the fence at the far side of the small pen. An occasional glance across the clearing toward the woods several hundred feet away convinced me that there was a drainage ditch about two-thirds of the way across the opening which ran at an angle into the woods. The pipe had to run into that ditch. I waited for night hoping I would not be taken from the pen before then.

Dark! So far, so good. The pen was lighted, but the lights shone in towards the bunker; they did not carry far into the adjoining clearing. Now all I needed was an air-raid. When it came, we darted into the bunker. I whispered to the others that I would need help. Two of them raised the pallet and I slithered into the pipe.... "God, no," I thought... "Just wait for the weekend." But by now the game was too real, and I wanted to beat it! "Slime! What if there's a snake in here? What if this gets smaller? What if ... what if...." I slithered on. After an eternity, I actually smelled fresh air, and then I was at the end! I lay on my back, and eased my head out of the pipe just enough to be able to see the guard tower. The others, after the air-raid drill, milled around a little faster, changed direction, made nine look like ten, and then caused a distraction. I could have sworn the guard looked right at me, but the light out there was not good enough to give me away. I'd been lying at the pipe's end for about five minutes, when the guys inside came through. First some bumping and shouting, and then wrestling match as if in anger. The guard fired warning shots with his tower machine gun, and then turned to sound an alarm for help. I bolted!

At first I was so cramped I thought my extremities would not function. Scurrying on all fours as low as possible in the marshy ditch, I headed for the woods about fifty feet away, expecting any minute to be caught in the glare of a search light or run down by guards. I made it to the woods and crashed headlong into the underbrush. It was thrilling! I'd have never believed I could have been so absorbed in what was essentially a game! By now, though, it was real, and I was going home! I came to a dirt road and saw a small light to my right. I was Superman, and there was my phone booth! I grabbed the field phone and cranked. A voice said "hello," and I said, "This is Lt. Kirtley and I've escaped." I was asked for a number on the box and told to wait. Within minutes I was in friendly hands, not knowing what to expect. I was taken into a large tent with a table and chairs and a large American flag hanging across one whole side. I know I had tears in my eyes and a lump in my throat.

I was interviewed about my escape and told I would be "debriefed" as if it was a real escape situation. Then I found heaven—a cup of coffee, an apple, and a peanut butter and jelly sandwich. This was, indeed, America! I was amazed at how difficult it was for me to describe the layout of the prison camp. We had those bags on our heads and marched in circles every time we moved from one area to another. I was asked the number and names of the other prisoners; I don't remember how well I did. After about an hour I was put back into the training as if I'd never escaped.

The rest is a blur ... we lost all track of time. Finally, we were standing in the main compound with those bags over our heads, Commie music playing, and the commandant again berating us "Yankee dogs." He paused, and the music suddenly changed to the American National Anthem! In a not so commandant voice, he said something like "What are you guys doing with those silly bags on your heads"? And like that, it was over. We pulled off the bags and stood there looking at each other with dazed looks on our faces, and then most of us actually cried. I couldn't believe that we had only been there for a few days!

There wasn't much reflection immediately. We walked out to some buses and returned to the civilized part of the base. We showered and went to the O'Club. I was surprised that I couldn't eat but about half of the steak I'd ordered. One beer later and I crashed. No bowling, no partying, no bravado. Just a bed with clean sheets for a humbled Navy lieutenant.

Our "drill" had ended late Saturday; I never knew if that was bad or good ... just done. Sunday we flew back to Vallejo for the next phase; for me that was some classes on small arms as I commenced the weapons training week. Was I different after SERE? I think so; I knew I could be broken; knew there were limits; wondered what my limits were; and swore I never wanted to find out. Years later, as I read the stories and books of our returned POWs, I cried for them; I have no idea how they survived the real horrors of those torturous years.

Well, two weeks into "small riverine craft operations" and I hadn't seen a river or a craft. Nor would I during my third week. I joined another group and we headed for Hawthorne, Nevada, home of one of nation's only legal whorehouses, and an Army facility with a firing range where we would learn to operate "heavy weapons." The whorehouse remained but a legend, as we spent every waking hour shooting real guns.

We fired everything from small sidearms (.45 cal. and .38 cal. pistols) and the infamous M16 rifle, to heavy machine guns (.50 cal., and M60, and 20 mm cannons). But I fell in love with what would be my weapon of choice for my whole Vietnam experience—the M79 grenade launcher. This little beauty was a single shot weapon about the size of a sawed-off shotgun. It had one barrel, or tube, and broke in the middle like a shotgun. With a distinctive "thunk," the M79 lofted a spin stabilized 40 mm grenade with uncanny accuracy for about 300 meters. It could also fire a close range buckshot round that would slow a stampede. Yes sir, when I got in-country I was gonna get me one of those. After the week in Hawthorne, I could not only counter insurgency and actively "SERE," but I could also fire each and every weapon available to the riverine sailor. So bring on the boats!

Again, had I not been a "special case," my training would have included all of the intricacies of the many variations of riverine craft in the brown water Navy arsenal. The make-up of the riverine forces was best described in a Navy information pamphlet from the Chief of Information in June 1968 entitled *The Navy in Vietnam.*

4. Riverine Training

> The Mobile Riverine Force (MRF) is a joint Army-Navy strike force designed for combat in a riverine environment. There are four types of river assault craft, all heavily armed and armored, the "Monitor," the Command and Communication Boat (CCB), the Armored Troop Carrier (ATC), and the Assault Support Patrol Boat (ASPB). The work horse of these craft is the ATC. Armed with an arsenal of short range weapons, each boat can carry a platoon fully equipped infantrymen almost anywhere in the Delta. With longer range fire power, the heavy gunfire support comes from the "Monitor." The ASPB, acts as a destroyer for the fleet, escorting the other boats up the rivers and canals. It also serves as a minesweeper. Both the Army and the Navy use the CCB as an afloat forward command post during operations. The little green fleet, along with its larger support ships (a Mobile Riverine Base) makes up the modern Mobile Riverine Force.[1]

A simplified translation of the above quotation is "Big slow boats with awesome firepower!" The ASPB or "Alpha" boat was the only new design, from the keel up, for riverine warfare. All of the others were conversions of World War II LCM6 landing craft. We'd all seen the films of those craft hitting the beaches of Europe and the troops pouring out. On all of the conversions the coxswain, or wheelhouse, was moved forward and armored with quarter-inch steel plate and bar armor—horizontal steel bars a few inches apart—to detonate rockets before they reached the steel plate. The coxswain house was then surrounded by gun turrets, housing either .50 cal. or M60 machine guns, 20 mm cannons, or Mark 18 automatic grenade launchers. The "well deck," or troop hole, was modified in various ways to create the ATC, the Monitor, the CCB, or, one craft not mentioned in the article, the "ZIPPO," or flame thrower. The other common conversion feature was the 18-inch thick, heavy foam reinforcement down each side of the craft at the water line. This foam was then covered with bar armor. The theory was that an in-coming rocket would be detonated by the bar armor and absorbed by the foam, thereby not allowing penetration to troops and /or equipment and machinery inside the craft.

On an ATC the troop well was covered by a steel flight deck for helicopter evacuation or resupply purposes. The front landing craft door remained operational. To create a Monitor, the door/ramp was removed and the bow (front) of the craft was rounded. A solid steel deck covered the troop well, and a 40 mm cannon or 81 mm mortar was mounted forward to provide heavy artillery.

The CCB was the floating "brain" of the riverine unit. It, too, had a rounded bow and a steel deck sealing the troop well. Beneath this deck, in the only air conditioned space in the riverine force, was housed the communications center; command and control of all operations was exercised from the bowels of the CCB—boat-to-boat, CCB to the mobile riverine base, and CCB to air cover and evacuation coordination points. Although the air conditioning was tempting, the CCB could quickly become a coffin if mined ... there was only one exit from the control room below decks.

The final LCM-6 conversion craft was the "ZIPPO." With two Army napalm flame throwers on the bow, and bladders of raw napalm in its belly, the ZIPPO was by far the most awesome, and feared, of the riverine craft in action. My experience in-country with the ZIPPO, described later in this book, would make anyone quit smoking.

To refer to the Alpha as a "delta destroyer" was somewhat of a misnomer. Actually, because of its weight when fully manned and armed, rather than cutting gracefully through the water, it plowed, leaving a wake that was devastating to life along the canals. When the Alpha stopped suddenly, a rather large stern wave would overtake it and wash across the rear deck, taking any loose belongings over the side. In fact, the first version had an open stern, and was actually swamped during testing, forcing the addition of a rear deck. The weight of the deck naturally drove the boat lower in the water, further exacerbating the situation.

The full extent of my riverine craft "special ed" was some classroom time watching films of the boats in operation, a walk-through of each type, and an overview of the U.S. Navy's Planned Maintenance System (PMS), as applicable to the craft (another not so funny joke later lost in translation). I also spent several hours in the Sacramento Delta training area, with the instructor conducting mock attacks on the officers and crews who were getting the full course of instruction on the boats. At this point, as I prepared to depart for Vietnam, I could have coined a famous question from a popular TV commercial, about my abbreviated training: "Where's the beef?"

Thus, with limited training and no relevant experience, I was off to Travis Air Force Base to go play my part in the enigmatic Vietnam conflict. I had no idea how far "outside the normal range of US Navy experience" my next year would be! I just knew I was now a Naval Advisor to the South Vietnam forces, going thousands of miles to give advice to a strange people, in a strange land, in a strange conflict, with all of my expertise gained in six weeks of special ed! It was April 1970; I was 26 years old, and slightly apprehensive, to say the least.

5

Here I Am... Take My Advice! (First Impressions)

By the time I lifted off from Travis AFB on a chartered airline (stewardesses and all), with over 100 wide-eyed, subdued members of all branches of the service, there were approximately 340,000 U.S. servicemen still in-country. Public opinion supporting an immediate withdrawal was increasing past 50 percent—a comforting feeling for those of us heading the opposite way. Communist strength in the South had gradually been rebuilding since TET 1968; and in Go Dau Ha, Republic of South Vietnam, fifty miles from Saigon, on the Vam Co Dong River, fourteen enlisted advisors and one lieutenant commander, USN, awaited the arrival of Lt. Richard Kirtley, new Assistant Senior Advisor to RID40 ... fresh meat!

The flight from California to Saigon took about twenty-six hours, with stops in Alaska and Japan. I sensed a mood shift in us all as we left Japan and headed for Vietnam. The years of newspaper and TV coverage, my Academy days when the names of the first alumni casualties showed up in Memorial Hall, and my days on *De Haven* off the coast, all raced in my head; I had absolutely no idea what to expect. "Will the plane be shot at as we land? Do we run to bunkers? When do I get a weapon? Who'll meet me there? Who even knows I'm coming? What am I doing here? Turn this plane around!"

"Look, the coast of Vietnam!" someone shouted. "O.K ... snap out of it ... get a grip." My heart was racing; God, I think I was scared. From the air, South Vietnam was beautiful—so green ... so peaceful looking; could all of the reported horror really be happening down there?

I barely remember the touchdown at Tan Son Nhut Airport. While taxiing to the terminal area I caught glimpses of tremendous numbers of aircraft, military and civilian, jets, props, and helicopters ... it seemed to go on forever.

We deplaned and walked quickly into a processing building. (I was "processed" in the service more than deli luncheon meat.) Those of us in the Navy were then bused to the Annapolis Hotel, the Navy's conduit to Vietnam duty assignments in the Southern regions. The bus ride is by now a blur, but it was my first glimpse of the teeming city; I did think that it seemed not so different from so many of the other Far Eastern cities I had visited during port visits on *De Haven*; the Philippines came to mind. There were just so many Vietnamese here!

Differences began to appear as we reached the hotel—the heavily sandbagged entrance with flak-jacketed marine guards was a big clue. Inside could best be described as a zoo. Realize that this was the Navy's gateway to the great unknown for all of the "first timers." The administrative burden alone was staggering. Once identified and assigned a bunk, I was told I could be there as long as a week—you guessed it, processing, i.e., getting uniforms issued (green fatigues and boots) and weapons ("I'd like to sign up for an M79 grenade launcher please. What's that, a three day waiting period for a background check?") Actually, I blindly accepted my M16 rifle, bandoliers of ammo, flak jacket and helmet, and, because I was an officer, a .38 cal. pistol and holster ... move over Audie Murphy and John Wayne.

The place was stifling. After two days I was going nuts. On day three I was called to the lobby; I had company. "Lieutenant Kirtley, I'm BM1 Mountain and this here is GM2 Scorpion; we're here to take you to Go Dau Ha; let's grab your gear, Sir." My God, I had arrived! Surely these two had been in Vietnam since the war started! Mountain was possibly the largest individual I'd ever met. Fully bearded, with a southern drawl, he hefted my duffel bag like it was empty, and off we went. Scorpion, on the other hand, was slim and wiry; dressed in camouflage and tanned almost black, he reminded me of a tightly coiled snake. I later learned that he had been a hippie in the Haight-Ashbury district of San Francisco, and volunteered for the Navy in Vietnam so he could legally kill somebody!

They signed me out like a piece of equipment and I was whisked out to a waiting jeep. "Lieutenant, this is RMC Creed, your leading Chief Petty Officer." "Hello, Lootenant; welcome to Nam. Hop in ... we have to didi; long drive before dark." I climbed in; another mental checkpoint at which I would have turned back if I could; too late. I wondered what "didi" meant? Perhaps I would know, if they had taken the time to send me to language training.

As I rode in the front passenger seat I glanced at Chief Creed. This was his second one-year tour in-country. I immediately was drawn to his rugged bravado—a cocksure attitude that would sustain me through my settling-in months. He had on green fatigue pants, a green tee shirt, and a stump of a cigar that he rarely removed hanging in the corner of his mouth, even when he talked. The most striking physical differences between me and these guys was my relatively pale skin, and the newness of my uniform, especially my boots! I wondered if they had ever seen Walt Disney's *Spin and Marty*, where the other boys "seasoned" Marty's new jeans upon his arrival at the dude ranch. My stuff needed seasoning quickly!

We made our way through endless streets, all alive with street people, and thousands in motion on, or in, the most diverse modes of transportation I'd ever seen. Small three-wheel taxis darted here and there, and bicycles abounded. The strangest mode was what appeared to be a combination rickshaw and motorcycle or bicycle. The seating area (for two) was mounted up front and the driver sat on the cycle seat behind. Lord, the passengers were actually the front bumper! Little did I know that one day that would be my chosen mode of transportation whenever I returned to Saigon.

As the traffic thinned and we moved into what appeared to be the suburbs, I realized that my three companions were so calm. Sure, they each held a weapon, but they seemed oblivious to our location in the world. I, on the other hand, tightened more internally with every mile.

Suddenly, Chief Creed pulled over and skidded to a stop; Scorpion and Mountain hopped out. "What's wrong? What's happening?" "Relax, Lootenant, they're just buying some fresh bread to take back to the base." Fresh bread? Fresh bread? I'm shittin' my pants and these guys just stopped for bread!? Three hundred and sixty-two days to go!

As we drove out of the city we passed Tan Son Nhut and I thought about trying for a space available/stand-by flight home. As we left the suburbs I was relieved at least to see that we did not enter any jungle. We were actually on Highway 1 from Saigon to Phnom Penh in Cambodia, a two lane highway which passed through miles of open land and occasionally narrowed as it squeezed through a village. The guys explained that day-time travel on this highway was fairly safe. There were lots of ARVN (Army of the Republic of Vietnam) troops along the way, and the openness made ambush a rarity. The only fear was of possible random sniping. We passed the turn off to Cu Chi, where there was a large U.S. Army base. I would soon learn to beg, pillage, and plunder there for the basic necessities of life.

Finally, we entered a city somewhat larger than any of the villages we'd passed. There was lots of activity—civilians scurried from shop to shop; there were roadside cafes where a mix of civilian and uniformed Vietnamese took refreshments. There was a lot of ARVN heavy traffic on the main street—trucks, jeeps, and even a large, truck-mounted howitzer of some sort. As we passed within feet of the crowds I noticed varied reactions. Most of the civilians did not even offer a glance; some ARVN soldiers seemed to stare, while others smiled and waved; and I got my first taste of the hordes of Vietnamese kids with their hands out, for anything—candy, C rations ... anything.

In the middle of town, we passed a major left turn that appeared to lead the main highway up to a bridge over the Vam Co Dong River toward the Cambodian border. The road, however, was barricaded, and we proceeded further and turned left onto a side road. The regular highway traffic seemed to run both ways on this amazingly small, dirt road. As the houses (actually shanties we called "hooches") parted, I saw the river ahead. We started across on obviously temporary pontoon bridge which allowed traffic only one-way alternately. I looked left, down the river and the necessity for the temporary bridge was obvious; the center span of the main bridge was completely missing! "VC blew it again a couple of weeks ago," said Chief Creed; "They blow it; ARVN rebuilds it; they blow it again." A strange thought flashed across my mind, "Glad I don't run the budget for the Vietnamese Department of Transportation!" All that came out was the first of many naive questions, "Can't they defend it?" "They try, but eventually, the VC get it every time." Scorpion added with a laugh, "They shot the poor son-of-a-bitch in charge of defending it this time." Me: "The VC shot him?" "No, the ARVN executed him in the field on the other side of the bridge. Some of us went up on our end of the bridge and watched!" Taxi! Saigon please!

The temporary road from the temporary bridge curved left and intersected Highway 1 a few hundred yards from the main bridge. Turn right and you headed west toward Phnom Penh, capital of Cambodia; the border was only ten miles west. The small piece of land marked by the arc of the temporary road as it turns toward Highway 1, between the road and the bridge, accommodated the Advanced Tactical Support

The remains of the bridge at Go Dau Ha, South Vietnam, where Highway 1 crossed the Vam Co Dong River. Highway 1 was the main route connecting Saigon, the capital of South Vietnam, with Phnom Penh, capital of Cambodia. The bridge had been blown up by the Viet Cong when the author arrived in Go Dau Ha.

Base (ATSB) at Go Dau Ha, home of Vietnamese River Interdiction Division (RID) 40. We drove through the makeshift gate in a makeshift wire fence, and I immediately felt like we had driven onto the set of *M*A*S*H*!

(Act 1, Scene 1: Lt. Kirtley arrives at Go Dau Ha ATSB. "Roll cameras! Action!" Close-up of the Lt's face as he steps from the jeep and begins to realize that this is his home for the foreseeable future! Priceless!)

6

The Big Picture

As I stepped from the jeep, it struck me full force that I knew little to nothing about my assignment. Remember, I was rushed through stateside training because of an urgent need; I was a special ed/special needs advisor. I had received no specifics at the Vallejo training center, only a historical overview, no one had briefed me about anything at the Saigon processing center, and I certainly had gotten no smarter on the ride from Saigon to Go Dau Ha. I had been briefed in Vallejo on the organizational structure of the Commander of Naval Forces in Vietnam (COMNAVFORV). However, I knew only a little about the organizational structure of the Naval Advisory Group (NAVADVGRP), of which I was a part, and even less about the newly evolving South Vietnamese Navy, to which I was to provide advice. I knew the basic objective of "Vietnamization" and "Peace with Honor," and that "ACTOV," Accelerated Turnover to the Vietnamese, was the name given to the Navy's role in the larger Vietnamization picture. My first thought when I heard the word "Accelerated" in our program was that the term too closely described our frantic turnover effort as a *retreat*. I also could not get the old saying "haste makes waste" out of my head. At the time of my arrival, at least those seeds of skepticism had not yet been planted in the minds of our allies.

In order for you to fully understand my going-in situational awareness, I will digress here to a *brief* historical overview of the Navy's transition from a "blue water" strategic force to a formidable "brown water" strategic and tactical force in the Vietnam Delta. My learning process on all of this was backwards, i.e., out of necessity, I first had to focus on the tactical roll of RID 40. What follows was learned mostly in hindsight. My intention is to provide here only enough for you to understand where my unit, RID 40, fit in the strategic picture at the time of my arrival. Only then can I dig into the tactical role and resultant frustrations in filling that role. With that said, I will not attempt here to describe in great detail the other two main types of boats in the brown water Navy and their capabilities ... swift boats and PBRs, but rather provide a brief description of each. Those boats and their history and heroic Vietnam performance can be found in numerous books and magazine articles written at the time and during the intervening years. Since Vietnamese RID 40 was a derivative of the U.S. Navy's Mobile Riverine Force (MRF), a quick look at their short but historic history is in order.

By 1965 it was evident that supplies for the Viet Cong units fighting throughout South Vietnam were flowing into the country from the east by sea along the coast, and by land from the west, through Laos and Cambodia. The U.S. Navy with all of its seagoing capabilities was basically helpless to stop those supply lines. Consequently, a plan was conceived to literally establish a barrier completely around South Vietnam by gaining and maintaining 360 degree control of water access into the South, and throughout the waterways from Saigon south. Shutting down the coastal access routes was relatively easy conceptually. First, utilize coast guard cutters, already possessing the speed and mobility to intercept small boats close to shore. The Navy, however, had no available assets to pick up responsibility where the Coast Guard left off—i.e., from the mouths of the rivers emptying into the Gulf of Tonkin, further in-country on those rivers, as well as the thousands of small canals easily used by the Viet Cong to move about unopposed. The Navy's answer was to develop two new types of boats designed specifically to pursue the VC anywhere they could go by water in the Delta. The first was the aptly named swift boat—conceived and built by modifying the design of an existing water taxi in Louisiana for support of oil rigs in the Gulf of Mexico. The speedy craft, with a top speed of 32 knots, was 50 feet long with a shallow draft and lightly armed with machine guns and a mortar. The first 50 boats arrived in 1965, and eventually, as the design evolved, there were additions to the swift boat ranks through 1972. Some swift boats captured after the fall of Saigon in 1975 are still in use in Vietnam.

The second new boat was designed for operation in the rest of the smaller waterways throughout the Delta. The Patrol Boat, River (PBR) was fiberglass with water jet drives to allow for access into the shallow, weed choked canals.[1] At 31 feet in length, PBRs were armed with machine guns and grenade launchers. The first boats entered service in Vietnam in March of 1966 and eventually they grew to a force of 250 boats.

With the swift boats and PBRs working to secure the waterways through small boat and junk searches by day and ambush setups to catch cross river/canal movement by the VC at night, the one remaining capability desired for control of the waterways was the ability to move troops by water to respond to emergent needs. The Navy's MRF was created in 1966 as a joint organization with the U.S. Army. The Navy controlled heavy assault craft would transport troops to hot spots in the Delta, and then provide weapons coverage in support, in conjunction with heavy close in air support, when available. The concept was developed rapidly; however, there was no time to develop an official military doctrine for MRF use in Vietnam. Therefore their missions and utilization were open to interpretation by the Navy, and ultimately the Vietnamese Navy after the turnover of assets. The U.S. operated the boats of the MRF from 1966 until the transfer of assets to the Vietnamese, which began in January 1969.

In November '68, the U.S. Navy's Admiral Zumwalt, then the Commander of Naval Forces in Vietnam (COMNAVFORV), launched "SEALORDS," South East Asia Lake, Ocean, River, Delta Strategy, a campaign, in conjunction with the turnover of operations and assets to the South Vietnamese, designed to cut all VC supply lines from Cambodia, and to put pressure on VC operating bases in the Delta. One key to the success of not only SEALORDS, but the MRF in general, was the addition of close air support from two very unique, surgically precise, highly decorated sources, i.e., armed helicopters of squadron HAL-3, nicknamed "Seawolves," and small fixed wing OV-10 Bronco aircraft, nicknamed "Black Ponies." These assets would prove to be my favorite friends in later ops with RID 40. By early 1969, SEALORDS had been extended all the way up to Tay Ninh, northwest of Saigon, completing a continuous line of patrols on the inland waterways from there all the way south to the Gulf of Siam.

In December '68 the operation west of Saigon had been officially named Operation *Giant Slingshot,* because it established bases on two rivers, the Vam Co Tay and the Vam Co Dong, whose extensions from their merge west of Saigon, continued NW and SW like the arms of a slingshot. The bases on both of these rivers were established to cut off a major VC supply route from the Ho Chi Minh Trail in Cambodia into the Saigon area through a protrusion of Cambodia called the Parrot's Beak. One of the Advanced Tactical Support Bases for *Giant Slingshot* was established in Go Dau Ha, originally as a U.S. Navy base with

U.S. Navy MRF boats operating from there. River Interdiction Division (RID) 40 was formed in late 1969, and the Vietnamese Navy assumed operational responsibility for its 14 MRF heavy assault craft. By the time I arrived in Go Dau Ha that fateful day in April 1970, the MRF boats were fully staffed by the Vietnamese Navy, but the base was still under the control of the U.S. Navy. It was here that I was introduced to my new boss, the LCDR Senior Advisor, and the fourteen Navy enlisted Advisors to RID 40. So, if all of that seems confusing to you now, please try to imagine what it was like for this totally naive, totally unprepared, young Navy lieutenant as I stepped out of that jeep!

7

Meet, Greet and Settle In

As I stood there by the jeep, in a slow, continuous, 360-degree turn, Chief Creed asked Petty Officer Mountain to take my gear to my "quarters," while he took me to put my rifle in the command bunker. He would then introduce me to the rest of my advisors in their "hooch." Apparently, my boss, the senior advisor, was at a meeting in Saigon and would return the next day. The Chief said he would also try to arrange for me to briefly meet the Vietnamese commander of the RID and his junior officers before the briefing for that night's boat ambush positions. In addition, he said we should probably stop by and meet the Master Chief in charge of the base. Apparently it was going to be a busy afternoon.

I should make it clear at this point that when I use the term "base," it's not what you are probably thinking. A typical Navy base, anywhere but in Vietnam, was acres of admin facilities, warehouses, living quarters, medical offices, commissary, exchange, piers, ships, etc., all surrounded by high walls, with entrance gates guarded by marines. The base at Go Dau Ha was an Advanced Tactical Support Base (ATSB), on about an acre or two of land, with equipment and facilities just sufficient to support the 250 Vietnamese sailors and the 14 river assault boats of RID 40. Again, keep the base in *M*A*S*H* in mind, but without the operating rooms.

The layout of the base was simple; there was a single dirt road (actually the entire base was dirt) from the gate to the waterfront. Along the left (north) side proceeding from the gate were three plywood, screen and corrugated-tin roofed latrine facilities; a large sandbagged ammunition bunker; and a dining facility (also plywood, screen and tin roof). The dining building serviced all personnel on the base, American and Vietnamese, officer and enlisted. It was operated by U.S. Navy personnel

The Advanced Tactical Support Base (ATSB), on the west bank of the Vam Co Dong River at Go Dau Ha. Located at the foot of the Highway 1 bridge, the ATSB was home to Vietnamese Navy River Interdiction Division 40.

assigned to the base Master Chief. Along the right side of the dirt road were a line of six or seven single story buildings (plywood, screen and tin roof). These buildings housed the base Master Chief's office and admin support, the handful of U.S. Navy enlisted base support personnel, supply storage, RID 40 advisors' quarters, Vietnamese enlisted sailors' berthing, and officers' berthing.

All buildings, except sandbagged bunkers, were raised off the ground on wooden supports. The berthing buildings were all identical, with steps up to a screen door entrance onto a screened room with a table and chairs, and whatever appliances the occupants desired, i.e., refrigerator, hotplates, coffee maker, etc. The rest of each berthing building consisted of two rows, front to back, of cots, with a footlocker at the foot of each. Between the last of the buildings and the waterfront was a small water tower and shower facility. The waterfront itself consisted of two large floating docks, each with a storage building. The heavy assault craft were tied parallel to the docks.

Along the South side of the base, behind the row of buildings, and against the fence running parallel to Highway 1 leading up to the bridge, were sandbagged bunkers for personnel cover in the event of enemy action against the base. The last of these bunkers, immediately behind the officers berthing, was larger than the rest and housed the command center, where the briefing would be held. Inside were three rooms; the first and largest held all of the communications equipment for both the U.S. advisors and the Vietnamese. The second room was a small office with a desk and some files for U.S. and Vietnamese use. The third room was a small berthing room, with two bunks, small shelves, and a footlocker, originally built for the U.S. commander of the squadron of U.S. boats operating out of the ATSB. I soon found out that the berth was now utilized by the U.S. Navy Senior Advisor and the Vietnamese RID Commander. My immediate concern was the location of my own "berth."

Chief Creed led me along the road toward the waterfront, pointing out each building or bunker as we walked. It was afternoon and very hot; I noticed there was not a lot of activity as we walked. We stopped in front of one of the buildings, and I was informed it housed our advisors. We walked up and into the screened common area, and into another world. As I stood there in my brand new green fatigues and shiny boots, I was surrounded by the U.S. Navy enlisted petty officer advisors to RID 40. If I had not known their service affiliation, I could never have guessed it. The 13 members of the group were either sitting at the table or standing behind it, in various stages of dress, none of which resembled any piece of a standard Navy uniform. Several had on extremely worn boots, while others were in sandals or flip flops. Long or short cut-off camouflaged pants, also extremely worn, were the uniform of the day. A few of the men were topless, some wore cutoff t-shirts, and a couple had camouflaged tops with sleeves rolled or cut off, open in the front. All were tanned. The Chief went around the room and introduced each man and his specialty, either gunner's mate, engineman, radioman, or boatswain mate, the obvious specialties needed for the unit's mission.

The heavily sandbagged command bunker at ATSB Go Dau Ha was the communication center for coordination with the boats of RID 40 and American air support assets.

The meeting was short, but I immediately felt comfortable and confident that these men, in spite of their ragtag appearance, were fully engaged in their assignment. As we turned to leave the building, one of the men asked the Chief if he forgot to tell me about my lieutenant bars embroidered on my uniform collar. The Chief said, "Oh yea, Lootenant, you don't want to walk around here, or especially on the boats, with these on; or else you become a prime target for a VC sniper!" Good advice. Holy shit!

We walked to the command bunker, where I got the quick tour. There was no sign of the VN Dai uy in there (Lieutenant). So we walked out and around to the front of the officers' berth building. Chief Creed stopped and asked if I spoke any Vietnamese. When I answered in the negative, he laughed and said, "Well then, this should be a hoot," and up the stairs we walked.

At the time, I had been in Vietnam for three days and had yet to encounter directly a single Vietnamese, military or civilian. First impressions are very important, no more so than in an advisor/operational command relationship. Given the circumstances, all things considered, my first encounter eased my trepidation, greatly. The Chief knocked on the screen door, through which I could see several Vietnamese men sitting around a table like the one in the advisors' building. I was pleasantly surprised when the response to the knock was an English "come in!" That was a good sign.

I entered with much the same feeling of overdress as when I met the advisors, even though these VN officers were not nearly so ragtag. There were five or six men present, three or four very young, maybe in their twenties. Each of them had on what appeared to be a casual working uniform, two-piece, grayish blue. One man was obviously older than the others, perhaps in his forties, with the same uniform pants on with a white t-shirt. I immediately picked out the RID commander, as he stood to greet me. He was probably a young thirty or so, fully dressed in the same uniform with lieutenant shoulder boards. He had a sincere, engaging smile, and I liked him immediately. I didn't know it then, but our initial handshake was the start of a year-long professional relationship and friendship. Dai uy Tinh and I would share much over the next year. Eventually he would come to call me by my first name, while I would always call him "Dai uy." To my great relief, Dai uy Tinh spoke very acceptable English, thus facilitating our ability to communicate clearly. It seems that the Vietnamese authorities, at least, realized that clear communication might be a necessity in the relationship.

The youngsters in the group were all fairly new naval officers, while the older man in the t-shirt was a former officer with the ARVN (Army of the Republic of Vietnam), recently reassigned to the Navy, and now the Deputy Commander of RID 40. He remained a puzzle to me for the entire year. He spoke no English, and though he smiled every time we were together, I always thought he held some secret. I was convinced that he was placed in his position to keep an eye on Dai uy Tinh and to be an informal communication line back to his former ARVN command organization. This feeling was driven by the fact that the VN Navy was still proving itself to the dominant ARVN. For some unexplainable reason I had a hunch, never proven, that this man also had links with the local Viet Cong. In reality, I look back now and suspect that many of the men in the VN Navy had some relationship with the VC. I am positive that the young ladies hired to clean the base, and who had the run of the base during daylight hours, were in fact VC themselves or, at the very least, VC sympathizers.

Just before leaving my meeting with the Dai uy and his staff, he showed me back to the row of bunks in the back portion of the building, and to what was to be my bunk. I made a mental note right there that my first objective was to move my sleeping arrangements into the back room of the command bunker. It had nothing to do with my VN bunkmates, but everything to do with my desire to have something better than plywood between me and enemy incoming rounds! This objective was by no means devious or underhanded. On the contrary, soon after learning that I was to be an Assistant Senior Advisor, I learned that the other senior advisor positions in the Naval Advisory Group (NAVADGRU) were lieutenant assignments, and the assistant positions were LTjg's (Lieutenant junior grade). I had already decided that at my first meeting with my boss in Saigon I would make it clear that I wanted to eventually, sooner rather than later, either assume the Senior Advisor role with RID 40, or be reassigned to the first available Senior Advisor position. If I was going to spend a year here, I wanted the same responsibilities as my peers. Fortunately, that situation soon worked itself out.

It was late afternoon when we left the officers' quarters, and Chief Creed suggested we stop in the mess building for a bite to eat. I was again pleasantly surprised; the mess facility, given the relative austerity of the location and the rest of the facilities, was more than adequate. While it was constructed like the rest of the buildings on the base, it was roomy and had a large seating area with picnic tables; a large, well equipped kitchen; a competent staff of U.S. and VN sailors; and what appeared to be a well-rounded menu, much like a cafeteria at home.

As we approached the food service line, I noticed a gathering of five or six U.S. Navy men at a table at the far end of the seating area. These were more obviously recognizable as U.S. servicemen than my advisors, in that they all had full green fatigue uniforms on. It appeared that the largest of the group was holding court with the others; in any case he was obviously in charge of the group. Chief Creed smiled his wry smile and said, "Good timing; looks like you'll get the chance to meet the Master Chief of the base." The only hint I got at the time as to the reason for his wry smile was when I commented that the food looked pretty good. To which the Chief muttered, "Yea, well, it could and should be even better." I let it go, and figured he would explain the comment later.

We sat alone and I realized I was famished. We chatted a little about each of our backgrounds; I hadn't thought much about our introduction in the jeep, so only during this conversation did it hit me that his title was RMC, Radioman Chief. I had thought for some reason that all of the enlisted advisors were gunners mates, electricians, enginemen or boatswains. My previous experience with radiomen on board my destroyer led me to believe that they were all pale, nerdy types, who loved to play with all kinds of communications gear. The fact that he was what we referred to as a "salt" and was on his second tour on river assault boats, the first when the boats were U.S. staffed, somewhat surprised me. I quickly learned that he was anything but nerdy, and he immediately became my right-hand man.

He told me a little about each advisor, and some general opinions of how far we had to go with the VNs. I asked him about my boss, the Senior Advisor, and sensed that the Chief respected him, but thought perhaps he was better suited for an office assignment; he may have used the term "straight arrow" also. He cut that conversation short and suggested that we have a quick chat with the base Master Chief. I realized that he was still in session in the same spot. I hadn't heard any of his conversation with his men, but it had been punctuated often by raucous laughter. We dropped our trays off and walked toward the group.

To say that this entire encounter was a bit strained would be an understatement. I noted that the Master Chief never stood up, and never came close to the customary salute when greeting an officer. There was no handshake. The greeting exchange between him and Chief Creed was short and cordial, though the words could not hide their mutual disdain. Our exchange was short, with the Master Chief suggesting that I come by his office when I had a few minutes for him to brief me on base operations. I thanked him, nodded to his men, who had not said a word, and walked away with Chief Creed. It was eerily like I had been in the presence of the Godfather, and that, if not careful, I might wake up with a horse's head in my bunk, or in this case, a water buffalo's head. In any case, I had a very uneasy feeling. It was evident that there was a mutual dislike between the Master Chief and his men, and Chief Creed and the advisors.

As we exited the mess hall, Chief, as I will refer to him from here on, suggested that I go and change into something more comfortable, like my new issue camouflaged pants and a green t-shirt. I welcomed that suggestion, thinking only that a quick shower would make it better. However, the Chief advised me that there would be a briefing within the hour in the command bunker with the advisors and the Dai uy, his officers and VN boat captains. I was excited about the briefing, and the opportunity to begin to understand more about RID 40's mission and the relationship between our advisors and the VNs.

8

Down to Business

The first thing I learned as the briefing started was that what had been the U.S. Navy's relatively short-lived Operation *Giant Slingshot,* had been renamed Operation Tran Hung Dao II, as more and more U.S. assets were turned over to the Vietnamese. The VN Navy, including RID 40, had big shoes to fill. In one year the U.S. Navy's *Sealords* had become one of the most successful naval campaigns in history. Of course, it was up to those of us in the Naval Advisory Group to make sure those big shoes fit comfortably.

As I studied the large map in the command bunker and began to follow the briefing, I realized that our location and the responsibilities of RID 40 were exactly the same as the U.S. role under *Giant Slingshot,* regardless of whether the boats were U.S. or VN. The operating area was still north and south of Go Dau Ha on the Vam Co Dong River, running along the Northern boundary of the Parrot's Beak. The other ATSBs on the Vam Co Dong and Vam Co Tay rivers were also operational as Vietnamese bases. And the two rivers still looked like a giant slingshot.

The objective was also the same: interdict the flow of VC supplies coming down the Ho Chi Minh Trail and through the Parrot's Beak in Cambodia, across the two rivers, into the Saigon area. Two distinct tactics were used. At night, all civilian boat traffic was ordered off the rivers, and all civilians were ordered to stay within their villages and small cities. That left everything outside of those refuges as designated "free fire zones," meaning that anything moving through those areas at night was considered hostile and should be stopped; there was no need to request permission to take such targets under fire. Since there were a limited number of boats available, there was a cat and mouse game played out every night. The boats of RID 40 would be sent into ambush positions each night along the river's banks, preferably where smaller but navigable canals ran into the river from the West, since most if not all VC supplies were brought through the area by water. Five to seven of the boats would go out each night and turn into position on the West bank at thousand-yard intervals. Each boat had one U.S. advisor aboard. The transits would be made at dusk, while the boats could maintain visual contact right up to the moment they turned into position. The crews would take a few minutes to set out a semi-circle of directional anti-personnel mines, called claymores, and then take turns standing watch all night. All boats could communicate with each other and with the command center. The advisors had their own radios and could communicate with each other and the Senior Advisor or Assistant in the command center. At first light, the column of boats would transit back to the base.

The second tactic was to have the boats that were not out on the previous night's ambush patrol the river north and south of the base during daylight hours in search of contraband. They would observe the civilian boat traffic, and randomly stop any suspicious boat and conduct a search. Meanwhile, the boats back at the base had maintenance as required, under the watchful eyes of a U.S. advisor.

My first night on radio watch in the command center was uneventful. Since we could catnap with one ear on the radio throughout the night, I was sufficiently rested the next morning to request tours of some of the boats with their assigned advisors, while I looked forward to meeting my boss later in the day. One more day marked off of my short-timer's calendar and 361 to go!

I went over most of the boats at the base with the advisors all morning, as much to get to know them, as to see the boats. By midday I was ready for a shower and lunch. I went back to my quarters, tried my hand at casual communication with a couple of the young VN officers with some limited success, and then went to experience a cold water shower. Following that, I got into some dry clothes and went to grab a bite to eat in the mess hall. I sat with a couple of my advisors, and couldn't help but notice the Godfather again holding court in the same location. I caught his eye and gave a quick wave, but got no response. I mentioned something briefly to the advisors, and one of them asked if Chief Creed had told me about the "steaks for contraband" racket. He hadn't, but I made a mental note to ask him: it would have to wait; it was time to meet my boss.

I hung out with some of the advisors in the front room of their hooch while I waited. Within the hour a jeep belonging to the base Master Chief arrived, driven by one of his men, with my boss in the passenger seat. I walked out and met him as he stepped out of the jeep. He greeted me cordially and seemed to be in a cheerful mood. He was in his full green tropical uniform, with the baggy, multi-pocketed pants down over jungle boots that still had a shine on the toe, and the bloused top fully buttoned just below the neck. He wore the black beret that signified "brown water" Navy, and I noticed that his LCDR insignia was still embroidered on his collar. In contrast, after one day, I had assumed the casual look, with camouflaged pants, a green t-shirt and a floppy jungle hat. My boss had a soft briefcase and a small handbag for his personal belongings. Chief Creed had joined the group and my boss asked him how things were going. With nothing of note, I was invited to accompany the boss to the command bunker.

We greeted the Dai uy, who was busy at the large map with his deputy, apparently discussing that night's ambush positions. My boss dropped his things in the back room on his bunk and asked me to join him in the small office. After a little more small talk about my first day on the job, he got right to the point. He had been Senior Advisor for over six months, and was just recently promoted to LCDR. While he was in Saigon at what I learned was a monthly meeting of the Tran Hung Dao Senior Advisors, he had discussed his desire to be transferred to Saigon to a vacant LCDR position on the Naval Advisory Group Staff. Both he and our boss, a full commander in charge of all of the Tran Hung Dao advisors, agreed that the position would be career enhancing for him. Before I could ask, he informed me that I would assume the role of "Acting" Senior Advisor to RID 40 pending a decision on his replacement. We had less than a week to transition. With my sights set on the Senior Advisor role, I could hardly hide my excitement. It occurred to me that either he and his boss didn't know, or had forgotten, that I was a product of special ed. I had a lot to learn in a short time if I hoped to step into the senior position permanently. Otherwise, they would fill the position with a more senior, perhaps fully trained, lieutenant, and I would spend my whole tour as an Assistant, while my peers carried the Senior title. That's not what I wanted the LCDR selection board to look at when my year group was up for promotion; I wanted and needed that Senior Advisor title. Meanwhile, I would glue myself to the hip of my soon to be ex-boss for the few days he had left with us. How hard could this be? The answer came soon enough; that night one of the RID 40 boats was attacked and sunk while sitting in ambush, and I learned a new term, "sapper."

8. *Down to Business*

The briefing was held as normal that late afternoon, and the boats proceeded to their predetermined positions. The crew set out their claymores, and settled into their quiet watch routine. Several hours before dawn, the advisor radio in the command center came to life, and the calm, soft voice said "Remittance, this is Remittance 2, over." (Remittance was the radio call sign for RID 40 advisors; I don't know how call signs were picked, but they were definitely random.) The Senior Advisor in the command center was Remittance, and each advisor riding a boat was designated with the same call sign and a number in order to identify the advisor and the boat in question. Again: "Remittance, this is Remittance 2, over." My boss, startled, clicked his handset and responded. "Remittance 2, this is Remittance; go ahead, over." "Roger, Remittance, be advised, we have just been sunk, over."

By now, the VN boat captain had contacted the VN junior officer on watch, with the same message, only several octaves higher. Immediately, someone was sent to wake up Dai uy Tinh. The command center sounded like the Tower of Babel! Almost immediately things calmed just a bit when it was ascertained by both nationalities that the boat(s) were not under attack, and that the crew of the damaged boat had been accounted for and there were no injuries. The crew was gathered on the riverbank by the bow of the boat which was still above water, and beached on the bank where it was originally positioned. They were directed to remain in that position and to be alert and ready to blow their claymores at the first sign of enemy approach. The other boats were advised to stay in position until first light, but to be vigilant in watching not only the approaches from the rice paddies and tree line along the small canal to their west, but also the water around the boats for possible sappers. Sappers are enemy combatants highly skilled in breaching defenses and wreaking havoc from within. They can crawl stealthily under barbed wire surrounding a base, or swim without scuba gear undetected for great distances underwater to plant explosive devices on water targets.

At first light, I joined Dai uy Tinh's deputy on a Tango boat, with the assigned advisor and Chief Creed, and we headed for the previous night's ambush position. As we rounded a bend in the river and our eyes continued to adjust to the scant light, we saw the bow of an Alpha boat protruding from the water up onto the river bank. Perched on top of the bow, radio in hand, was Remittance 2.

We beached the Tango boat next to the partially sunken boat

and picked up the crew. It did not take long to establish the method of attack. There were no shots fired because apparently there were no other VC in the immediate vicinity. Somehow a single sapper had managed to approach the boat undetected and plant some sort of makeshift explosive device on the boat's hull, beneath the water line, adjacent to the engine compartment. The sapper was long gone when the device

Armored Troop Carriers (ATCs), referred to as Tango boats, were the work horses of the Mobile Riverine Force (MRF). Heavily armored for protection against rocket and small arms attack, and bristling with weapons, it could carry the fight to the NVA/VC in the form of ARVN troops in the well deck. The ATC, like most of the MRF craft, were converted World War II landing craft.

detonated. In all likelihood the sapper approached and departed by small sampan on the small canal, hidden by the tree line, left the sampan out of sight at the mouth of the small canal, and had only a short underwater swim to and from the boat.

As we proceeded back to the base, I couldn't help but wonder how the VC knew our ambush positions well enough in advance to plan and execute the attack. We were all very glad that whatever explosive was used was not strong enough to destroy the boat and injure or kill the crew.

9

The Master Chief and Other Loose Ends

It didn't take long with my boss to figure out that the available staff job in Saigon would have been his choice from the beginning of his tour. Apparently, he had never had any desire to be out and about the Delta; the open position had been a Godsend. It also became evident that he had never gotten comfortable with the laid back atmosphere among the advisors. In any other position of command I was sure, he would have been every bit by the book. He was very pleased with the professional knowledge of the advisors, and their ability to gain the trust of the boat captains and their crews. However, he appeared to be uneasy about them "going native" in order to gain that trust. He believed deeply in a strict definitive advisor–VN relationship. He also was obviously a strict authoritarian when it came to officer–enlisted relationships, and had struggled with the necessity to be closer than normal with the advisors, given the austere environment, wartime situation, and their small-fish-in-a-big-sea situation. He and the advisors had to ensure one face to the VNs, and that single face had to project the absolute necessity of the advisory effort if ACTOV was to succeed.

His final point about the advisors was that he was almost certain that some of them smoked marijuana. Apparently, weed was in great supply for anyone wanting it, and was common among the VN sailors. He told me that he hung out occasionally outside of the advisors' quarters at night, and on several occasions was sure he smelled pot. I asked the obvious question, i.e., had there been any incidents where he thought that pot had affected, or caused any harm; he thought not.

I finally asked him about the base Master Chief, explaining my observations and first impression; I held back the question concerning the steaks. My boss was aware that there was tension between the

Master Chief and the advisors. Only a short time back, the ATSBs, including Go Dau Ha, had been all U.S. Navy facilities, completely run and staffed by U.S. personnel, with the exception of contracted services from the Vietnamese civilian pool. In that situation, the Master Chief could function in a more standard role, with clear division of authority and responsibility. Now, two things irritated him immensely.

First, the evolving shared responsibility with the Vietnamese; it was clear to me already that the Master Chief disliked the Vietnamese and felt degraded to have to provide for their welfare. The thought of eventually having to turn the base, his base, over to the VNs hung over him. Second, he had a deep disdain for the advisors; they had no respect for him and he hated their laid back, seemingly undisciplined lifestyle. I got the feeling that my boss liked him. I hesitated, but finally asked about steaks and booze. All my boss said was that the advisors claimed the Master Chief was taking the best meats, steaks in particular, and trading them to Army units operating out of Cu Chi for liquor and weapons, especially enemy weapons, all for the benefit of him and his men. According to my boss, it was all unsubstantiated and not his business; end of discussion.

The next few days went by quickly; I went out on one night ambush, and that went off without a hitch, largely because there was no enemy contact. Otherwise I stayed glued to the hip of my boss and absorbed as much as I could from him. His curious, perhaps strained, relationship with his advisors was never more evident than the day he left. There was no gathering of advisors or VN officers, and no speeches. On his last day he simply made the rounds and said individual good-byes and good-lucks. I did notice that he did not stop in to say anything to the Base Master Chief. Then he was gone; I looked down at my hands, and sure enough, he had left me holding the bag.

One of the loose ends he left me was the preparation and submission of what he called an "End of Tour Award" for one of the advisors who had completed his tour and headed home a couple of days before my arrival. I had written a few award recommendations, but was not sure what an "end of tour award" entailed. So I sought the advice of Chief Creed. He told me that all Navy personnel completing an in-country tour received an award, either the Navy Achievement Medal, Navy Commendation Medal, or Bronze Star. There was an extremely blurry line between the criteria for those awards, especially in a combat zone. However, the criteria for the Achievement Medal, the lowest in the hierarchy of these three awards, clearly stated that the performance recognized "shall be of such merit as to warrant more recognition than is possible by a fitness report or performance evaluation, but which is not significant enough to justify a Navy Commendation Medal or higher."

Since I had never met the subject of the proposed award, I asked the Chief for his recommendation. He left no doubt that if it was up to him, there would be no award. The subject was apparently disgruntled, never wanted to serve in Vietnam, only grudgingly did his duties, and couldn't wait to leave. Naturally I informed Saigon that there would be no award recommendation. Imagine my surprise when I was told that at a minimum I must recommend an Achievement Medal. My concern was that this practice dramatically and negatively impacted the very foundation of the award system. Awarding the Achievement Medal to undeserving sub-par performers only meant that deserving individuals were elevated to the Navy Commendation Medal, and those truly deserving that award instead received the Bronze Star. Thus the esteem associated with the Bronze Star was seriously degraded. Besides, any service member who set foot in Vietnam, and whose breath fogged a mirror, already automatically received a "Vietnamese Service Medal" from the U.S. government, and a "Vietnam Campaign Medal" from the South Vietnamese government. I declined to submit any additional award.

So there I was, not yet a shot fired, neck deep in my first battle, and it was all "friendly fire"! My revolution quickly spread, and soon the phrase and the practice of "end of tour awards" disappeared. The episode was quickly forgotten as we focused on the war in the delta of South Vietnam, but like so many things in life, what goes around, comes around.

10

Organization and Ground Rules

I asked Chief Creed to get the advisors together around the table in their quarters about an hour before dinner. I had several topics I wanted to cover, and I was sure, now that my predecessor was gone, they had their own talking points to cover. I made no notes; I knew exactly what I needed to get across. I already was comfortable with the group, and my first assessment was that they were all dedicated and skilled, even though I knew that in their hearts they wanted to be operating the boats themselves. I knew exactly what they felt; it was hard to put your life in the hands of inexperienced replacements. So I decided to make that the first subject of discussion.

It was a great meeting! I explained that I was acting in the role of Senior Advisor, would be working to secure the title permanently, and certainly counted on their support to make that happen. Of course my success and their success went hand-in-hand. I didn't know how long we would operate with the current situation, but as of that meeting I made Chief Creed my acting assistant. I assured them I had been quick to learn in my previous afloat Division Officer position that, while I was certainly in command organizationally, I was also a student depending on them to be my teachers in all things associated with their profession. Besides the establishment of a chain of command, I discussed several other topics needing their full understanding and support. Those topics were: the advisory role, marijuana use, alcohol consumption, and the relationship with the Base Master Chief.

The most important thing for them to keep in mind as advisors was that they were no longer operationally combatants; the conduct of the war was now the responsibility of the Vietnamese. We would not be conducting any offensive operations against the VC/NVA; we were armed for self-defense only. This was hardest on the men with previous tours in-country with U.S. operating units. It would not be long before Chief Creed and I put that advisor/operator distinction to a test.

The pot discussion was a one-way conversation; I told them how it would be, and that I expected their cooperation. Basically, I knew that pot was readily available anywhere in Vietnam. Hell, it could be purchased cheaply pre-rolled in cigarette packs. I proposed a deal: I would not (could not) give them permission to smoke pot at any time, period. On the other hand, I knew that some of them would smoke it on occasion. Given that situation, I gave them my word that catching them smoking would not be one of my major objectives; I would not be lurking at all hours to catch anyone smoking pot, nor would I be conducting random searches of their belongings. Certainly we had no ability to use blood or urine tests to capture the guilty. I frankly had too many other things on my plate. In return, I asked them to pledge to me that they would *never* smoke any pot while working on the boats, or going on daytime search or evening ambush. After that meeting, I don't know if they all smoked, or if none of them smoked, but I never had an instance in which I suspected that pot use had affected their performance or contributed to any operational errors.

Alcohol use was another issue entirely. Strict interpretation of military justice told us that drinking on duty was strictly forbidden and was a court-martial offense. The rule was especially clear and important while operating on a Navy vessel. However, the situation in Go Dau Ha was different. Granted, I could have just said there will be no drinking. (Hint: never make a rule that is unenforceable.) Every serviceman in Vietnam had what was called a "ration card" specifically to limit the amount of liquor and cigarettes that anyone could buy on a monthly basis. The primary concerns were personal abuse and selling the merchandise on the black market. That seemed hardly a concern for the advisors of RID 40, since their opportunities to buy liquor were extremely limited. Only on the rare occasion they may have to go into Saigon, 50 miles away (but might as well have been 500), or when going on R&R. (Rest and Relaxation; each service member got one week of R&R out of Vietnam in some exotic location of their choice during their one year tour.) The question then became what to do with their liquor at the base in Go Dau Ha. The waters were further muddied by the fact that apparently the Base Master Chief considered this a U.S. Navy Base, where he established standard working hours for his men and watch-standing assignments after those hours. Therefore, if it was after working hours, his men not assigned a watch station were authorized to consume alcohol, with the only stipulation that they never got intoxicated. Most evenings there was a poker game, with alcohol, going on in the Master Chief's quarters.

Again, given the situation, I established my guidelines. Each man could keep his drink of choice locked in his locker. No alcohol was to be consumed during daily working hours, or on the day that the advisor was scheduled for night ambush. As long as those rules were followed, I even tolerated a couple of advisors being regulars at the Master Chief's poker games. As it turned out, the alcohol situation became a whole lot easier, and more fun, after the base was turned over to VN control, and the Godfather and his men were gone. More on that to come.

I opened my last topic wide by asking about the advisors' relationship with the Base Master Chief. Actually as it turned out, while the Master Chief and his men seemed to hold the advisors in disdain, the advisors seemed to have no issues with the Master Chief and his men, at least as far as their responsibility for base operations. As long as their quarters were cleaned by the VN-contracted service folks, and there was food in the mess hall and a movie at night, life seemed pretty good. So, I threw the elephant into the center of the room: What's all this shit about trading steaks for booze and weapons? It turns out that the explanation was simple, though very disturbing, and most certainly illegal. Understand that the U.S. Navy and now the U.S. advisors in the field, while supported by the U.S. Navy, ate *extremely* well. More than anything else, steaks of very high quality were in abundance. Why not, they are the favorite of most hungry men! The accusation, somewhat surprisingly reluctantly delivered, was that the Master Chief would regularly take the best steaks from base cold storage and trade them to any unit from any service anywhere near Go Dau Ha, be they Army, Marine, or other Navy, passing through. In return the Master Chief would take the buyers' ready supply of liquor or war souvenirs, like VC or NVA weapons or other contraband. Rumor had it that the Master Chief had in his possession a Russian made AK-47 rifle, the most prized souvenir of all to any serviceman in Vietnam. In addition, he was suspected of selling the items to the highest bidder. Wow! Is that all? I took the matter under advisement.

I decided shortly thereafter to simply confront the Master Chief directly about the rumors. However, before I could approach him, I stumbled right onto a trade transaction in process. Within a day or so of our meeting, I was walking down to the boats, and noticed a small army truck parked by the mess hall. I recognized two of the Master Chief's men, but not the two U.S. Army men. Sure enough, they were loading boxes from the mess hall into the truck. To say they were taken aback when I walked up to them directly would be an understatement. The confrontation itself was fairly uneventful but the aftereffect was not. The boxes were clearly marked as frozen steaks, making my questions and direction simple. I asked if we regularly supplied the Army units in the area with food, knowing the answer would be "no." I asked nothing about the details of the transaction, but told them I would much prefer that those steaks be served to our folks, and that the two gentlemen were very welcome to stop in for a meal the next time they had business at our base. I asked that the steaks be returned, and wished all four participants a good afternoon. Word spread like wildfire! I returned from my business down at the boats and asked Chief Creed if he would like to join me for a bite in the mess hall. If I recall correctly, he said something like, "Maybe we can have a good steak for a change!"

I wasn't surprised that the Godfather's court was in session, and I could guess the subject. I only hoped that retribution was not consistent with the Godfather scenario. In a few minutes their session broke up, and the monster of a man sauntered my way, with a sardonic sneer on his face. "Lieutenant, it seems that we have some business to attend to." I asked him to join us, knowing that he really wanted me to follow him to his place. I told him that I wanted Chief Creed to listen in, which let him know immediately that I was not alone in this, and that in all likelihood his little side business was over. I could read all of that in his immediate change in demeanor.

I won't belabor the point; the discussion was one way, I let him know how this would play out. If he wanted a fight, I would call for an immediate investigation, which would cause tremendous disarray for the entire base. Neither of us wanted that, especially given the likely outcome for him. I told him that with the exception of the transaction I had personally witnessed earlier that day, the rest of the evidence, although apparently extensive, was all hearsay, and that I had no desire to go into Perry Mason mode at the expense of my already overwhelming responsibilities. So, with Chief Creed as my witness, I told him that for the remainder of his stay at Go Dau Ha, any and all of his side business was to cease. In return, no allegations of misconduct would be brought, and he could go home with reputation untarnished and most probably a Navy Commendation Medal for his service. Since he did not work for me, I would not be responsible for any award recommendation. Keeping in mind our location and the abundance of weapons around, not only did I rely on Chief Creed's participation in the discussion as a life insurance policy, but I also put it right out on the table, seemingly in jest. I told the Master Chief that I had documented a summary of the accusations and a potential witness list that would find its way to the authorities in the event of my demise! And then I laughed and slapped Chief Creed on the back, leaving just the right seed of doubt in the Master Chief's mind.

The base turnover to the Vietnamese took place within a month or so after that encounter, and in the interim there was a cool, standoffish professionalism between me and the Master Chief. Everyone regularly ate steak, and no water buffalo head showed up in my bunk!

11

Spend Half a Tour in Go Dau Ha and Whaddya Get?

As my first month slipped into the history books, I was feeling fairly comfortable with the little things, i.e., the RID 40 mission, the daily routine, the advisors' relationship with their counterparts, and the departure of the Base Master Chief without incident.

Go Dau Ha reminded me of one of those small Texas towns along old Route 66 which grew where they did out of necessity. To call it a city in 1970 was a stretch; perhaps a large village, a hamlet, or a small town, but not a city by any means. Go Dau Ha was also not a liberty port for my men, nor had it been for the U.S. Navy men serving here before Vietnamization. There was nothing there that catered to Americans. The city survived on net fishing and small commercial businesses that provided services or sustenance to each other, and the throngs passing through, heading to and from either Saigon, Tay Ninh or Phnom Penn, Cambodia. The good news was that Go Dau Ha did not seem to be a haven for the Viet Cong, nor a place from which they would overtly strike at the small Navy base just over the bridge to the west. The city of Tay Ninh was about 18 miles north of Go Dau Ha, and was the capitol city of the province. It was a bustling city with lots to offer tourists in better/safer times.

In the months I spent at the Go Dau Ha base I ventured into the city twice, both times accompanied by Dai uy Tinh, and both times were most enjoyable. Though I will tell you that I was on edge at all times just considering the location; I conjured up numerous ways that I could be had by the bad guys; if they wanted me, those were my most vulnerable times. My first visit was a very pleasant surprise at the invitation of the

Dai uy. We were chatting one day in the mess hall, and he asked if I had ever eaten Vietnamese food; I had not. He said that at the first opportunity we would remedy that. Several days later, he found me in the command bunker around noon, and said "let's go to lunch!" Amazingly, my first thought was "what do I wear?" I was already used to the stand down uniform of the day, i.e., camouflaged pants, a green t-shirt, and boots or flip flops; certainly not appropriate for off base dining. So for the first time since my arrival, except for a Saigon run, I donned my green fatigue pants, jungle boots, green t-shirt and newly added black beret. Nothing on my uniform identified me as an officer.

Outside we hopped into his waiting jeep, and with a slightly elevated heart rate, I was on the way for my introduction to VN food. I did not remember such trepidation when first introduced to authentic Japanese food in Tokyo, or authentic Chinese food in Hong Kong! I did actually chuckle when I remembered being asked by the CO of my ship, heading into Hong Kong harbor, what they called Chinese food in China? I couldn't imagine. He had laughed and said, "Food!" I supposed that, to the Vietnamese, what the Dai uy and I were after was also just "food."

The city was a beehive of activity, with civilian, commercial, and military vehicles of all sizes, trying to make their way through a sea of pedestrians. I could have reached out and touched the crowd, but worse, I thought, they could touch me. Dai uy suddenly pulled over onto what I thought was a pedestrian way, especially because of the short exchanges between him and several members of the foot traffic. We were only a few steps from his objective, a small cafe with a counter and several small tables. Without consulting me, Dai uy walked up and engaged the proprietor in a discussion I assumed was about me and my first taste of Vietnamese food. The proprietor seemed very pleased.

My first lesson came with a cup of VN coffee, and I was hooked! Outside of the major cities, many of the small villages had no electricity and therefore no refrigeration. As a result, for years they ground coffee beans and brewed a remarkably dark roast coffee. Milk and sugar were replaced with condensed milk which requires no refrigeration. It was amazing; the combination was delicious. The proprietor/waiter then came to the table with what looked like small spring rolls, a small leafy lettuce, and very small sliced tomatoes. My attention was drawn to a small bowl of innocuous looking liquid, brownish red in color. I followed the Dai uy's lead; he picked up a small spring roll, a slice of tomato and rolled it in a leaf of the lettuce. And then, he dipped it into the liquid and devoured it in two bites. "Now you," he said with a smile, as the proprietor looked on amused.

Uncertain, I wondered what kind of meat might be in the spring roll, but did not want to insult my host. I first picked up the bowl to smell it. "No! No! Don't smell first!" cried the Dai Uy, "if you do, then you never try it!," he laughed. So I boldly plunged my wrapped delicacy into the bowl, lifted it to my mouth, and bit off about half. It changed my culinary life! I had just been introduced to Nuoc Mam—Vietnamese fish sauce. I won't belabor the point, but I will tell you that VN Nuoc Mam at that instant became, and still is to this day, my favorite dining condiment. It is also a favorite of my wife and kids! I will leave you with this warning: do not smell or eat pure Nuoc Mam straight out of the bottle; it needs some doctoring as only a true Vietnamese can show you. Second, *never* ask or research how the best Nuoc Mam is made.

We finished with something else I could not identify that was equally delicious, and I realized that I was truly relaxed for the first time since my flight lifted off en route to Vietnam. I even tried a deep fried grasshopper with a peanut where the belly used to be. All in all, it was one of my best days in Vietnam.

My second trip into the city of Go Dau Ha was actually arranged by what I call the "Hearts and Minds" office of COMNAVFORV. It had arranged a nice photo op one afternoon at a local elementary school. Dai uy Tinh and I joined the principal in handing out diplomas. Again, I experienced rare joy and relaxation as child after child smiled, laughed and giggled their way across a small makeshift stage and grasped their paper in one hand and my hand in the other. I experienced a few moments of what I think actually won some hearts and minds. It is such a shame that those moments could not have become the norm.

There was one other place outside of the base that became a favorite of mine. A few miles north of the base by water was a functioning rubber plantation, which I gathered had been French owned before their demise, and had somehow remained viable after the French departed. There was apparently an unwritten peace among the owners, the South Vietnamese military, U.S. forces, and the VC. After my first introduction by Dai uy Tinh to the operations manager or owner (I was never sure which), I had an open invitation to stop in any time for refreshments and light snacks. I have included pictures from my first visit. Curious, but the number two man, perhaps the foreman, was always in black pajamas,

The author handing out graduation certificates at a local elementary school graduation in Go Dau Ha.

the uniform of choice for the VC. I gathered it was because he could go either way if things got bad. I am convinced also that after dark, when the good guys were gone, the plant manufactured the classic, heavy duty rubber sandals favored by the VC; I never asked.

I spent a lot of time with my counterpart, Dai uy Tinh. Thank the good Lord that his English was good enough for us to communicate. He too was pleased with the working relationships between our men on the boats. I noted that everything we discussed about operations was tactical, but as long as we remained in Go Dau Ha, with the exception of our brief support to a May incursion into Cambodia, we did nothing strategic. We both understood that we were a small, but important piece of a

The author (seated center) enjoys a meal as a guest of the management team of the rubber plantation just north of Go Dau Ha on the Vam Co Dong River.

much larger puzzle, but we stayed focused on our role. The boats set up ambush positions every night in random locations and performed surveillance, and search and seizure during the day. I was still in learning mode, so it did not bother me yet that as a senior "advisor" I had offered no advice. I began to think more about why the night ambush positions had yet to encounter any crossings. Even though in my hurried prep for this assignment I had received no detailed briefings on enemy activity levels in our area of responsibility on this stretch of the river, in general I knew that American units operating out of the *Giant Slingshot* bases had certainly had their share of contact, especially just to our south. I decided to dig deeper into the differences between our situation, tactics, etc., and those of the previous American units operating in this area.

I knew very little about what was happening outside of Go Dau Ha since my arrival in-country. Keep in mind that we had no social media with today's instant news, and as advisors we did not even receive news provided to regular U.S. forces in-country. For a short time we did have

The author jokes with the chief of security at the rubber plantation about the latter's being able to "go either way" in his black pajamas," the favored uniform of the Viet Cong insurgents.

a junior Naval intelligence officer working out of the base, but most of his intelligence was more Army/ARVN centered, and rarely, if ever, had actionable specifics affecting RID 40. For instance, in late April '70, President Nixon had authorized the last combined U.S./VN river operation—an incursion into Cambodia to disrupt VC/NVA base areas in order to buy time for the U.S. withdrawal. I was unaware of the initial surge, a combined armada of more than 100 river craft proceeding up the Mekong River, well south of our operational area, toward Phnom Penh, Cambodia. Shortly thereafter, in mid–May '70, with little notice, several of our RID 40 boats joined the VN boats just to our north on the Vam Co Dong at Tay Ninh.[1] Those boats supported the ARVN push into Cambodia as part of the overall Nixon-approved operation. Although the ARVN troops reached the Ho Chi Minh Trail, the boats of RID 40 stopped well short of that, and in fact saw no actual enemy contact, but only the aftermath of the ARVN push. Within a week the boats returned to Go Dau Ha, and rejoined the non-productive interdiction effort.

There was, however, one thing that came out of RID 40's participation in the Cambodian incursion that had a dramatic and lasting effect on my Vietnam tour of duty; that was the discovery and rescue of "Rat." It is a story that deserves telling here, just as it happened then ... at the most unexpected of times. To the VNs, Rat was a potential meal—probably tough by American standards, but, with a little "Nuoc mam" fish sauce, a welcome change from their daily rice ration. To me and my other American advisors Rat was a symbol of survival in an alien environment; he really shouldn't be living here, but then again, neither should we.

Rat's first American encounter was with BM1 Mountain; as it turned out, that was the key moment for Rat in ensuring that there was a rest of his life. Petty Officer Mountain, "Tiny" to his friends, was advisor on one of our TANGO boats proceeding into Cambodian, northwest of Tay Ninh, in support of the Cambodian Incursion. Because of very recent NVA/VC hostilities along this stretch of river, Tiny, the other advisors, and the VN sailors on all the boats were in a high state of tension, if not readiness. Remnants of recent firefights scattered the banks—smoldering hooches, blackened trees, abandoned bunkers. Anxiety was high; trigger fingers were itchy.

The average VN sailor rarely saw combat action much beyond the "whoosh—bang" of a B40 rocket attack, followed by his own devastation of plant life anywhere in the vicinity. The chance to don soldiering gear and mop up after the ARVN was too much to resist. The Tangos and Alphas were beached at a smoldering village, and several VNs cautiously proceeded away from the boats. At that point, at least in the mind of one young sailor, he was John Wayne or Audie Murphy in one of those American movies we showed occasionally at the fire support base. In a stealthy crouch he arrived at the first grass "hooch" still standing. Deftly laying his M-16 at his feet, he grasped a Frag grenade in his right hand and the pin in his left (after failing to release the pin with his teeth). In one swift motion he pulled the pin, pivoted, rolled the grenade inside the hooch, and flattened his back against the outside grass wall. It was technically perfect, save for the construction material of his objective. With the explosion, smoke and grass went in every direction, the VN in only one—straight for the boats! Rolling, screaming, grabbing his back, and yelling Vietnamese obscenities, he retreated. By now his shipmates had passed their initial shock, and were overcome by the black humor of it all. The young VN would live to fight again, but would surely alter his style.

Shortly thereafter, Tiny, having recovered from his own fit of laughter, strolled up and around a bunker. Peering inside he announced, without fear or excitement, "Hey, there's something alive in here!" He crouched for a moment, and then stood. Tiny stood about 6 foot 6 and weighed in excess of 280 lbs.; fully bearded, he was an awesome yet gentle presence. Lost to the casual observer in Tiny's cupped hands was a small black living thing—recognizable only upon close examination as a puppy. Now I don't mean a roly-poly, under the Christmas tree, Norman Rockwell puppy; I mean a scrawny, skin and bones, concentration camp emaciated, Vietnamese/Cambodian, "there ain't even any rice to eat" puppy. The black skin was

The author holds the tiny dog "Rat" just a few days after his rescue from an enemy bunker just across the border in Cambodia. "Rat" became the protected mascot of the U.S. RID 40 advisors.

as dry and thin as paper, and torn in places; one back leg was broken. Here was a living creature more miserable than we were!

The thought of keeping a pet dog—a pet of any kind—in this environment was just absurd enough to be tempting to us. So, to the dismay of Dai uy Tinh and his men, we dubbed Tiny's find "Rat," for obvious reasons, and declared him our official mascot. While I was not sure if the concept was understood by the Dai uy, I urged him to explain to his men that Rat was now a protected species; he was not to be fattened up as a future delicacy, and woe be unto any of his men who threatened Rat in any way.

Tiny splinted Rat's broken leg and we used our first aid kit to treat his torn skin. I secretly wondered if he had any chance to survive—and if so, for what? Rat spent the remainder of that river excursion resting as comfortably as possible in the chest pocket of Tiny's fatigues. Tiny nurtured him on water and soda sucked from his fingers, and a little rice and chocolate candy as he gained strength (human babies don't own the market on chocolate-stimulated diarrhea). Back at the base at Go Dau Ha, we expanded his diet as soon as possible to include steak and beer ... the point being that the toughest dogs we remembered back home survived on handouts from kids or overturned garbage cans.

Amazingly, Rat quickly flourished and as he grew, the pitch black color seemed to split, and he soon resembled a dog in zebra's clothing! He enjoyed the run of the base, and the Vietnamese honored our "hands off" request. Rat most enjoyed spending afternoons under the poker table in the advisors' hooch, or, when the heat was unbearable, sleeping on my cot in the rear of the air conditioned command bunker. Tiny quickly lost interest and Rat's upbringing naturally fell to me and Chief Creed—not because of our seniority, but because we were both softies whose childhoods had included canine companionship.

The Cambodian incursion was initially considered a success; early estimates were that NVA planning and logistics were set back anywhere from six to 12 months, depending on the information source. Historians would later debate those assessments, and argue that within a month or two the NVA and VC had substantially resupplied what was lost. Those early assessments really didn't matter, since the U.S. press called the incursion an "invasion" and accused Nixon of "widening of the war" while pledging withdrawal. The Kent State riots and shooting deaths in May added fuel to the growing fires of dissatisfaction. To put things into perspective, I was unaware of the incursion and RID 40's planned

The author shows off a happy, healthy "Rat" after his care and feeding by the U.S. RID 40 advisors.

participation until preparations were underway to provision our participating boats. I would somehow have to broaden the scope of my own intelligence about future plans outside of the norm.

In the interim, beyond just taking care of the needs of my advisors, and working with the Chief on their boat assignments, I was not really in any position to give advice or add value to the overall operation. I satisfied myself that the Chief and our advisors, given their experience, were more than adequately filling that role. Dai uy Tinh seemed satisfied that when he needed anything, I was able to provide it.

During my second month I was informed that I had been named Senior Advisor, and that a new assistant was "in the pipeline," which

I assumed was the regular, full-length training for advisor duty. I also assumed that all Navy officers assigned to combat positions were volunteers. Think again on both counts. Near the end of May, the new Assistant Senior Advisor, a Lieutenant j.g., arrived in Go Dau Ha, and he was not a happy camper; nor was he a volunteer. He had absolutely no desire to ever serve in Vietnam, and when he received his orders, had made it clear that if he must serve in Vietnam, he wanted a staff assignment. He wanted nothing to do with a combat role, and the ride from Saigon to Go Dau Ha had solidified that position. He too had been given an abbreviated training program because of the immediate requirement. Most of all he did not like the Vietnamese people. He sank even further into his morass when he learned he was in a community berthing situation with the VN officers.

My only chance to salvage the young officer was to ignore his discontent and have him shadow Chief Creed's every move. I hoped that by observing the Chief and me, he would absorb our dedication, motivation and desire to create something sustainable out of our situation. I would not let him or the Chief see my own gnawing doubts. I thought it would be a while, though, before my assistant became a contributing member of the team, if ever. The fact that someone in the advisory personnel assignment business would fill my Assistant Senior Advisor position—a position critical to the success of the ACTOV program—with a candidate so unwilling to participate says much about either the Navy's commitment to ACTOV or, far more likely, the growing unavailability of qualified personnel willing to volunteer to be sent into what they now viewed as a losing game. Maybe, just maybe, the more talented and qualified for the advisory assignments were also the ones in touch enough with the politics of it all to avoid it at all costs? What does that say about me? Years later, and I still seem to always buy high and sell low.

12

Another Day Older and Deeper in Debt

The Viet Cong and North Vietnam regulars had recovered from their decimation during the TET offensive, so why weren't we making any contact? I would hold that concern for a while and just observe. Meanwhile, as the tedious schedule of daytime patrols and night ambushes proceeded without incident; the sinking of our boat became history and tensions relaxed. At the lowest working level, on the boats, my advisors, each with their own individual talent, never let up in their effort to change a culture at its roots. At that level, and still at mine, neither the VN sailor nor the advisor realized that the end game had already been decided. By all appearances, the U.S. was still committed to the two–Vietnam outcome, and perhaps at some levels still believed it possible. However, remember that by 1969 the North firmly believed that "victory was in the offing."

In hindsight (a term used far too frequently in assessing the Vietnam conflict), senior "leadership" from either the U.S. or South Vietnam must have seen that the plans for Vietnamization (and ACTOV) barely allowed enough time to accomplish operational turnover, but were far too short, and without the necessary assets, to sustain the all important repair, maintenance, and replacement requirements for a self-sufficient South Vietnamese military.

Actually, there was at least one small subset of folks somewhere down in the maintenance support organization of the Navy who realized that the mechanical performance life of the river assault craft would be very short after turnover if the South Vietnamese Navy could not be convinced to adopt the U.S. Navy's philosophy of planned maintenance. In 1963, the U.S. Navy introduced its Planned Maintenance System (PMS), covering maintenance requirements, standard procedures, and common practices, which not only ensured continued readiness of its ships, but also provided more accurate manpower projections. In simpler terms, regular equipment maintenance over time not only ensured availability of equipment when required, but also extended the life of the equipment. The concept has been so successful that it is still in use in the U.S. Navy today. Proof of the system's value was found in the fact that, except for the Alpha boat, the heavy assault craft of the U.S. Navy's Mobile Riverine Force were converted landing craft from World War II. The fact that those boats continued to operate successfully in the severe environment of the South Vietnam Delta was attributed to the performance of regular systematic maintenance on the equipment. It must be realized that the development, implementation, and evolution of the PMS was accomplished over many years, and it was a complete change of organizational mindset for the Navy.

Unfortunately, at the time of the turnover of our riverine assets, there was no such mindset in the Vietnamese culture, and certainly not in their fledgling Navy. On the contrary, in the new South Vietnamese Navy, if a piece of equipment was operating, it was considered Number One (#1), and should not be touched, except to push the start button or pull the trigger. When the equipment suffered a failure it was deemed Number 10 (#10), and should be replaced. That concept was expensive enough when applied to small, inexpensive spare parts. However, the VNs applied it essentially to all operating equipment.

Shortly after my arrival, I learned that the U.S. Navy was in the process of translating all PMS material relevant to our heavy assault craft, and as far as I knew, to all other Naval assets being turned over. While I cannot begin to estimate how many man-hours were expended on that process and at what expense, it had to be significant. One of many problems the translators faced was that there were multiple technical terms in the U.S. manuals that had no corresponding word in the Vietnamese language. In those cases, the English word was left in place. In every one of those situations it was left to the advisor to explain. After several months of anticipation and delays, at last the day came for introduction of the Planned Maintenance System to the VN sailors of RID 40. Dai uy Tinh and his officers had been somewhat indoctrinated, and their participation in the implementation was paramount. In order not to drag out this ugly story, I will just tell you that it did not go well. The VN sailors for the most part were not interested in this new philosophy, and strangely showed less understanding of the English language than usual whenever being pushed to use the materials. My advisors were very frustrated, and in many cases ended up doing the maintenance themselves. They, of course, could not read the translated material, and had no way of checking its accuracy.

In short order, much of the documentation began to disappear, first from the individual boats, and finally by the boxful from locked storage. If RID 40 had remained in Go Dau Ha, I am certain that there would have been a very unpleasant audit in our future. Both Dai uy Tinh and I would most likely have taken the fall. As it turned out, we were soon to be packing up and moving the entire RID to the South. Rumor had it that our destination was the U Minh Forest, long a stronghold of the Viet Cong. The fact that there would be no home base for quite a while, left any hope of serious maintenance to a planned stop at the repair facility in Dong Tam, en route to points south. In Vietnamese terms, the Planned Maintenance System itself was "Number 10."

Meanwhile there was no lack of random drama and comedy on a daily basis in our lives. It just seemed to come from all sides when least expected. At the time of each, I rarely thought about the individual effect on our operational success or failure, if any. It is almost surreal now to look back and see how bizarre the totality of events sounds when played back. Perhaps we allowed daily events to prevent us from dealing with the "elephant in the room," the withdrawal of America from the conflict. During the next several months in Go Dau Ha, the basic operational schedule proceeded unencumbered., and through it all I continued to wonder why we were not interdicting anyone. I was more and more convinced that after each daily briefing on where to set the boats in ambush, there were leaks to the VC, faster than the leaks to the press today out of secret Congressional Committee testimony. I expressed these concerns quietly in confidence to Chief Creed. As you will see in a later chapter, the Chief and I tried to rectify this potential security breech.

However, first let me share a little of day to day ACTOV in Go Dau Ha.

In Vietnam there were always things around that could kill you. The most obvious, of course, were the personal weapons of all parties, when aimed at you on purpose. Because there were no front or rear lines drawn, and also because the VC were indistinguishable from the friendly forces and civilians (sometimes one and the same), there was always the chance that you could be a victim of the war at any time.

Besides the direct offensive way to die, there were all sorts of leftovers that could get you. I will share two such examples.

When I had first accompanied my predecessor into the small office in the command bunker, I noticed that what appeared to be a large mortar round was being used as a doorstop. When asked, he said that it had been there when he arrived. The departing U.S. squadron commander told him that it was a communist (Russian or Chinese) 82 millimeter mortar round, apparently a dud from a previous encounter. With that, it was passed from one bunker resident to the next. I have included the requisite warrior photo that we all had taken with the souvenir. Several weeks later, a Navy bomb squad explosives expert came to the base at my request on another issue. While I was briefing him on my request, he kept glancing over at the mortar round–doorstop. When he finally asked about its origin and I told him what I knew, he calmly asked if I could clear everyone out of the bunker please and wait outside. That sounded rather ominous, so I naturally complied.

The next thing I knew, he was gingerly walking the round toward the front gate, while calmly telling all bystanders to give him a wide berth. He proceeded out of the gate and diagonally away from the base on a raised paddy wall. He finally stopped, laid the round on the ground and backed away. He returned to his vehicle and retrieved a small radio-detonated explosive device. He walked back out to the round, attached the device, and returned to where we stood. After yelling "Fire in the Hole," he detonated our souvenir with a blast that would have certainly taken out the command bunker and all inside. I think I soiled myself, if not literally, then surely figuratively!

That was not even the reason for my call to the ordinance disposal folks; there was an equally dangerous situation that had played itself out two days before. By way of background, in an earlier chapter describing the various weapons we fired at the Navy's range during my training, I dwelled on the M-79 grenade launcher. Ever since the fire support base had been in existence at Go Dau Ha, an untold number of folks had stood watch in the small tower or simply enjoyed weapons "training" in small groups. Just like me, the favorite of everyone was the M-79. Hundreds of rounds had been fired out into the abandoned rice paddies north of the base. What nobody thought about was the small percentage of rounds that were duds. As such, they could lay dormant for months, maybe years, waiting for an unsuspecting, curious person to step on it or grab it for a souvenir ... *Boom*!

The author shows off "dud" communist mortar round, later determined by an ordnance expert to be extremely dangerous. It was safely detonated by the expert and witnessed by shocked advisors who had also posed with the shell for macho pictures.

Two days before the expert was called, the Dai uy sent for me to come to the front gate ASAP. He and one of his officers were engaged in animated discussion with an elderly man and his granddaughter, who appeared to be about ten years old. Then I noticed the focus of the excitement. The granddaughter carried an open basket, filled to the top with unexploded M-79 grenades! I knew it probably wasn't wise for her to have them, but I had yet to have the real danger explained, i.e., the volatility of the rounds. Apparently the old man and his granddaughter had been exploring the abandoned paddies, perhaps dreaming of someday bringing them back to life. They had repeatedly come upon these unknown objects and thought they might be of some value to the folks at the base. The Dai uy translated and instructed the young girl to gently place the basket on the ground where she stood at the side of the approach road, and then back away. When the immediate danger had passed, I suggested that the Dai uy give them something of value for their concern. I was thanking God for preventing what could have been a tragedy. The disposal expert detonated those grenades in the same spot he destroyed our souvenir. Twice we had literally "dodged a bullet"!

As opposed to a fragmentation hand grenade or the M-79 grenade, a concussion grenade is exactly that ... its damage is done from the concussion of the explosion; there is no shrapnel. The real value of a concussion grenade is when your target is underwater. In that environment the force of the concussion is magnified many times. Anyone close underwater will be rendered harmless, with burst eardrums, concussion, loss of consciousness, etc. We used concussion grenades like every brown water unit before us in Vietnam, to protect the boats from underwater swimmers/sappers. Our sentry on duty around the boats at night would walk around the floating dock and throw concussion grenades into the water at random times. They were a huge deterrent, and, like any explosive device, dangerous when not used appropriately and carefully.

We got used to hearing the muffled thud of the grenades throughout the evening, but on two separate occasions, the value and the danger associated with the grenades was made evident. On both occasions we heard an explosion by the waterfront that was louder than the normal underwater blast. The first time it happened, we rushed down to the floating dock to find a couple of VN sailors shining flashlights on a body in the water about twenty feet from the dock. They got a small boat and went out to investigate. They dragged the body around the end of the dock and up onto the riverbank. The damage done to this swimmer was far beyond that of a concussion grenade. The sentry swore he had thrown one grenade as usual, but was shocked by the secondary explosion. The body appeared to be that of a young man, probably in his teens. His entire chest was blown open; I had the awful thought that it looked like a real life version of the game of Operation. We didn't hear the full, sad story until the next day, when an investigative team went over to the city and found the truth.

A team of Viet Cong had sneaked into the city under cover of darkness; they must have picked their target family ahead of time. They invaded the family's home and kidnapped every member. They next threatened to kill the entire family unless the teenaged son swam across the river under cover of darkness, and planted a makeshift bomb on the hull of one of RID 40's boats. When he returned the VC would detonate the explosives and leave the family unharmed. Unfortunately for the teen, the makeshift bomb had been made from a handful of unexploded, unstable M-79 grenades. He had them strapped to his chest for the swim, and the concussion grenade had triggered the explosion before he could reach the boats. The rest of the family was left unharmed and the VC had vanished.

A week or two later, we eerily had the same start to another concussion grenade incident. This time when the first men reached the floating dock there was no sign of the sentry. A search was started on the dock and all boats tied to it. After a few minutes there was moaning apparently coming from between the inboard boat and the dock. There was a few feet of space between the dock and the boat created by bumpers hanging on the dock side. Flashlights revealed the guard in the water but struggling. It took several men to grab his clothing and pull him onto the dock; the sight of him was devastating and heartbreaking. His left hand was gone, from the wrist down, and his left thigh was blown open exposing the bone. We had no doctor or corpsman assigned, so he was taken to the nearest VN medical station by helicopter as quickly as possible. His life was saved, but with the loss of his hand and his left leg, which could not be saved. It was later determined that he had been randomly throwing the concussion grenades as directed, but one of them hit the side of a boat and bounced back onto the dock. He panicked and tried to pick it up and throw it again. However, it blew up as he held it next to his left leg while standing up. He survived only because there was no fragmentation.

Over the next couple of days, there was a lot of discussion about concussion grenades. In part of the discussion it came up that the VNs were using many times more of the grenades than the Americans had used. No mystery, said several of my advisors at once. Since the inventory and issue of the grenades was turned over to the VNs, they had started using them to fish! Hell yeah! No more cumbersome nets to haul in. They would take the boat to a known fishing spot, throw in a concussion grenade, and then scoop the stunned fish as they floated to the top. Who needed my advice?

Speaking of advice when you least need it—you've heard it a million times: "We're from the Government (or Front Office) and we're here to help." And you know how that works out. Vietnam was no different. Fortunately, in the Naval Advisory Group, the senior staff in Saigon were normally very good about leaving the guys in the field alone, as long as we were doing our jobs. Besides, all Senior Advisors in the field came together once a month to exchange information. Not only did I like that interface, but I also loved getting into Saigon for a couple of days a month; more on that later. However, on the rare occasion when a Saigon "staffer" decided to audit the war fighters, my job was to run interference.

In most cases inspections or audits, by necessity, focus on the negatives and the ways to "fix" what's not broken. However, I don't mean to hurt feelings, but it was my opinion that, with very few exceptions, auditors/inspectors were ego and power driven, and loved to inflict pain. They came from broken homes, were bullied in school, and wanted to get even! They never retired, but went to work for the IRS. Again, there were exceptions, but I rarely saw one. In Vietnam, when in the field with any combat unit in a hostile, or potentially hostile, environment, the last thing you needed was "help" from an auditor or inspector.

My first experience with this issue came a couple of months into my tour. We received a visit from a new in-country commander from the COMNAVFORV staff in Saigon, purported to be on an administrative visit for orientation purposes. I guess they just wanted him to see the river assault side of the Advisory Group. Let me set the scene and explain the difference in the unit cultures first. The folks stationed in Saigon were barely aware there was a war beyond the city limits. They lived in American maintained hotels converted to accommodate them comfortably; they worked in air conditioned offices and ate in restaurants, not mess halls. They had cocktails, beer or wine before and with dinner, and perhaps a liqueur after. Their laundry was done for them, and they wore casual khaki uniforms; they were clean and well groomed. The war came to them the day after the action in the *Stars and Stripes* newspaper or on Armed Forces Radio.

I have already given you somewhat of a picture of life for advisors. Let me remind you. They lived and worked in the heat—oppressive heat; they ate in a mess hall and slept in bunks in an open plywood and screen building, with no privacy. This was only those lucky enough to have had a base with those accommodations. They took cold showers when the water truck filled the tank, or bathed in rain-filled craters from past B-52 strikes. They cut each other's hair when it became too shaggy. Sometimes they lived on their boat for days or weeks at a time on extended operations. They wore remnants of cut-off uniforms to combat the heat, and they wore bandanas to hold their hair back and to keep the sweat out of their eyes. They always had loud music playing, mostly Creedence Clearwater Revival.

So, I was in the command bunker, in my sandals, cammy pants, green t-shirt, and hair longer than regs, but trimmed with scissors above my ears and across the back of my neck. I was looking at area maps with Dai uy Tinh when one of my guys came in and told me the helo was inbound. I excused myself from the Dai uy and went outside to greet our guest. I knew he was a full commander as soon as he got off the helo, because his clean and pressed working khaki uniform displayed the insignia on the collars. The mirror finish on his shoes was dulled by dust settling from the landing.

He was not smiling when he walked over to me and saluted, obviously expecting me, as the junior of the two of us, to have initiated the salute. I offered my hand instead, and told him that salutes out here make you a prize target. That realization made him shrink a bit. I led the way through the gate and down the hot dusty road toward the water. The sweat was already showing on his khaki shirt. I told him that before I showed him around, I would brief him in the command bunker, the only air conditioned spot on the base. AC was required for all of the electronics, not for our personal comfort. We went into the bunker and, after a quick intro to Dai uy Tinh, we sat in the adjacent office. Our club/bar was a work in process, so I offered the Commander a drink of water.

After just a few minutes of small talk, I determined that he actually didn't consider this an inspection or an audit, but rather a familiarization visit since he was to join the staff in some operations position. With that knowledge, I relaxed, let down my defenses and smiled; he did not. We were his first trip outside of Saigon, and he was obviously not happy to be here. Soon I realized that he would be happy just to stay in the sandbagged, air conditioned bunker, and be briefed from the maps. He showed no interest in getting out and about. Another thing I noticed was his clear look of disapproval of my appearance; he didn't say it outright, but it was there. The proof of that came soon enough.

We had been talking about the organization of the advisors and the RID, the simplicity of the mission, etc. (I even included my concern about our lack of interdiction contact.) At that point, my First Class Engineman knocked and excused himself; he asked if our guest was ready for his look at the boats. At the moment all I could see was the look of disbelief on the Commander's face. In front of him stood one of the brightest, hardest working, dedicated petty officers I had ever met. But the Commander saw only a deeply tanned, shirtless sailor in beat-up jungle boots and cut-off shorts. He was covered in a mixture of sweat, grime, and grease, and displayed a shaggy mop of hair, roughly trimmed out of his eyes, cut over the top his ears, and nearing pony-tail length in the back. The Commander did not respond, so I told my EN to go on back to his boat, and that we may or may not meet him there.

No sooner had he left us, when the Commander shook his head and asked, "Is that man in the United States Navy?" I laughed and said something like "of course he is; who else's Navy would have him?" He did not smile when he muttered something about "disgraceful." Well, I was pissed, but calm. "Come with me, please, Commander." I could see his resolve start to shrink as soon as the heat hit him at the bunker exit. He asked where we were going, and I just asked him to bear with me. We encountered Chief Creed on our way down to the boats, bare chested and sweaty from working on the Ski Boat, with the stub of a cigar in the corner of his mouth. A quick introduction did nothing to mellow the Commander's disdain for our appearance. We hopped on and across an Alpha tied next to the dock, and up onto the rear decking of the Tango tied up outboard. One of the Tango's two Marine 225 HP diesel engines was running, and the deck plating was all off, allowing access to the engines. My EN and his VN counterpart were wedged in close to the idling engine, engaged in hand signaling over the noise. When they saw us, they hopped out and my EN stood there while his sidekick went to tell the Boat Captain to cut the engines. By now my man looked as if he had spent the day getting a motor oil massage in a sauna. But the smile never left his face. He looked at the Commander and asked if he wanted a tour of the boat.

I stopped him there and said to the Commander, "Sir, the temp in the sun today is over 100 degrees. I don't know what it is down there by the engines, but I could guess. One of the engines on this boat is down and the VNs want a new one. My man's job is to convince them that these old engines can be repaired, and that they will last forever if maintained. He is fighting a culture where if something works, it's Number One, so you don't touch it. When it grinds to a halt, it's *Number Ten*, so the Americans will get them a new one. So my EN here was on this boat all night on patrol, and has been here all day trying to fix the engine, while explaining the concept." If he is lucky, he might get an hour to catch a nap and some dinner before getting ready for another night in ambush.

"So," I continued, "I will make you a deal, Sir. If you will join him for the rest of the afternoon down there just observing the engine repair, and then join them on the river tonight in their ambush position, when you get back in the morning, I will personally drive this man the 50 miles to Saigon and stand there in the enlisted quarters while he showers and gets a haircut. I will acquire a new set of fatigues for him and new-issue boots, and drive him back here, just so he can meet the standards of the next newbie from headquarters who comes out to visit for an afternoon. Otherwise, Sir, please don't judge me and my men on our field appearance." My EN could not contain his smile, and he excused himself to get back to work. The Commander said nothing, so I suggested we take a quick walk around the base and return to the comfort of our bunker. As we walked, I pointed out what there was to see, and then we returned to the bunker. His helo was ready, so I walked him out to the gate. He stopped and turned to me, looked me in the eyes and started to salute; he caught himself, and offered his hand; I may have seen the twitch of a smile as he thanked me for a very enlightening afternoon. With that, he got on the helo and was gone. I never heard a word about his trip report. I guess it's a good thing our club wasn't open yet.

One of the most commonly used terms in Naval slang, "cumshaw" means to obtain something you need through other than the normal means, either deviously or ingeniously; for instance, trading something of value to someone in return for something you need. When the Base Master Chief traded steaks that were not his to trade in return for liquor and war souvenirs, that was not cumshaw. However, when Chief Creed found the opportunity to acquire a mini-gun for our base defense tower, Dai uy Tinh and I both approved the trade of a case of steaks; the mini-gun was for the common good. RID 40 advisors broadened the term cumshaw to include the "theft" of something the group decided it needed more than its owner. Petty theft for personal gain was still unacceptable.

Perhaps our biggest and most useful item gained under the stretched definition of cumshaw was a 2½-ton truck, "borrowed" from the Army, without their knowledge, for the duration of the war. We justified this procurement because the Army had more trucks than they needed, and all we had was a jeep assigned to me. The truck was found, keys in the ignition, by Chief Creed and one other advisor, at the huge

Army fire support base at Cu Chi, about halfway between Saigon and Go Dau Ha. We often used the Cu Chi base as an oasis when traveling to and from Saigon. The big truck would greatly enhance our cumshaw capabilities in the future. The funniest thing is, the Army sentries at the gate actually climbed in the back while conducting a search of the truck when our guys drove it out.

As soon as the truck arrived at the base, my guys set to work on a conversion effort. Using grey paint, also obtained through previous cumshaw, they painted the truck haze grey and stenciled "U.S. Navy" on each cab front door. A creative serial number was stenciled under that on both doors, and we were in business!

One of the first large "procurements" using our new truck was a complete pallet of 4 × 8 foot sheets of plywood from Cu Chi. I even convinced the driver of a nearby forklift to load it into our truck. We had decided to convert one of the unused buildings on the base into a bar and club worthy of our advisor status, and the plywood was our first real requirement. The raw plywood became classy wallboard by running a blowtorch slowly over it, and then finishing it with a coat of varnish. We gradually outfitted our club with the fruits of our new cumshaw definition, until it was so realistic you could step out of Vietnam and into a great replica of a redneck bar in rural America. With the addition of acquired bar stools, tables and chairs (hauled in our getaway truck), the bar became the hangout of choice for the advisors, and I used it to host any infrequent visitors. The funniest of all was the first and only visit from my boss, Commander Steve Van Westendorp.

Steve (as I came to know him after Vietnam) was one of the best bosses I ever had. On this occasion I set him up for some fun. His helo circled the base and landed just outside of the gate; I met him as he disembarked in a cloud of dust. As we walked through the gate he asked if he could please get something to drink (meaning water or such). I took that as my cue, and said, "Sure! Let's step right in here to the bar." As we approached the converted building his expression told me he was trying to process what I just said so I hit him with a preemptive, "Don't ask, sir!" As I opened the door and we stepped inside, his eyes had to adjust to the dim lighting. He slowly did a full 360 degree turn before he simply mumbled, "What the...?" What he saw was a scene out of an old movie: my almost rotund electrician in white apron wiped down the bar and asked in a booming voice, "What'll it be, Commanda?" There were four of my advisors in a staged poker game at one of our two large

The author unwinds with sailors of Vietnamese RID 40 in the U.S. advisors' club, which was finished entirely with "cumshaw" material, mostly from the Army base at Cu Chi, west of Saigon.

round tables, plus one hunched over the bar on a recently procured bar stool; and two more playing darts on the other side of the room. The effect was perfect; Steve was stunned speechless! Since we were on duty, he was served a glass of water. I welcomed him; all of the advisors gave a round of applause, and after he said a few kind words, we were ready for his base tour. Heading for the exit, Steve asked in a halting voice if he had imagined seeing a water skier on the river between the base and the city as they circled prior to landing. I answered in a deadpan voice, "Not your imagination, Sir." I explained,"It's not safe to ski north or south of the city." From the moment I took the Commander into our bar, he was putty in my hands. Next I explained the ski boat.

13

The Kenner Ski Boat

There was one more boat in the RID 40 armada that I have yet to describe, mainly because, at first thought, it is not associated with riverine warfare. When the U.S. boats were turned over to the Vietnamese, the package deal included a Kenner Ski Barge; it had an open body, flat bottom, with a fore and aft bench seat running down the middle, a driver's console with steering wheel and throttle and a driver's seat all the way in the rear. It was powered by twin Johnson 40 HP motors. However, the main distinguishing attribute on this boat was its .50 caliber machine gun mounted in the bow. When I arrived, the care and feeding of the ski barge had been assumed by Chief Creed. It was used during the day for junk search, or for inspection and maintenance of the assault boats. My immediate thought was that it was a perfectly useful asset just waiting for a champion, a role I assumed. I contacted a Navy friend in the States who I knew to be a serious water skier, and asked if he would pull together a set of skis and all necessary associated equipment. I had him ship the equipment to me under the guise of Welfare and Recreation, and we picked it up in Saigon. Obviously water skiing quickly took the top spot on the list of our downtime distractions. It was a bizarre scene, the boat speeding back and forth in front of the city with crazy Americans on skis, dodging sampan traffic, and all the while the man on the .50 cal. kept his eyes on the nearest shoreline or suspicious boat. Even though it was perfectly safe during daylight hours within the confines of the city on one side and the base on the other, I had nightmares about having to notify anxious parents that their son was shot off of water skis on the Vam Co Dong River! Again, skiing was a rare downtime stress relief, and certainly not the norm.

When he was ready, Chief Creed came to me with his proposal to counter the leak of information about our ambush positions, and it centered on the Kenner Ski Barge. He had a friend who was a Navy Seal, and the two of them had a plan: would I be willing to listen if his friend could get a few days to come to Go Dau Ha and assist? Without hesitation, I agreed to the visit, and also to keep this between me, the Chief and his friend. A week or so later the three of us sat over coffee in the mess hall while I listened to their simple, but brilliant plan. If our suspicions were true, then the VC would wait on the nights they were ready to move supplies across the river until they were told if the ambushes would be north or south of the bridge. They would then pick a crossing point on the river in the opposite direction from the boats.

The Chief's plan was to put three people in the Kenner—black- and green-faced, of course, and heavily armed—including plenty of

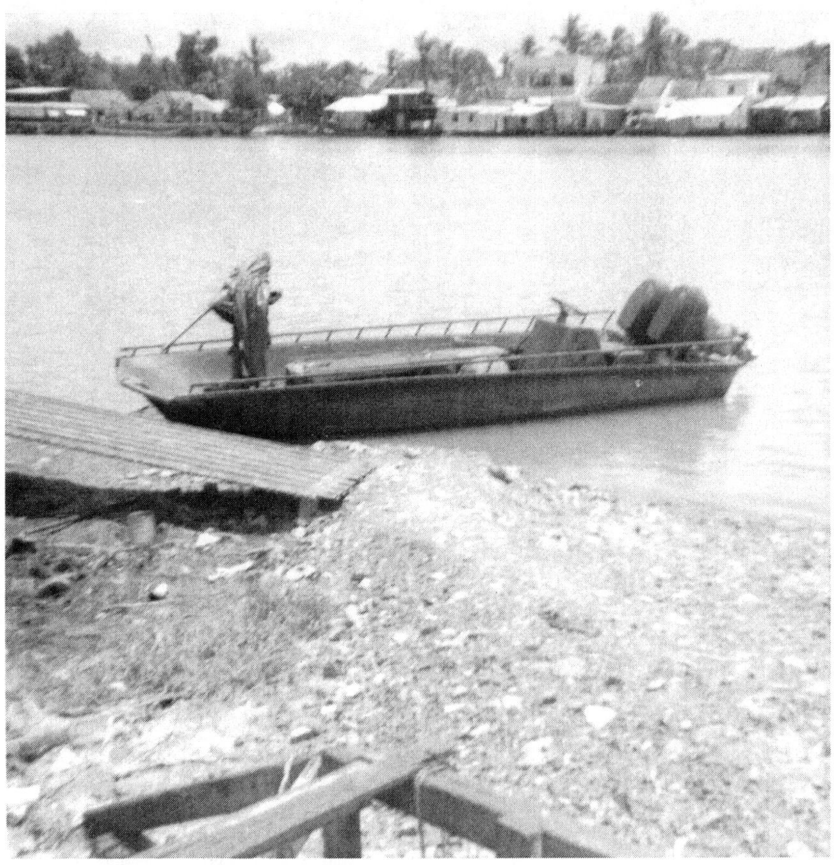

The Kenner Ski Boat, ready to go for fast river patrol, junk (small boat) search, night ambush, and recreation on occasion.

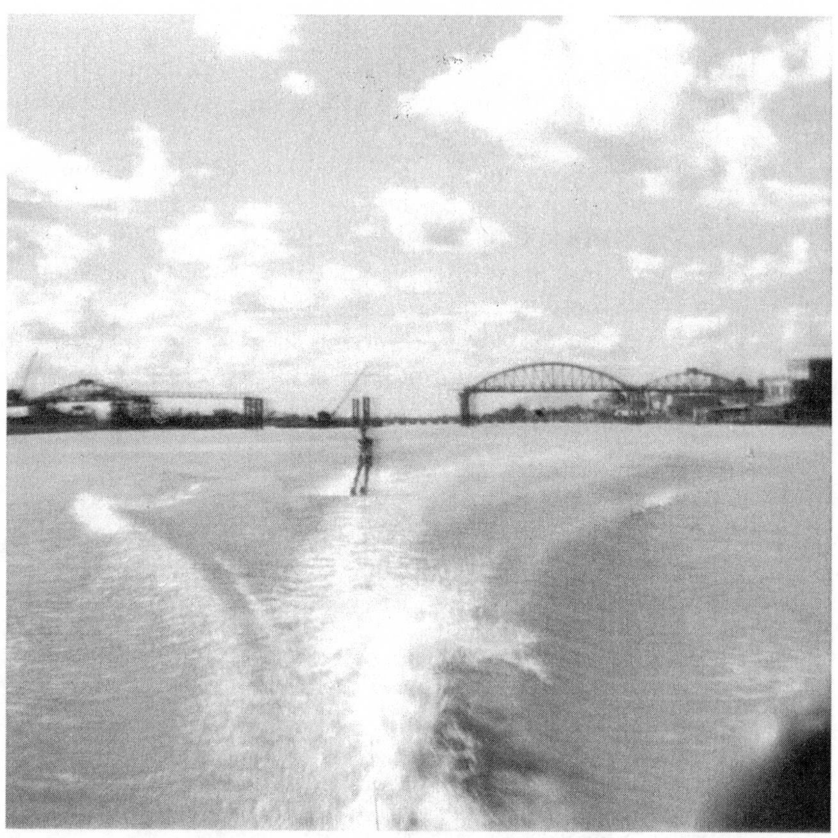

The Kenner Ski Boat, being utilized as its designer intended, with remains of Highway 1 bridge at Go Dau Ha in the background.

Claymore anti-personnel mines. As the assault boats left the base and proceeded either north or south, the Kenner and its crew would follow, but would slowly drop behind. Then the Kenner would reverse course and proceed in the opposite direction. The crew alone, with my knowledge, would predetermine a prime location near an obvious potential crossing point at the mouth of one of the east-west intersecting canals, large enough to move small boats laden with contraband. For safety reasons, not to mention that we were, after all, advisors, I decided that I would have to brief Dai uy Tinh; I trusted him.

I gathered from my discussion with the Dai uy that even though he agreed with the concept, he thought anyone would be crazy to want to be in the Kenner under those circumstances. Only then did I inform him that I would be the third man on the team, at least for the first few missions. One final change was that we would make the U.S. advisors on the assault boats aware each evening of the planned ambush position for the Kenner.

Since we only had a couple of days with our Seal expert, we decided that the evening of his second day with us would be our first time out. I knew that both the Chief and the Seal were not convinced that this untested and inexperienced LT was the best choice for their third team member. However, I made it clear that our unorthodox plan was my responsibility, and that if anything went awry, I would take the heat. My still reluctant assistant would man the command bunker radio. We finalized our decisions on what arms and ammunition we could safely carry; it was close on the 50 cal. because of the weight of the gun and its ammo. We decided that its value outweighed the risk, and that weight and its adverse affect on speed were not as important in a stationary ambush position as its firepower.

After the briefing the next day, we drew curious looks as we finished last minute preps, and then eased out to follow the big boys. We had decided to save the face and hand painting until out of sight. Three painted Rambos in a small boat bristling with guns would be too much. Chief Creed reflected the calm of a seasoned veteran, and what can I say about a Navy Seal who believes that sitting in a ski boat on a canal all night in hopes of an ambush encounter with VC infiltrators is his R&R? As for me, I think they both knew that my external bravado was barely concealing a combination of excitement and fear. I would never have been a part of this venture with any other two men.

We backed out into the river as the sun was just setting in the West, and we idled as the heavy assault units pulled away from the base and headed south. Chief was at the controls, and me and our Seal companion sat on the center seat facing opposite sides just behind the 50 cal. We eased in behind the last boat and followed as it passed under the recently reopened Highway 1 bridge. Just as we passed close to one of the bridge supports, Chief once again throttled back the engines and swung the ski boat slowly around 180 degrees and brought us adjacent to the bridge support, momentarily out of sight from the town, but more importantly, out of sight of anyone on the base. After a few minutes, as dusk was falling, Chief brought us from under the bridge, and after slowly clearing both the base and the city, he got us up to a nice cruising speed. We passed the rubber plantation, which had several lights on in the quarters, and shortly thereafter Chief and Seal easily located our planned ambush position.

We pulled into the West bank and tied the boat under overhanging palms, parallel to the shore, heading back to the South (and the safety of the base). We were about 100 feet south of a small canal coming into the river from the West; a canal just large enough to accommodate small junk passage. From our position in the tree line, we had an open view across rice paddies directly to our west, and a full view of the river. We would be unable to see anything move in the canal until it reached the river. We quickly set out our Claymore mines in a semicircle around our position, and then moved to our predetermined positions; Chief stayed in the boat to watch the river north and the tree line south and to handle the 50 cal.; I was in the tree line merely a few feet south of the boat listening for movement from the south (most unexpected), and across the paddies from the west; our Seal was just north of the boat in the tree line listening for movement in the canal. Oh, and I had my M-79 grenade launcher and an ample supply of grenades.

Now stop and think about this scenario; I was a twenty-six-year-old Navy Lieutenant, highly skilled and qualified as an afloat officer on a seagoing Navy combatant. However, I was not a Marine or a Navy Seal, nor had I ever been trained to act like one. At the time, though I might still be wrestling with my responsibilities as Senior Advisor, I was damn sure that sitting on a river bank in camouflage, face painted green and black, hand on the squeeze triggers to five or six Claymore mines, in the company of a vacationing Navy Seal and a salty Navy Chief, waiting for an unknown enemy, in the dark ... was definitely NOT one of my responsibilities! On the other hand, I had this surreal memory of me and my best friend Skip, in the sixth or seventh grade, sitting in a pine grove, BB guns in hand, waiting to ambush an imaginary enemy, in one of the many war game scenarios we thought up.

Suddenly, I was snapped out of that vision by a slight tugging on the wire leading out to one of my Claymores; was that rustling movement? Another slight tug on the wire! I was mere seconds from squeezing the triggers when all sound and movement stopped, no more tugs on the wire. I sat there perfectly still for I don't know how long until I heard slight movement behind me, and realized that it was light enough for me to see Chief approaching. That meant that there would be no interdiction that night; this war story had an uneventful ending. I told Chief about my "almost" a few hours back, and we crept slowly out to the Claymore location, only to find that some number of hostile rats had nibbled on the Claymore wires until they found them alien and inedible. The realization that I almost blew all of my Claymores and our ambush cover on a couple of rats was very sobering. I would have most certainly made someone's wall of shame!

Undismayed by our lack of contact, and with one more night of Seal companionship left, we determined to go out the next night and try again. I was much more at ease during our preps, and actually had a little swagger now that I was finally a veteran of a night in the bush. The evening initially went the same as the night before, except the boats went north and we headed south. Once we tied the boat at our chosen spot, I noticed that the scenario, with us just south of the juncture of another small canal, was identical to the previous night, and we set up the same way.

It was another long night, and about an hour before dawn I was convinced that this night also would not be my baptism by fire. Suddenly the Chief crept quickly and silently to my location, whispered that our Seal had movement in the canal, and apparently low voices there also. Without being certain how many, if any, hostiles were approaching, the Seal decided against the use of Claymores. We would both move closer to our boat and set up to engage on the river side. Chief had a night vision scope and by now we could barely make him out in the remaining darkness. I still could see nothing on the dark river, but Chief turned his back to the river and made a sign indicating four people, and then a paddling motion. We had previously agreed with Dai uy Tinh that anything moving west to east in the free-fire zone, away from the city limits, under the cover of darkness, required no approval to engage. The three of us had also previously agreed that with the exception of the use of our Claymores, Chief Creed would initiate any offensive contact.

Now, as I squinted in the predawn half dark, I made out a dark shape gliding slowly south, but it was still too dark for further details. We would rely on Chief and his night vision to make the call. When the movement was directly east of our position, and I had just started thinking it was nothing, Chief opened up with the 50 cal., followed seconds later by the rapid fire of some modified Russian weapon the Seal carried. I immediately went night blind! Between burst, Chief snapped me out of my shock by yelling, "Lootenant, *the M-79*!" Oh, shit! That was me! I tried to follow the tracers from the 50 cal. to their impact point in the river because I could see nothing else. I leveled the M-79, and heard the distinctive "*thump*" as the grenade left the barrel, followed shortly by a satisfying "*boom*" somewhere to the East! Again, *thump ... boom*! I was on a total adrenaline rush by now; kicking some ass! Until Chief yelled, "TOO HIGH! HITTING OPPOSITE TREE LINE!" So I was wreaking all of my devastation on the hapless palm trees on the opposite shoreline.

By the time I adjusted to at least hit the river a couple of times, Chief yelled to stop firing. He asked the Seal and then me if we were OK. I told him yes but still couldn't see shit! It hit me that we had received no return fire, so either the surprise and magnitude of our attack had caught them unprepared, or we had been shooting at shadows. By the time we gathered our gear, it was light enough to see clearly, though we certainly could not expect to find anything by then in the swiftly flowing river. So, with Chief's visual of four men on a makeshift raft, Seal's confirmation that there was definite movement, and my acknowledgment that I had seen something shadowy moving south until my blindness onset, we reported contact and termination of an enemy river crossing, with estimated four enemy dead; unable to find anything at first light due to the flow of the river.

I was still wired as we headed back toward the base, and I could tell that even my seasoned companions were pleased that our plan had apparently borne fruit. At the base we bid adieu to our Seal, who specifically insisted that he not be mentioned as having ever been there. After I thanked the Chief and he ribbed me about my providing covering fire on the east river bank, and I went to shower and notify my boss of our successful innovative use of the ski boat to combat possible leaks to the VC about boat ambush positions. The reply later that day was far from what I expected. Instead of praise, I was chastised; as it turned out, rightfully so.

In no uncertain terms, I was reminded that we were in *advisory* positions, and that there were to be no U.S. missions of any kind. Specifically, there would be no ambush in the future without full Vietnamese participation. We tried to maintain our enthusiasm by asking the Dai uy to assign one of his men to ride in the boat with us but not touch anything. Chief and one other advisor went out several nights after that, with a VN in the boat to make it an "advisory" effort, but the thrill was gone. Besides, Dai uy Tinh was never convinced that he had a leak in his ranks, although he had no idea why we continued to have no interdiction contacts.

Aside from skiing a couple of times, I enjoyed driving the boat on occasion to give visitors a look at things from the river; it was welcome respite for a staffer to get out where the action was. I gave up driving it altogether after a mishap caused by a mechanical failure set back goodwill efforts in Go Dau Ha. I was taking one on the Dai uy's men across the river, as a favor, for him to pick up something from a contact in the city. Crossing the river and dropping him off in the vicinity of his destination would save him time, and gain goodwill ... or not.

Sparing you the suspense: As I approached the city in a spot where houses of questionable stability sat over the water on rickety supports, I deftly followed the finger pointing of my passenger as he guided me to his rickety house of choice. I was by now very cocky in my ability to approach a position at more speed than advised, only to plunge the controls down into reverse, resulting in a dramatic sudden stop, followed by a gentle assist boost from the stern wave to glide to a full stop precisely at desired mooring spot. However, on this occasion, as my passenger stood to wave to his expectant friend, I plunged the controls for reverse and another impressive display of my prowess. To my surprise, the connective mechanical cable snapped, so the boat remained in full forward motion, only now at full open throttle. The jolt threw my passenger to the deck, but he looked up just in time to see his friend and others scatter as we hit the first "shack" at full speed. The boat proceeded up and through the first structure, and took out several more before coming to rest deeply imbedded in the village of Go Dau Ha.

As the residents surveyed the damage, and I tried desperately to disappear, a radio call to the Dai uy brought assistance from the base. After the necessary apologies, a team of volunteers, American and VN, spent a week rebuilding what was totaled. This incident was not reported, and besides, I had a VN in the boat making it an advisory effort.

We did in fact use the boat again in what I could stretch into a Vietnamization/ACTOV support role, at the tail end of a most bizarre intel gathering story. You recall during my earlier description of SERE training, the very controversial interrogation technique called "water boarding," used by U.S. Intelligence agencies sometimes on high value prisoners, known to have information that might possibly save American lives. It was controversial, but apparently valuable. However, after years of debate, the United States announced to the world during the Obama administration that water boarding was, by definition, torture, and that we would forever cease using it. But in my opinion the

Vietnamese had a far more insidious method of extracting information. I'll tell you going into this description of events that I would spill my guts if even threatened with this method.

One morning I was walking back up from the boats toward the command bunker, when Chief approached me looking pretty excited about something. He said, "Lootenant, have you seen the ARVN method of interrogation yet?" I told him that I had not, so like a little kid going to peek at the presents under the tree early on Christmas morning, the Chief told me to hurry with him into the command bunker. There were two ARVN soldiers at the bunker entrance, and they stepped in front of us, blocking our entrance, Chief said something that sounded like "Me Dai uy," and I thought to myself that wouldn't work, i.e., telling them he was a lieutenant. One of the men motioned for us to stay there while his partner turned to go inside. I mildly scolded Chief for telling them that he was a LT. He laughed and told me that "Nguoi My" was Vietnamese for "American"; the"My" is pronounced "me." We both laughed, because I had heard what I thought was "Me Lt"! I was thinking again how nice a little language training would have been.

The second ARVN soldier came out and waved us inside, where I immediately heard angry yelling from the small office to the right. I worked my way over to the door by Dai uy Tinh. Now I could see three tough looking men in the uniform of the ARVN. They were leaning in over a wiry little VN who was tied to the chair with his arms pulled behind him, around the chair back and tied there. There was no doubt in my mind that he was Viet Cong; what else? He was tanned and dirty, with a mop of black hair in disarray, and dressed in a ragged black shirt. I moved to get a better view of the questioning, and noticed that the prisoner's pants were pulled down around his ankles. I leaned to Dai uy Tinh and asked him why his pants were down. He told me that he was VC and the ARVN wanted him to lead them to his weapons stash. However, the frantic little man was desperately denying that he was VC; the ARVN interrogator was going to make him talk. I was not prepared for what I saw next.

The obvious senior ARVN yelled something and one of his men hurried out of the office and out of the bunker. Meanwhile the prisoner's demeanor had changed from denial to defiance; he sneered at the interrogators, but said nothing. Very quickly the third man returned and he was holding a field telephone, the kind with a hand crank on the side. The crank is turned rapidly to develop enough charge to power the phone. As he handed it to the lead man, the prisoner showed signs of curiosity; for all he knew they were calling his mother!

Things changed quickly after that. The two men who had been standing outside were called inside, and immediately kneeled down on both sides of the prisoner and pulled his knees apart. Recognition that this was not to be a call home must have hit the prisoner at this point and he began a useless effort to struggle against the ropes and the two me at his side. One of the original three stepped in and dumped a cup of water over the prisoner's privates. When the startled prisoner looked up, he realized what I had just realized, and fear and panic set in. He was looking at one interrogator holding the field phone in one hand, with his other hand on the crank; the third man held two wires leading from the phone, one in each hand. It was evident to the prisoner and me at that moment that he was going to experience an early Christmas, with his "chestnuts" roasting on an open fire! He desperately jerked his head left to right, and screamed what I gathered were at first obscenities, but then I thought must be pleas for mercy.

Not one of the interrogators seemed to hear or care, as the man with the wires moved in, kneeled down and reached between the prisoner's legs with the wires. The man with the phone yelled something and turned the crank slowly a few turns; the response was instantaneous. The prisoner jerked, stiffened and let out a high pitched scream. The crank man yelled something and then really got cranking! That's when I left the bunker. I was pretty sure that if that man had any info about a weapons stash, he would be giving it up soon. I can only imagine what the faint-of-heart protestors who forced the cessation of water boarding by U.S. Intelligence would say about the field phone service.

I was standing outside of the bunker with Chief Creed, discussing what we had just seen, though he was not as shocked as me (no pun intended), since he had seen it before, when Dai uy Tinh came outside followed closely by the lead interrogator. It seems that the prisoner had given them some info about a weapons stash at a village south of Go Dau Ha, and would lead the ARVN to the village and show them the hiding places. Apparently RID 40 boats could get them to the mouth of a smaller canal leading to the vicinity of the village. The ARVN wanted to know if we could come along in the Kenner and take a few of them with their prisoner into the canal as far as possible. I immediately had my doubts, but Dai uy Tinh said that he intended to go along, and that the village had never been considered VC friendly in the past. Besides, it wasn't too far from the main river. We would leave immediately in order to ensure that there was no time for leaks to precede us. Chief looked at me and said he would drive; I was still young and ambitious enough to say that I would accompany the Dai uy. With that, Dai uy Tinh went to ready a couple of the RID 40 heavies, and Chief and I enlisted the help of another advisor to mount the 50 and gather the weapons we could carry. We had to keep in mind that we would probably have no less than ten people in the ski boat.

The transit was uneventful, but when I realized how narrow the small canal was, I started to rethink my decision to come along. However, as they moved the prisoner to our boat and we all readied for the transit to the village and the search, youthful exuberance once again took over. I had decided to carry my M-16 rifle this time, thinking that if anything happened while we were in the boat or within the confines of the village, I would have more flexibility than with my M-79. I breathed a lot easier when I realized that the canal did not traverse jungle, but rather cut through rice paddies. Anyone standing in the boat had a clear view across the paddies both north and south. There was a constant stream from the prisoner's mouth, as he seemed very willing to share, as long as there were no more phone connections utilizing his gonads.

We had not gone far when it became obvious that proceeding further would have gotten us to a point in the narrowing canal where we could no longer turn the boat around. It was quickly agreed that we would secure the boat and proceed on foot. One of the ARVNs would stay with the boat. As we debarked and stood on the bank, we could see the edge of the village not more than half a mile further along the canal. Smoke from cooking fires rose in the calm air. So, we hiked. I have thought about this venture many times in the years since, and in every instance there is not one time that I could justify the potential risk. In every war story ever told with a similar situation, we were the hapless troops walking into a set up ... an ambush, with no additional cover or backup.

In hindsight the whole thing was slightly anticlimactic. There was a quick moment when the stories of the My Lai massacre flashed through my mind, but they were put to rest by the stark differences in the circumstances. This village was not far out in the jungle in a remote location like My Lai, nor was it suspected of harboring Viet Cong. In addition, we were not a group of stressed out, worn out, U.S. soldiers like those involved with My Lai, who had been constantly patrolling, getting ambushed and booby trapped, and watching their buddies die horrible deaths. Those troops entering My Lai were a time bomb waiting to go off. On the contrary, we were a strange mix of ARVN, VN Navy and U.S. advisors, following a desperate VC, who was just trying to keep from having his balls on the wrong end of a long distance call.

The villagers, mostly elderly, did not seem particularly surprised as we entered, and if they recognized the prisoner they didn't let on. They did get agitated when gathered in the village center and berated by our lead ARVN. Dai uy Tinh said he was accusing them of hiding weapons for the VC, and that he expected their cooperation. Of course, they all knew nothing, so they were ordered to remain in their group while the village was searched. The ARVN followed their "guide" from hut to hut, overturning pots and baskets, and looking under floor rugs and mats inside each hut.

In the end, the search revealed what appeared to be small amounts of various supplies hidden long ago, and perhaps forgotten. There were several stashes of rice buried under mats in huts, and some hand grenades discovered in holes beneath earthen pots, but search as they did, berating the prisoner at every false lead, they found no weapons beyond the grenades. After chastising the villagers and accusing them of being VC sympathizers, the ARVN reluctantly admitted to Dai uy Tinh that their "VC" was not a big player, and that he had probably not been in that village for several years. We returned to the boat with its napping sentry, and made our way back to the base. We were thanked for our willingness to help, and then the ARVN and their bedraggled guest departed by jeep. We were never told where they came from or how they had captured their prisoner.

14

Saigon

I saw Saigon when I arrived in-country, when I attended monthly Senior Advisor conferences, and once to meet my brother before he flew home. Regardless of what those folks located permanently in Saigon tell you, during the years 1969–1970, they hardly knew there was a war going on. There had been several notable VC terrorist bombings in Saigon in the early 1960s, including a couple targeting billeting for U.S. personnel. However, by the time of my arrival in 1970, the memory of those incidents had faded, and Saigon could have been any bustling Oriental city with a population over two million. The city's biggest problem was its exploding population growth and the resultant exhaust fumes from the thousands of motorcycles jamming the streets. While most U.S. servicemen stationed in Saigon were vigilant, some even wearing flak jackets to and from work, for those of us from anywhere outside of the city, Saigon was an oasis, a safe haven to conduct our business and then relax and enjoy perhaps one night of good food and entertainment.

Truth be told, during my first visit back to Saigon, about a month after my arrival in-country, I was unfamiliar with the city and remained on edge. I had come to connect with my older brother, Bill, a U.S. Army captain, who was flying home to the States. He had served about 10 months of his one-year tour, but was being sent home early due to my assignment in-country. We were the only two surviving sons in our family, having lost a younger brother to leukemia in our teens. In addition, our father had passed away only months before, so the Army took brother Bill out of harm's way. We stayed in a Bachelor Officer Quarters (BOQ), modest by any account, but after all we were in a combat zone. It had two-man rooms, no air conditioning, and common showers on each floor. The BOQ was also meant to serve as my accommodations for future business trips into the city. However, I would soon learn that one need not live under such rudimentary conditions when on short stays in Saigon.

So brother Bill flew home the next day and I headed back to Go Dau Ha, soon to be the Senior Advisor, hence my future regular ventures into the city. I had been driven into Saigon in my jeep, accompanied by two of my advisors, who I assumed had stayed in similar accommodations for enlisted personnel. However, on the return trip to Go Dau Ha, as they discussed their previous evening, it sounded like we had been in two different cities. After checking their weapons and leaving the jeep at Advisory Group Headquarters, I learned, they had gone on liberty, or "hit the beach" in Navy terms. When they asked me where I had stayed, they laughed at my reply, and one said something like, "all you officers are alike." The more I pressed for details, the more astounded I was by their replies. It turned out that they had stayed at the President Hotel in ChoLon, Saigon's China Town. A modest room with a window air conditioner cost them $10 American, and (I thought now they were just baiting me) there was a rooftop pool, restaurant, bar, and large area with multiple pool tables and a bevy of young Vietnamese ladies. "Yeah, right!" I said and laughed. They looked at each other and shrugged; that was the end of that discussion.

So, as previously discussed, I soon was officially named Senior Advisor, and my new Assistant, though not happy to be there, began to accept his assignment. When June rolled around, and I prepared for my upcoming conference in Saigon, I took Chief Creed aside and asked him if he was aware of the President Hotel in Saigon, and had he ever been there. I knew that he would rather spend his time in Go Dau Ha, looking after the Advisors and the boats, than spend any time in Saigon. However, he told me that the stories were entirely true about the accommodations. Though troops permanently assigned to Saigon rarely if ever stayed at the hotel, they did frequent it in their off time, but as far as he knew, there were no restrictions on outsiders, on temporary business, staying at the hotel.

In hindsight, I should have asked a lot more questions. But I was a young Lieutenant, new in-country, overwhelmed with my new responsibilities, and totally unfamiliar as yet with organizational accountability for enlisted or officers whose duties took them from place to place. That included whether or not I was free to secure my own accommodations in Saigon. The Chief added that he had heard that the President had been French owned, but with their ouster, the hotel had passed into

VN ownership. I decided to look into the setup on my upcoming Saigon trip.

At that time, and until the time of this writing, I believed the story of French ownership of the President Hotel, passing to South Vietnamese private ownership. Only recently have I pursued more details, which it turns out are sketchy and rare. I was able to find a public call-out from a French journalist to any veteran who could provide information or photos of the hotel. The writer indicated that research showed that the hotel was built by the U.S. Army in the 1960s as enlisted quarters, and had remained as such until at least 1968, after which there is no more documented history. Whatever its origin, all I can tell you is that in 1970, the President Hotel was staffed and operated by Vietnamese civilians, with no sign of U.S. or VN military involvement.

The only other evidence of its existence I could find was a freelance video posted to YouTube on September 29, 2017. It is a 15 minute tour without narration of the hotel, which has apparently been vacant since 1973. Though everything looks structurally the same, including the top-floor empty pool and the large room that housed the pool tables, restaurant, bar, and dance floor, the building shows the toll taken by 44 years of disuse and total neglect. It was the eeriest feeling to experience that tour through the lens of a camera, and to recognize every location. I could literally close my eyes and see myself there in 1970. Even more strange is the fact that there is now a notation on the video's webpage that comments have been turned off to protect minors.

As I prepared for my next Saigon trip, I made the decision to rotate the men who would accompany me on each trip to Saigon. There were always two men with me in the jeep, one driver and the other literally "riding shotgun." Now that I understood more about the potential for those men to unwind for a night, I considered the overnight a valuable treat. Upon arrival for my first conference as Senior Advisor, we left the jeep in secured parking and checked our weapons, and I instructed the men to meet me back there at noon the next day for our return to Go Dau Ha.

I attended my conference that afternoon, which consisted of introductions, highlights from the field (still an absence of any reports of interdiction), current or upcoming special events or missions, etc. During the course of the afternoon I ascertained that my peers were all staying in officers' quarters, as was my plan. They would most likely enjoy steaks and wine atop the Brink Hotel/BOQ, which housed officers permanently stationed in the city. Not only could patrons of the

Brink enjoy good food and good company, but from that vantage point they could often see real time evidence of the war being played out. They could be mesmerized by distant tracer rounds piercing the night ... red from U.S. guns and green from the enemy.

At the close of the meeting, I was feeling adventuresome, so I left my small carry bag of overnight needs in a locker, and went outside to place my life into the hands of a local driver. That day it would be a taxi, but in the future I would join my men on wild races through the city on the front of motor scooters, in a small seat at road level. For now, I planned to go and see for myself the President Hotel, and its apparent allure. I paid little attention as the driver had known right away how to get there. After a relatively short drive, the driver announced that we had arrived at the President Hotel; he actually grinned broadly, pointed at the hotel, and said, "You like!"

15

The President Hotel

I devote a complete chapter to life at the President Hotel because it reflects the extremes experienced by many of our men in Vietnam, including me, if we made that choice. It is a sad truth that this scenario played itself out for hundreds of service members during the years of the Vietnam War. While six-month deployments had long been a "normal" part of Navy life, the one year Vietnam tour was new and different; it took a huge toll on personal lives. During that year the service member missed one of everything... Christmas and other holidays, birthdays, anniversaries, and perhaps even the birth of a child. They sought replacements to fill those voids, something other than the constant ugliness of the senseless war.

I walked into the lobby of the President Hotel that late afternoon, telling the clerk at front desk that I was not staying, but only going up to check out the restaurant and bar. I took the elevator to the top floor, and a million miles from the war.

I stepped out into a small hallway outside of the entrance to the offerings of the roof, and was immediately taken by the sweet sounds of the Beatles, so different from Creedence Clearwater Revival. While CCR set the mood for the canals of the Delta, the mood here was set by the likes of the Beatles, the Rolling Stones, and the Animals. On the rivers and canals, the "rolling on the river" of CCR's "Proud Mary" sustained us, but here, it was the Stones' "(I Can't Get No) Satisfaction," the Beatles' "Come Together," or the Animals' "We Gotta Get Out of This Place."

I walked through the entrance into another world. The room was already a sea of activity, the entire center of which was pool tables. Most tables were occupied by young Americans, most with a beer and some with a cigarette. The uniform of the day appeared to be a green t-shirt, loose at the waist, over green fatigue pants, and jungle boots. There was no sign of rank. With few exceptions, every man was accompanied by a lovely young Vietnamese lady. Before I could take in any more of the sights, a nicely attired Vietnamese lady, slightly older than the rest in the room, approached and took my arm. With a big smile she welcomed me, and asked if this was my first visit to the President, to which I replied "Yes." She then offered to show me around. As we walked, she asked me a curious question, "You officer?" Without thinking, I replied, "Does it matter?" She laughed, and we continued to walk. I would learn soon enough that the distinction between officer and enlisted was well known here, especially the difference in income!

We walked past the bar, skirting the pool tables, to the open-air restaurant. I looked at the menu, which had pictures of enticing food choices, and menu offerings with English descriptions. I would most certainly try dinner here; the hook was set! Next was the enticing outdoor pool, surprisingly crystal clear, but almost devoid of swimmers. There were a number of servicemen in bathing suits around the pool on lounge chairs. As with the pool players, each man was in the company of a young lady, and to several I wanted to suggest "Get a room!" We strolled back into the large, open pool table room, where, with the timing of a seasoned professional wrestling tag team, we were joined by one of the many young ladies, who took my available arm. Without asking, my hostess smiled and said, "Mai Ling will take good care of you now."

Mai Ling was very attractive and tantalizingly dressed. She spoke hesitatingly in broken English; I gathered that she wanted to sit and get a drink. I convinced her that I couldn't stay, and that I only came in for a quick dinner and a beer. I thanked her and walked to the restaurant, and was seated at an outside table. As one of many firsts that day, I was introduced to "33" beer, "Ba Muoi Ba," Vietnamese beer. I finished the beer and ordered garlic crab and a second beer. The crab was awesome! Similar to, or the same as, the Chesapeake Bay blue crab, with the shell removed and the center inside body parts cleaned out; the rest was sautéed in garlic butter. They were now reeling me in; there was no fight left in this fish! I finished, paid for my dinner, and was leaving the restaurant with every intention of leaving the hotel and going to my quarters for the night; I had a resumption of the advisors' meeting in the morning.

I was almost out of the large room when I heard two loud voices behind me, I could have sworn were calling, "Dai uy! Dai uy!" I turn, and there came my two guys from Go Dau Ha. The rest, as they say, is history. Thrilled that I had found the hotel, the men insisted that I join them for a beer ... an invitation I should have declined. However, at the same time, having heard that I was an officer, the hostess had come over with renewed interest in me as a patron. She not only seconded the invitation, but brought the first three beers on the house.

I found out the next day there was another very good reason that all three of us were being wooed ... we were Navy, and the Navy still had money near the end of the month. Turns out that, in Vietnam, Army paydays were once a month, so by the last week or so in a month, the hotel's regulars from the Army were broke. Whereas, the Navy paid its personnel every two weeks, so that left things pretty much to Navy folks in Saigon during the last week of every month. Well, the one beer turned into a pool challenge, which turned into more beer. At this point, a more mature and savvy Naval officer might have started to worry about the Navy's "fraternization" policy, which forbade personal relationships between officers and enlisted personnel. However, that policy was usually used to discourage dating relationships between the sexes, and not occasional social mingling after work as a group. At the time, standing down for a night from the war in Saigon, I didn't consider a few beers and a pool game to be violating the policy. That was soon the least of my worries.

As the night wore on, it seemed only natural that we would be joined by Mai Ling and her friends. The final pool game led to one more beer on the outside deck. When I finally decided that I should get a cab back to my quarters, my two guys convinced me that this was not the time of night, after several beers, to be heading anywhere. Besides, I could sleep in an air conditioned room with a shower for $10 U.S.; any other services would be additional costs. We all stood in anticipation of the evening's end, when the hostess joined us. I noticed that any patrons who had been playing pool or enjoying drinks without the company of the ladies had all apparently left at a reasonable time. Now I saw only couples and most of them were drifting away arm and arm. At this point the hostess suggested that my men go ahead and retire for the night, and that she and Mai Ling would make sure that I "was taken care of" ... wink, wink. From there it happened smoothly and quickly; the hostess handed Mai Ling a room key, said something to her in Vietnamese, and then said to me, "You go with her now; she will take good care of you." I was surprised that there was no mention of money. I felt strangely like Lieutenant Cable in *South Pacific,* and I half expected the hostess to depart while singing a verse of "Bali Ha'i."

15. The President Hotel

The next morning when I woke up there was no sign of Mai Ling. I showered, and went down to the lobby, expecting to check out. I handed the clerk my key, and he smiled, and said, in near perfect English, "Have a nice day, Lieutenant." Now there were two unanswered questions: why had no one asked for any money? and how did the clerk know I was a lieutenant? Those two thoughts stuck in my mind through the morning meetings. I needed to have a serious chat with my guys when we met to head back to Go Dau Ha. One thing I had decided was that my one night accommodations in Saigon every month would be at the President Hotel.

Life and our lack of interdiction success went on unabated at Go Dau Ha through July and August. Chief Creed and the other advisors had formed growing relationships with the individual boat captains. While the Planned Maintenance concept was slowly withering, there did seem to be more of an acceptance of responsibilities by the Vietnamese, and an effort to work side-by-side with the advisors, rather than just observe. Because of the slow progress, I decided that being able to operate and maintain without being interrupted by VC- or NVA-initiated firefights was probably a blessing for this fledgling group. I hoped we, with Dai uy Tinh's continued support, could get some cohesion before we "went live."

Meanwhile, back to Saigon. After the first afternoon of my next advisor conference, I grabbed a taxi to the President. This time I checked in to grab a room for the night, knowing that there would be no lame attempt to wander out at closing. I went to my room and got into the "uniform of the day," cammo pants, green t-shirt, and this time I wore flip flops, a sure sign that I had bought into the program. Again I heard the music, and again it was the Beatles. I stopped at the entrance to the main room and noted that, just like the previous month, there was a decent scattering of servicemen, but the place wasn't packed. Now I was aware of the reason ... the Army was broke again! As I had promised my men, I brought two different advisors with me, and I saw across the room at one of the pool tables that they were both fully engaged, with pool, "33" Beer, and lovely ladies helping with their cues.

What happened next was unexpected to say the least. The same hostess from the first night approached; by now I figured she was more than a hostess, but rather was in "command" of everything on the entertainment floor. She smiled and gave me a kiss on each cheek. She had been followed over by what seemed like half of the ladies in the room, and before she said a word, the beautiful bevy opened the questioning all once. "Dai uy, you bring same men as before? I like very much!" "You numba ten, Dai uy; you only bring two men!" "Next time you bring my man back, Dai uy!" "Why you not bring alla your men? They all need good time!" I felt like a U.S. president at a press conference! After a minute or so of this, the hostess held up her hand and shhh'd them. She said something to them in Vietnamese, and they hung their collective heads and wandered off, but not without at least one parting shot, "You numba ten, Dai uy!" The hostess asked if I would like a beer or something stronger, as she led me to the nearest table. I asked for a beer, and within ten minutes I understood everything. I was absolutely correct about the Army money impact on end of the month activity. However, what I hadn't thought of was the boost they would get near the end of each month from even two Navy men from the field with hundreds of available dollars saved through months of nowhere to spend it. I'm sure that she hoped I could bring in even more patrons with money, but it was clear they would be happy with even two big spenders every month. I say "two" big spenders instead of "three" because it was becoming clear that all I had to do was show up with my two guys every month and my accommodations would be free. However, I insisted on paying for my room, and told her that she must understand that my men were free to spend their evening in Saigon as they chose. She smiled, and said, "That OK; I know what they choose!" She got up to leave the table and I asked if Mai Ling was there. She smiled, and said, "No worry about Mai Ling; you wait." For a fleeting moment, as if carried by the music, my mind drifted; it ran about a two-minute rerun of my life since I first flew to Japan and reported aboard the *De Haven*. During that excerpt from *This Is Your Life, Dick Kirtley,* I tried to make sense of how in the hell I ended up here, in this situation. It was not in any of the recruiting materials.

The spell was broken when a pair of small hands came from behind me and softly covered my eyes. First I flinched, but then reached up and slowly lowered the hands and turned around. Nope, my dream must still be running, because there stood an angel. I had never seen a sweeter vision; she was drop dead gorgeous! Here again, I will skip the details of the evening, but it turns out that her name, although not her given name I'm sure, but her "stage" name, was "Frenchy," for obvious reasons. She was half French and half Vietnamese, having drawn the best qualities from each. The short of a very long story is that for that evening, and every other evening I chose the President Hotel for my Saigon accommodations, Frenchy was to be at my beck and call. Since coming to Saigon that first time, I had gone from God-fearing man to pimp.

Just to show you that I was still able to draw the line somewhere and say "no," later that night, as we headed for my room, Frenchy asked me softly if I wanted some "can sa"? Can sa is Vietnamese for pot, but she was talking about pot cigarettes, already rolled, cut and packaged; I politely declined. Later that night, as I was drifting off, there was a soft knock at the door. She got up, went to the door and opened it a crack. After a quick exchange in Vietnamese (again, just a little language training would have gone so far), she shut and locked the door. When she came back to the bed, she told me that we must be quiet and stay in the room for the rest of the night. I pressed her for the reason and she said that "some VC going up to use roof for something; no sweat, by morning they be gone."

The next morning when I woke to shower, not only were the VC gone, but so was Frenchy. It made sense; no need to pretend this was something it wasn't. I couldn't help but wonder why such a beautiful, sweet young lady would lead this life. The more I thought about it, the more I realized that for her, there probably was no choice. She was more than likely fathered by a Frenchman before the French military was defeated at Dien Bien Phu in 1954 and forced to leave the country, probably including her father. Growing up, she would have been scorned by the Vietnamese as a half-breed. So at this point in her life, she had two choices: to grow old by age thirty, perhaps homeless, selling trinkets on a street corner, or to sell herself into a life with shelter, food and someone to look out for her. I am not justifying any of this; but I do think I understood it.

Once again, the next day after the conclusion of my morning meetings at Advisory Group Headquarters, I met my two men at the jeep for the drive back to the base. Before I leave the confessional, there is one more thing. Since each of my monthly trips to Saigon allowed two of my men the run of the city for 24 hours, I issued them a challenge. We were building our club and bar with the stolen plywood, but we would be in desperate need of bar stuff ... stools, table lamps, wall decor, beer mugs, shot glasses, brass bell, etc. My challenge was that each man must "cumshaw" something to add to our bar decor; simple as that. There was nothing these guys couldn't do or obtain with a little motivation. So, the jeep heading back to Go Dau Ha was heavily laden. As far as I knew at that time, RID 40 would be in Go Dau Ha for the duration of my tour, and I would be making these overnights every month, so we might as well take advantage of the "shopping" opportunities.

On the way out of Saigon, we had to pass the sprawling Tan Son Nhut Air Base where we had arrived in Vietnam, and, God willing, would leave sitting upright. We had a little time, so I told the guys I wanted to stop in the Officer's Club to see about a cumshaw of my own; it would only take a minute.

I cannot tell you the feelings of shock and anger I suffered over that next half hour. Keep in mind that we are in a war zone, so the splendor of the club left me almost speechless. The men let me out and I walked in wearing my combat greens. The lobby was plush, but the bar blew that away! Tables with white tablecloths and small candles spread out in front of a magnificent long bar, with glass mirrors on the wall behind it for the entire length. I guarantee you that nothing in here came by way of "cumshaw"! My intent had been to slip in, get a beer, and hope for a nice enough mug or glass to be worthy of our new club. Well, slipping in was not going to happen; I stood out like a sore thumb!

Every man in the room, this early afternoon, was in spiffy looking sports shirt and slacks or in a washed and starched uniform with not a smudge, and without fear of wearing their rank. The bartender was right out of a movie, with a starched white shirt, a red bow tie, and a sharp looking apron. Feeling very out of place, I slithered up to the end of the bar and caught the bartender's attention. I ordered a beer; my cover was blown, but I was still going for the beer glass! As I sat there trying to make myself small, a gentleman walked in wearing a nice shirt, slacks, with gold watch, and a nice gold neck chain. All in all a good-looking guy, a lot older than me judging by the gray at his temples. I had no idea if he was civilian for military, but if he was in the service he damn well outranked me. He looked slightly miffed about something and he slid up to the bar right next to me but without a glance. By now I was really pissed off. Everybody in this place was making the same combat incentive pay as me, as my men, or the soldiers patrolling the jungles ... the same combat pay! I didn't want to be there any longer, so I was just going to guzzle the beer, hide the glass under my fatigues, and be gone.

It did not go down exactly that way. Just as I was guzzling the last bit of my beer, this rube next to me looked at his gold watch and at the tables and small dance floor, and then back at his gold watch. The last golden drop was crossing my lips, as he looked distractedly at nobody in particular and said, "I can't believe this, the combo was supposed to start by now." All I could take; last straw! From mouth to bar top, without even thinking, I brought that beer mug down as hard as I could. It shattered and left me holding the glass mug handle, as I yelled way too loud, "God damn it, just rough it tonight!" It was an E.F. Hutton moment, and then I turned and left the bar and the club without another word. I didn't get my beer mug, but my glass mug handle and that story went a long way in the not so fancy RID 40 Advisors' club bar, a long way from the glitter of Tan Son Nhut!

For the next few months, the routine was only broken by the random incidents previously described. The boats patrolled the assigned operating area north and south of the bridge during the day, and sat in ambush positions every night. At the base, it was boat maintenance and training, including cleaning of unused weapons. My advisors played cards at the "club" in the evenings when not out on ambush, wrote letters home, or caught up with an hour or so of sleep every now and then. My Assistant had reluctantly accepted his circumstances, so I had him shadowing each advisor in turn, learning everything he could about their expertise and about the boats they kept running. And once a month there was Saigon. Above it all was the continued lack of contact with the VC/NVA, but it did not seem to concern Dai uy Tinh. He had no interest in utilizing the Kenner's potential for surprise ambush at night.

I had begun to formulate several possible theories on why we were seeing no action, either enemy or friendly initiated. The first and most probable was that the NVA and VC on the Cambodian side of the Vam Co Dong in the Parrot's Beak area had all pulled back to avoid contact with the American backed ARVN incursion in May. Even if done in an orderly fashion, it would take them time to reestablish their infrastructure to facilitate the flow of men and supplies once again. The second possibility is that most of the contacts before our arrival had been because the establishment of the ATSBs along the river had been new and disruptive (as was the plan), and the boats were accompanied by Army units which were dropped into the action quickly as required. The third possibility, my original concern, was that the nightly ambush positions were compromised by VC sympathizers within the ranks of our VN Navy folks. However, at this point I was beginning to think that, if I was lucky, I might just finish my year in Vietnam without ever being on the other end of a hostile shot fired, and I was OK with that.

16

Change Is Inevitable

Sometime in late September or early October 1970 I got word from Dai-uy Tinh that he had been told to start preparations for RID 40 to leave Go Dau Ha and move south in support of a pending operation. At that time he either had no further details or wanted to wait until I was briefed through my chain of command; he didn't have to wait long. At our next Senior Advisor meeting in Saigon I was briefed that we should start preparations to leave Go Dau Ha with RID 40 for points south. We had less than a month to prepare.

Although RID 40 was part of the "Mobile" Riverine Force, that definition had not yet been tested; i.e., while operating from the base in relatively docile Go Dau Ha, both the South Vietnamese and my advisors had become somewhat comfortable, perhaps almost complacent. Becoming "mobile" meant exactly that—culling out only that which was essential to move aboard the assault craft permanently for an unspecified length of time. Such an effort might be compared to cleaning out a college dorm room after graduation. Since we had no idea if and when we would once again operate out of a base, we were forced to throw out the unnecessary or pack it up for a one time chance to ship it home from Saigon.

Speaking of Saigon, this change in assignment would bring an end to my monthly sojourn at the President Hotel. As my next trip would in all likelihood be my last, I was forced to pick the two lucky men who would accompany me. In fairness, I had to pick two who had yet to experience that overnight escape. I think those who had made the trip with me over the past five months cried themselves to sleep when they realized they would have no chance for a teary farewell.

While bidding adieu to the ladies at the President Hotel was going to be disheartening, I was soon confronted with a more monumental issue. Chief Creed took me aside just days after we learned of the

The author and his counterpart, Dai uy Tinh, RID 40 commanding officer, at a birthday party for the author. Dai uy and his men teamed with RID 40 advisors to throw the party.

pending move, and asked me simply, "What do we do about Rat?" OMG! Lost in the overwhelming preparations for the move was the future of our dog Rat. Over the past few months he had become one of us, wandering the base without fear, sleeping under the table in the advisors hooch or in the "club," and most nights crashed on my bunk in the command bunker. Now we were in a near panic, knowing that he could not live with one of us on the boats, nor could we abandon him.

I won't keep you in suspense: American ingenuity saved the day! We would just call his tour of duty over and send him to the States. Like any other mobilization problem, this one needed a plan, including recognition of roadblocks and formulation of steps necessary to overcome them. The first obstacle was that he could not fly internationally without the requisite rabies shot. The solution was obvious, yet complicated. We knew that the Air Force security folks at Tan Son Nhut had a guard dog unit, so it followed that they must have veterinary services. Once again leaning on the art of cumshaw, the Chief and I with one other who was closest to Rat loaded him into the jeep early one morning and headed for Tan Son Nhut. Also on board we carried a few items of potential barter value, including a communist AK-47 assault rifle donated by one of our own. That alone should surely buy Rat his shot. Fortunately Rat slept under a blanket going through the Tan Son Nhut gates. After that the trade went off without a hitch. The rifle was handed over in return for Rat's rabies shot and the supporting paperwork. I don't recall the required waiting period before Rat could fly, but it was completed before our return for his flight.

Before returning to Go Dau Ha we found the commercial airline that would handle his flight and learned the necessary details. We made arrangements for a proper crate, but as yet had not decided on a destination. That one was easy; Chief Creed's family had a large farm in West Virginia, and he assured us that Rat would find a good home there. So it was settled; just prior to our departure from Go Dau Ha, we would drive Rat back to Tan Son Nhut for his freedom flight.

Our departure date seemed to be fluid, but in late October, Dai uy Tinh informed me that we would be leaving Go Dau Ha in about two weeks. We would proceed to Dong Tam, a large ARVN base, which included a MRF boat repair facility. The base was located on the Northern branch of the Mekong River, near the city of My Tho, about 40 miles SW of Saigon. The site had been built by the U.S. on reclaimed swampland in late 1966, to be used as the U.S. Army's base camp for control of that region of the Mekong Delta. The U.S. Navy's MRF was formally created there in 1966 to operate in concert with the U.S. Army. The base had been turned over to the ARVN in late 1969, and it continued to house the repair facility for MRF boats. Thus our planned stopover in Dong Tam was to get the RID 40 boats a much needed overhaul.

According to Dai uy Tinh, after repairs and outfitting in Dong Tam, we would move south to the small city of Ca Mau, 175 miles south of Dong Tam, at the Southern edge of the U Minh Forest. From Ca Mau, we would support an invasion of the U Minh Forest. Apparently, South Vietnamese President Thieu had proclaimed that he would "spend Christmas Day 1970 in the heart of the U Minh Forest"!

16. Change Is Inevitable

The U Minh was a vast, mostly uninhabited swamp area in southwest Vietnam, between Ca Mau and Rach Gia. Often referred to as notorious, it was rumored to harbor VC and NVA forces for years. My guys had heard a story that in 1952 a brigade of 500 French paratroopers dropped into the U Minh, never to be heard from again. I have since verified that tale.[1]

By 1968 the U.S. Navy's Mobile Riverine Forces, in support of the larger Operation Sealords, had taken control of the South Vietnam Delta, with the exception of the U Minh Forest. Now there would indeed be another attempt to take control of the Forest. Only this time it would be attempted by the combined forces of the South Vietnamese Army (ARVN) and units of the South Vietnamese Navy Mobile Riverine Forces, supported by U.S. air support. RID 40 had been picked as one of the MRF units to support the operation.

Having our priorities in order, we soon headed back to Saigon, and tearfully put Rat on a flight to West Virginia. Funny, with all of the uncertainty surrounding our own immediate future, all I could think at the time was "Please, Lord, watch over Rat and get him safely to West Virginia." His departure left a hole in my heart.

17

Round 'Em Up and Move 'Em Out

Things happened quickly after that, but we did manage to get everybody's excess personal gear packed and ready for shipment to the States. I attended one more advisor meeting in Saigon, where I learned more about the magnitude of the pending operation. It was in fact true that President Thieu was tired of hearing about the U Minh being a haven for his enemies; it was actually an embarrassment to his government that such a sanctuary existed in his backyard. It appeared to me that he intended to use half of his Army if necessary, supported by up to four of his riverine assault units, every personnel-carrying helo in his inventory, and U.S. close air support, including Huey Cobra gunships and Marine Corps OV-10 Broncos.

The intent was to stage everything at sites outside of the U Minh, and launch an overwhelming two-pronged pincher attack. Learning from the French disaster, the ARVN troops would not be dropped into the forest to fend for themselves. Instead, there were two areas chosen in the Northern and Southern ends of the forest which would almost instantaneously become artillery fire support bases. First, artillery would soften up those areas. Immediately after the artillery barrage, U.S. aircraft would drop specially developed bombs for clearing helicopter landing zones and artillery emplacements in otherwise overgrown jungle areas. Troops would then be brought in by helo to secure the cleared area, while hundreds of workers were flown in, with some heavy equipment to start expanding the clearings. Finally, field artillery, lightweight 105 mm howitzers, would be ferried in and set up around the clearing perimeters. Their versatility allowed them to fire standard rounds up to seven miles in support of the infantry, but also to fire anti-personnel rounds, called "Bee Hives," packed with hundreds of metal flechettes. These rounds would be fired nearly horizontally to stop onrushing enemy troops.

The plan was to continuously send troops out from those bases in ever increasing circles on search and destroy missions. Both locations were located beside navigable canals, accessible from Ca Mau in the South and Kien An in the North. The river assault groups would operate from those two cities to establish control of the water accesses to each base, in order to allow for the movement of troops and supplies. RID 40 was to be the lead unit to enter the forest from Ca Mau in the South.

That evening, I held my own briefing, minus any details of course, with the ladies of the President Hotel. As before, two of my first-timers were with me. All I could say, of course, was that we would probably not be returning to Saigon. Since they of course had no idea what we did or who we did it for, all it meant to them was lost revenue. Although, I must say that, in my humble opinion, not only would we be missed by the "Mamma-san," but Frenchy truly seemed hurt by the news. I was able to give three of the men one more trip into Saigon with the truck to deliver and ship personal belongings from Tan Son Nhut.

While my jeep was to stay in Go Dau Ha and be assigned to the Senior Advisor of our relieving unit, nobody in authority was aware of our unofficial truck. Dai uy Tinh had managed to commandeer a couple of smaller trucks to transport some of RID 40's excess equipment to Ca Mau, and he was thrilled with the addition of our 2½-ton truck. The one stipulation was that it would be driven by one of my advisors. My firm belief was that if I just turned it over to the Vietnamese, we might not see it again. Never mind that we had acquired it in much the same way.

So, in early November 1970, much to the credit of my 14 advisors, all 14 boats of RID 40 got underway from Go Dau Ha for the first leg of the trek south. If we could hold things together until we reached Dong Tam, still a U.S.-run repair facility, I thought we just might get the boats ready to fight. With Dong Tam about 70 miles south of Go Dau Ha, I figured it could take anywhere from 10 to 14 hours, at our slower Tango boats' maximum speed of 4 to 7 knots (4½ to 8 m.p.h.), depending on engine performance. In any case I fully expected us to run the engines at less than maximum and take two days to reach Dong Tam, traveling during daylight hours; at least that was my position from an advisory perspective.

However, Dai uy Tinh said that time was of the essence and that we would travel the first day at the best speeds possible, and slow our speed after dark, but proceed through the night. The first two-thirds of the trip would be on open river in daylight—but the last third, which he wanted to transit at night, consisted of narrow twisting canals, with small villages along the way. Navigation would be by spotlight on the front (bow) of the boats. All I could do was tell my advisors to get some rest during the daylight transit, and prepare for a long night with radio in hand, ready for anything.

The daylight transit went off without a hitch, and if you consider that we did not engage any enemy combatants that first night and did arrive in Dong Tam by daybreak, you might call that part of the trip a success also. However, I feared that we had lost a lot of "hearts and minds" along the way, judging from the shrieks from the canal banks as we plowed past small villages, and the debris stuck in the armor on the bow and sides of the boats ... fragments of rickety piers and tattered fish nets. I don't think that "we're from the Government and we're here to help you" was well received by the locals along our overnight track.

18

Dong Tam

Dong Tam, as previously described, was a beehive of activity, the most important of which to RID 40 was upkeep on the heavy assault craft. The approach to getting the most out of Dong Tam for our boats, while very successful, turned out to be much more different than planned. The plan was for the VNs to formulate work packages for their boats, while the advisors would assist in getting as much of that work done as possible. Again, the end was achieved, but not nearly within the normal means. Most of the necessary work on the boats was documented and driven by my advisors, with little input from the VNs. However, when it came to armament it was entirely different. Dai uy Tinh had become aware very soon after our arrival that many of the craft tied up nearby had been all but abandoned by their VN crews, who for the most part were off to see family or other personal activities. As a result, the advisors on those boats had to spend extra time away from the boats, running down maintenance actions.

Thankfully, unbeknownst to me at the time, Dai uy Tinh made a deal with his staff and sailors. They would all be granted the next afternoon and evening off for personal business, if they remained with their boats overnight and through the first morning. What his men pulled off by the next morning was nothing short of miraculous. They essentially staked out boats from other units, waited until they were vacated, and slipped aboard. There they deftly "lifted" whatever weapons they determined would replace or supplement what they had on their own boats. Thus, while my advisors went above and beyond to bring the boats up to top performance mechanically, the VNs ensured that the boats of RID 40 were the best armed in the Delta! And to be sure, Dai uy left not one of his boats unattended the second night. He also made sure that I was unaware of the entire arms raid until we were well away from the scene of the crime.

That first night showed us all why the base at Dong Tam had earned the nickname "Mortar City." We had heard that the base had essentially become a practice range for VC mortar teams, and that night we were reluctant spectators. Shortly before midnight as we drifted in and out of restless sleep in various spaces around the decks of the boats, we were rousted by the sounds of explosions, not real near our location but definitely not from friendly fire. Because we had no place to seek shelter, no bunkers, we decided to seek the highest part of the superstructure for the best vantage point. Since the base and the surrounding wetlands were all flat, we didn't have to get very high up to see everything.

What turned out to be a fairly regular mortar attack was thankfully uneventful, especially for those of us on the boats. It seemed that these events were always sporadic, randomly placed, and short lived; that night the boats were not targeted. We watched what would not cut it as a Fourth of July fireworks event, and were pleased to learn that there had been no casualties. In discussion the next day with some Americans stationed on the base, I learned that the real purpose of these attacks seemed to be for harassment only, and apparently it worked. At the start of any such attack, those on the base stopped whatever they were doing, including grabbing that desperately needed couple of hours' sleep, and ran to their assigned sandbagged bunker until the "all clear" signal. At that point, the VC objective had been met. Besides, their mobile mortar teams had no desire to stay and fire from a stationary location, making themselves targets for any air support nearby. It could also have been the VC's desire to return some of the pressure that they felt being hunted every day. That is, turnabout is fair play.

One particular incident during our two days in Dong Tam that stuck with me long after was a simple encounter that actually startled me because I was so unprepared. On the second day of our stop I had gone aboard a U.S. Navy repair ship anchored by Dong Tam. It had been two years since I saluted the flag on the stern of the USS *De Haven* and departed for my assignment at Patuxent River; two years since experiencing the wonderful protocol and camaraderie shared by officers serving on a U.S. Navy ship. One part of that camaraderie was the gathering for meals in the wardroom of the ship. The wardroom was not only where the officers dined but it had the atmosphere of a gentleman's club. Here traditions called for civil interface, and absolutely no discussions about religion or politics.

For the three regular meals of the day there were usually two "sittings" depending on the complement of officers aboard. The first sitting traditionally was with the Commanding Officer at the head of the table accompanied by the more senior officers on his staff. The second sitting of the more junior officers was sometimes more relaxed, but within the bounds of the same tradition. When a ship is deployed, especially to a combat zone, the bonds grow the strongest. Although the meals are taken in working attire, the wardroom members were still expected to be in clean, pressed uniforms, and to be well groomed to Navy standards.

As I approached the quarterdeck, the place on deck where you actually step aboard the ship, I remembered protocol, and turned toward the stern of the ship and saluted the American flag there. Then I turned and saluted the Officer of the Deck, responsible for proper and orderly boarding and departing the ship. Continuing protocol, I requested permission to come aboard, which was granted. I had planned to simply visit with the Repair Officer, and perhaps see some of the repair capabilities. What I did not expect was an invitation to join him for lunch in the Wardroom. The first sitting would be just starting, so I could meet the Commanding Officer and the other department heads.

We reached the door to the wardroom, and the Repair Officer opened it and waved me in. Once again I was smacked with the realization of just how far "outside the normal range of U.S. Navy experience" I had wandered. It was as if I had stepped out of Vietnam and back into the Navy I had signed up for. The wardroom was like so many I had seen before, with a nice decor, comfortable couch seating on one side, TV mounted on a shelf (no flat screens yet), pull-down movie screen at the other end for the evening movie, and a serving counter with a pass-through window from the kitchen. The room was dominated by a large table running from left to right (port to starboard), with a white tablecloth and full place settings. Wardrooms at that time were supported by the officer staff with monthly dues, based on the desires of the group as to the budgets approved for food and amenities. Because of the time spent in the wardroom, especially when deployed, most officers wanted and therefore supported a well appointed wardroom, and this one was no different.

The first sitting was obviously just underway, as no food had yet made it to the table. I'm sure that the ten or twelve officers seated there had seen many "River Rats," as brown water Navy men were called, come and go. Therefore they showed no reaction to my appearance. I on the other hand could not have felt more conspicuous. I was wearing cut-off, unofficial, camouflage pants; jungle boots; and a green t-shirt, holding my black beret in my hand. My hair was too long, trimmed with scissors at the neck, but over my ears, and I had not showered in about four days. As if no one had noticed, the Repair Officer introduced me to the Commanding Officer first, and then to the group as a whole, and said that he had asked me to join them for lunch. The CO shook my hand and said "Great!," and indicated a seat at the table.

I was speechless for a moment and didn't move, not for any other reason than the fact that it drove home just how far removed I had become from the reality of the Navy, and suddenly I missed it. I snapped out of it before anyone really even noticed, and had already decided that I would not stay to eat. While I probably would have enjoyed the fellowship, it came down to one thing.... I did not want to touch anything! I even laughed and made a joke about feeling like Pigpen in the Charlie Brown cartoons. Without fanfare I thanked them all for the invite and for the reminder of shipboard life and wardroom warmth, but I declined to stay. The Repair Officer walked me back to the departure deck, where I once again thanked him for the support to our boats. We exchanged good wishes and he returned to the U.S. Navy and I stepped back into Vietnam.

The only regret I had was missing the opportunity for a real American meal. When we pulled in the lines and left Go Dau Ha, we also left the support of the U.S. Navy for our subsistence. For the foreseeable future we would subsist on the Vietnamese "economy." I put that in quotes because where we were going, and for most of the trip to get there, we would see nothing in the way of commercially available sustenance. The one staple that was in great supply aboard all of the boats, or in small villages along the way was rice. All meals taken aboard the boats included a large bowl of rice, sometimes by itself, and other times with some strange vegetable. Rare, if ever, were we going to see any type of protein ... until we decided to invest in the local economy. It was simple ... the Vietnamese were essentially broke, receiving a pittance for pay, and sometimes nothing; but they had rice. The advisors, on the other hand, had money and no place to spend it. So, each advisor struck up a deal with a VN boat captain, agreeing that the advisor would provide funds for the boat crew to secure whatever they could at every opportunity, which turned out for the most part to be some locally harvested fish, and on occasion a scrawny chicken. To their credit, the VN sailors could create something enticing out of very little and the ever present rice. While I fully expected to grow an increasing aversion to rice, I actually acquired a liking for it which persists to this day. At every village or small city along the way excitement surrounded the return of the shoppers to their respective boats.

19

Ca Mau—Gateway to the U Minh

After three days of attention in Dong Tam, the fourteen heavy assault craft of RID 40 left in fair to good working order, and more heavily armed than when they arrived. We headed south for Ca Mau, roughly 150 miles from Dong Tam, depending on the chosen route. Dai uy Tinh shared the planned transit route with Chief Creed and me on a map of the Delta. It appeared that we would continue southwest for about 40 more miles until we hit a branch of the Mekong River, which flowed from Phnom Penh, Cambodia, to the South China Sea. As this major river passed into South Vietnam, it split into branches resembling the fingers of a hand on the map, the individual fingers spreading out to reach the sea at various points along 50 miles of coastline. A smaller river, the Bassac, also flowed from Phnom Penh, south of and parallel to the Mekong, through South Vietnam and into the South China Sea. Once into South Vietnam the name of the river changed to the Hau Giang, but at that time, and for simplicity here, I refer to it as the Bassac.

The result of these rivers and their tributaries was the formation of the rich, fertile Mekong River Delta of South Vietnam. When we reached the first, northernmost branch of the Mekong we would proceed west upriver about 50 miles, to the point at which that branch flowed very close to the Bassac. At that point we would literally make a U-turn to the South, pick up the Bassac, and proceed down river toward the sea for about 60 miles. At that point we would turn south on the final leg ... a smaller canal, but a straight shot to Ca Mau, albeit another 75 to 80 mile jaunt. If you're thinking that the math doesn't add up, you're correct. We were going to travel about 225 miles of river and canal to accomplish the 150 mile trip to Ca Mau. Averaging speeds of anywhere from 5 to 8 miles per hour, we were looking at 30 to 45 hours, not including stops. Once again we put our collective fate into the hands of the Vietnamese.

It was unsettling enough for me to have lost control of my own destiny, but I tried to imagine the state of mind of my mom. She now had one son safely back in the States, but was clueless as to the whereabouts of her second son. During my time in Go Dau Ha, she was only a week or so behind in knowing what I was up to, depending on the travel time of my letters home. There was no instant flow of personal news over any sort of social media. I had managed a short phone call with her on my last trip to Saigon, and had not done her state of mind any good by telling her only that we were moving from Go Dau Ha, and would be living on the boats for a while. I had no idea how or when we would even get mail into the Vietnam-to-home flow again.

Late in the afternoon of the first day out of Dong Tam, just before reaching the Mekong River, all of the boats stopped at a small village. There was a small pier but the boats were far too big and heavy to tie up to it, so the crews tied them to trees on each side. Dai uy Tinh informed me that we were invited to eat with the chief and the village elders. I welcomed the chance to stretch my legs, and looked forward to the experience; what could possibly go wrong? I walked with the Dai uy through the center of the village to a small building, with a covered area outside of the entrance. I could see from outside that the building was quaint, with dirt floors and open windows. There was a wooden table outside of the entrance, under cover, with five or six elderly Vietnamese sitting around the table.

As we approached, the man at the head of the table rose, and greeted Dai uy Tinh; they exchanged what I guessed were pleasantries, given the smiles and laughter. Dai uy said to me that this was the village chief, and that he, the elders, and the rest of the villagers were honored to have me as their guest. We sat down in adjacent seats, and Dai uy Tinh went through the painstaking introductions. This group included the Chief, the village security chief, and four other elders; they were the village government. Dai uy did his best to facilitate small talk, translating enough tidbits, I think, to establish a bond built on mutual hate of the Viet Cong and NVA, and a great appreciation of America's support in their freedom fight.

In what was apparently a rare offering of their appreciation, they had slaughtered a chicken and prepared a meal in my honor. The Dai uy explained that they would stretch the one chicken by chopping some of the meat and mixing it with green "lettuce" and chopped nuts, rolling the mixture in rice paper, and deep frying it.... AHA, spring rolls! They would boil the carcass for soup, which would also contain vegetables and spices. I missed whatever would happen to the rest of the meat. When the rolls and the soup were served, I was very pleased that the small rolls were accompanied by a local version of Nuoc Mam (fish sauce).

I was doing fine with the meal, and I nursed a warm beer that had been given to me from Dai uy Tinh with a smile. We finished our meal and the plates were cleared by several women. It was late afternoon, I was pleased with the "event," and expected us to say our goodbyes; but the Dai uy had other plans. As he explained things to me, the Chief and his elders simply smiled and nodded. Dai uy said that as the honored guest, I was in for a special treat. At that, there was some light clapping and cheering as a plate was placed in front of me; I looked down and almost gagged. Staring up at me with dead hollow eye sockets was the head of the chicken that we just had for dinner! As the clapping and smiling continued, Dai uy explained that the head of the chicken—more precisely, the cooked brains of the chicken—was a delicacy. In addition they were believed to bring good luck to the honoree. Anywhere else I would have thought that I was being "punked," in which case I would have laughed it off and been done with it; but they were serious. When I balked, Dai uy said, "Not really so bad; just pick up with fingers on both sides by eye sockets, put bottom with neck opening to your lips and suck brains out!" This was not going away, and stalling just made it worse. So, in one motion, I grabbed, lifted and sucked! Final marks: Presentation 10, Shock Factor 10, Texture 1 (OMG!!!), Taste 3. Any more discussion and even after all these years it still might come back up!

Evening over? Guess again; the trap had been set. A woman came to the table and placed what looked like a mason jar almost full of a clear liquid and two small glasses in front of the village chief. It hit me that the glasses were the size of shot glasses, just as I saw Dai uy Tinh exchange a quick smile with the Chief; I was about to be had. The Chief poured a small amount of the liquid into each glass, pushed one over to me and smiled. Dai uy Tinh, also smiling, said, "Village Chief want to have drink with you." I asked him what was in the jar and Dai uy Tinh replied, "It OK; they make own." It took a few seconds for me to realize that I was staring down the barrel of a shot glass full of Vietnamese moonshine ... white lightning.... "Hooch!" Not wanting to disrespect the host, I reluctantly agreed. Glasses raised, "cheers" in two languages, and down the hatch.

HOLY MOTHER OF GOD!!! I had just swallowed liquid fire; I could trace its path through my body by following the burn! A line from the old song "Love Potion Number Nine" flashed in my mind, "I didn't know if it was day or night…." I remember thinking, strangely late in the process, that I wasn't poisoned, because the Chief had also downed his shot. As I fought to catch my breath, I noticed that everyone else was laughing, and the Chief was pouring another drink. Surely this was for a similar toast with Dai uy Tinh. Wrong again. Before I could say a word, Dai uy Tinh said, smiling even more broadly than before, "Now village security chief want have drink with you." All I could do now was give the Dai uy a look that said, "I know what you are doing, and I will get even." And so it went around the entire table, with each of the elders exercising their civic duty to have a drink with their naive young guest. In the words of Willie Nelson, "Turn out the lights, the party's over."

While I did not disrespect my host, who, by all accounts, was honored and could not have been happier with our visit, I certainly was guilty of conduct unbecoming an officer! No, I was not raucous and rowdy, nor did I get mean and pick a fight. However, I have no recollection of the final shots of hooch, or my return walk to the boats. In fact the next thing I saw was daylight! I was on the deck of the command boat, the sun just up over the horizon behind us, and we were slowly making our way west on the Mekong River!

It was night when we managed to make the connection with the Bassac River and once again head southeast. Several hours before sunrise we stopped at a tactical support base in Long Xuyen, about 30 miles from the Cambodian border. The base had played a major role in support of the U.S. Mobile Riverine Force in 1966 and '67 during Operation Game Warden, an operation to deny the Viet Cong movement on the canals of the Delta. By the time we arrived, the base was supporting the South Vietnamese riverine forces operating close to the Cambodian border. We would take on some fuel and supplies at Long Xuyen and top off at Can Tho, 50 miles further to our southeast. I wandered around and looked at some of the boats that had taken part in the recent Cambodian incursion and they had taken a beating. While we were not going in that direction, history told us that we could see some of the same in the U Minh Forest. Dai uy Tinh did not want to give his young and mostly inexperienced sailors too much time to see the results of VC attacks on the other boats, so it was a short stop and we headed for Can Tho.

Our stop in Can Tho was also brief, which was unfortunate. The support base there was larger, with facilities for Army and Air Force, as well as ARVN and VN Naval Mobile Riverine Boats. There was a small club which I visited in order to find perhaps some interesting conversations with U.S. personnel, not only for casual conversation but also to pick up any news about what was going on elsewhere. As it turned out, most of the buzz was about the impending U Minh Forest operation.

I was engaged in conversation with a group of U.S. Navy Seals when I noticed a friend and classmate from the Naval Academy walk in alone. I recognized him immediately; he was a former Navy football player, and he stood there tall, neat and proper in his officer khaki uniform, clean shaven, and his haircut was up to Navy standards. I, on the other hand, was looking more ragged than any time since arriving in-country. He caught my wave, but even as I crossed the room he had no clue who I was. Needless to say, even when I got close enough for him to recognize me, there were no man hugs.

We both only had a few minutes, but I would have traded places with him right there. He was an admiral's aide, on a fact-finding trip. Well, if he had the time, I had some facts for his admiral; but my facts would not have made anybody's report. How about a one-liner: this whole Vietnamization thing is a sham! Never mind; with the few minutes we had we just caught up on how we each got there, and then it was time to go. As he walked away, headed back to the real world, I reflected a few minutes on the different choices he and I had made to both be passing through Can Tho, South Vietnam, in 1970, under such different circumstances.

Years later we met under the Class of '67 tailgate party tent outside of Navy's football stadium at our 10th reunion. We touched on that brief encounter, and it became clear to me in that instant that, to him, the Vietnam experience had been just another duty assignment, helpful, of course, when reviewed by promotion selection boards. Don't get me wrong; I don't begrudge him that feeling at all. I only wish sometimes, in hindsight, that I could have just let my *De Haven* Vietnam experience suffice for my own promotional benefit. As I said at the opening of this book, while I don't feel emotionally scarred by my Vietnam experience, my patriotism was most certainly scarred. I take that back; my faith in our elected officials was severely damaged.

19. Ca Mau—Gateway to the U Minh

Amazingly, all of our boats were still running as we made the turn off of the Bassac and headed down the very narrow, very straight 75 mile canal to Ca Mau, our jumping off point for the U Minh campaign. Here is as good a time as any to tell you that since the direction to pack and prepare to leave Go Dau Ha I received at my last senior advisor meeting in Saigon, I had received absolutely no information or guidance from any U.S. source, not strategic or tactical, about the upcoming campaign. In addition, I was also not sure what Dai uy Tinh's source or chain of command was. At this point, we were along for the ride.

As we neared the bustling city (big village at that time) of Ca Mau, it became evident that as sure as Dai uy Tinh and his folks were of the route to get to Ca Mau, they were equally unsure as to where to go once we arrived. Ca Mau lies at a confluence of canals, and even in 1970 it was literally built out over the water more and more as we approached the confluence, and the navigable portion of the canals narrowed. There was much confusion and yelling in Vietnamese between the Dai uy and his lead boat commander about which way to turn. The resulting indecision was disastrous for some of the locals. Not only were the assault craft big and slow, but they were also cumbersome. Any momentum, even at 5 or 6 miles per hour, is difficult to stop. By the time the lead boat captain realized that he had taken the column down a narrowing canal, there was no longer room for one of the large boats to make a smooth turnaround. He had gradually slowed his boat and the others were now stacked close behind. When he stopped, the other boats veered left and right as they tried to stop, and they began to crush the fronts of the rickety houses hanging over the water. Fortunately, in order to ensure that this did not become an "Ugly American" scene, I had radioed all of my advisors and directed them to disappear somewhere on the boats until this fiasco was over. In a public relations disaster, right on the doorstep of a VC stronghold, most of the civilian structures along some two miles on both sides of this tributary received major structural damage. Starting with the last boat in line, each one had to do a back and forth (fore and aft) pivot until they had turned 180 degrees to reverse direction.

By the time the column was turned, the Dai uy's men had ascertained the right direction to our destination, the small support base, which turned out to be about one quarter the size of our base at Go Dau Ha, with earthen walls and a few buildings like those in Go Dau Ha. There were a couple of floating pontoons recently added from a base that had been destroyed by a VC attack the month before, just about 25 miles south of Ca Mau on the Gulf of Siam. The remaining PBRs at that location had been turned over to the Vietnamese, and by early December 1970, as RID 40 readied itself for a run into the U Minh Forest, the last remaining U.S. Navy patrol boats were turned over to the Vietnamese. Previously, all heavy assault craft of the Mobile Riverine Force had been turned over, meaning that December 1970 marked the end of the U.S. "Brown Water Navy." The South Vietnamese "Brown Water Navy"[1] was now the largest in the world.

20

"Haunted Forest— I'd Turn Back If I Were You!"

The name of this chapter, and in reality the theme of my second six months in Vietnam, comes from the sign that greeted Dorothy's friends at the edge of the Haunted Forest in *The Wizard of Oz,* as they marched bravely toward the stronghold of the Wicked Witch. I had originally thought that the plan was for us to carry ARVN troops into the U Minh to arrive at the point where the southern-most of the two fire support bases was being created, immediately after the initial defoliation. However, as I mentioned, the ARVN troops were going to be airlifted into the cleared areas, followed by the "landscapers," and then the howitzers. Simultaneously, the exact same scenario would play out from the North.

In the meantime, our boats, and the boats from a RID at the support base in Kien An at the North entrance to the U Minh, would be loaded with basic supplies to initially outfit the two fire support bases. The RID mission, therefore, from the kickoff of the operation was to carry a load of supplies to one of the two bases, offload, remain at the base for several days to provide security on the canal side of the base, patrol the area immediately north and south of the base during the day, and insert troops near suspected VC locations as requested. In addition, simply by their very transiting of the canals to and from the bases, the RIDS were keeping the waterways open for "friendly" use.

So if I looked at my first seven months in Vietnam as a baseball rookie's time in the minor leagues, it was apparent that I had been called up to the big leagues and the games were underway. We got word from Dai uy Tinh on the evening before the operation was launched that we would head up the canal into the U Minh the next morning. Hopefully, in view of the sheer magnitude of the equipment and manpower that would be focused on the two locations chosen for insertion, little or no attention would be paid to the boat convoys entering from the north and south. The best news for me was that Dai uy Tinh had been informed that shortly after we got underway, I would be contacted by our air support, in the form of two OV-10 Bronco "Black Ponies." Since they were American assets, they would utilize my radio frequency and my call sign "Remittance." It took me a while to get here, but the scene for the opening paragraph of chapter 1 is now set.

The term "firefight" stirs the memories of most veterans—and in most cases the memories are not fond. Before I delve into the details of my first firefight and the initial performance of RID 40 sailors, I should briefly describe a textbook firefight as taught at the Naval Inshore Operations Training Center (NIOTC), and as usually carried out by American riverine forces operating in Southeast Asia.

It must be noted that few, if any, firefights involving riverine forces were initiated by the good guys on the boats. The vast majority were kicked off by a VC rocket or small arms attack from ambush positions along the canal or riverbanks. In the classic scenario, a column of heavy assault craft would be progressing at 5 to 8 m.p.h. The relative hostility of the area of transit would determine whether or not the column had air cover overhead. For the sake of the textbook scenario, assume that a pair of OV-10 Broncos ("Black Ponies") would be circling in the vicinity, in radio contact with the commander of the boat division, who himself was in radio contact with each individual boat commander. This was the plan for our initial sortie.

The tension or calm, again relative to the hostility of the area, would be suddenly broken by the "whoosh" of B40 rockets followed by their explosion either against the boats or on the opposite bank. Small arms fire might or might not accompany the attack. Immediately the boat under attack would notify the division commander; weapons of all caliber would be brought to bear on the perpetrator's location. Fifty caliber fire from Alphas and Tangos would rake the jungle; M79 grenades would bring down small trees and foliage; 20 mm cannon fire would devastate the area. In addition, if a "Monitor" was present in the column, its 40 mm cannon, 20 mm gun and 50 cal. machine guns would literally shred the jungle vegetation like a Cuisinart. Finally, if the column were fortunate enough to have a "Zippo"—the napalm unit with twin flame throwers—it would literally rain fire for 300 feet inland, the flaming napalm dripping from the foliage onto anything hiding below.

While all of this devastation occurred (within seconds of the initial attack), the division commander would be giving somewhat simple guidance to the circling "Ponies": "Pony Zero Five, this is (Call Sign); we are receiving fire from the right bank at boat number three!" Within minutes, the two Ponies would deliver pinpoint devastation in the form of rockets and mini-guns as they paralleled the riverbank just above the treetops. The object was simple—keep the ambusher pinned down with initial return fire; burn them out if you had a "Zippo"; and finish the job with the "Ponies." Variations of this scenario were played out daily for years on rivers and canals all over South Vietnam; and then came "Vietnamization."

First, "state of readiness" took on a whole new meaning for the sailors of RID 40, since they had seen no actual combat. Most of the time it meant turn down the radios and put the rice bowls away. I was nervous but comforted by the fact that two very calm Black Pony pilots had established contact with me and were circling overhead. They had flown in as promised shortly after we got underway, and immediately put me somewhat at ease. My radio had come to life, "Remittance, this is Pony 05; me and my wing man, 07, will be flying your cover this morning. We've numbered your boats 1 through 14 from the lead boat; if you have trouble just let us know the boat number and the side of the canal, over." Me: "Roger, Pony 05, understand; thanks for coming; Remittance out." That was easy and those guys sounded like they were out on a Sunday picnic.

On our boats, behind every weapon was not a seasoned U.S. Navy gunner's mate, but a young, inexperienced Vietnamese farm boy, impressed into this hastily formed Navy. While the scene preceding the firefight in this case appeared the same, all similarity ended with the first B40 rocket! Immediately every Vietnamese sailor within reach of a weapon began to fire in whatever direction the weapon happened to be pointing—left, right, up, down, in the water, in the trees, in the air! With their too-big GI helmets rattling around on their heads, they continued the 360 barrage until, as Johnny Horton sang, "the barrel melted down." Seeing this "dome" of gunfire, the Black Pony pilots in the area immediately moved away to safety!

Enter the calm young warrior lieutenant; I keyed my radio and, as stated in the opening paragraph of chapter 1, came the following: "This is Remittance! We're taking shit down here ... where the hell is our air cover?" Calmly back, "Remittance, Pony 05, we're here, just out of range of your guys; have 'em bring their fire down into the jungle at least; when you are ready, we just need boat number and side, thanks, out!" By now, of course, the one or two VC who had launched the rocket attack were either long gone or safely crouched in a "spider hole," laughing their asses off at the havoc they'd wreaked. Aha, but enter the Zippo! I hoped the bad guys were old enough to smoke!

Even to the layman, including myself, the operation of the flame units was mechanically uncomplicated. Within a ring just in front of the napalm nozzle, a cloud of gas was emitted, and a series of sparks kept the gas ignited. Through this ring of fire the raw napalm was projected and ignited to then rain fire from the heavens.

In the absence of "planned maintenance" by the VN sailors, their employment of the Zippo in our first major encounter was anything but devastating. As related to me later by my advisor on the Zippo, at the height of the frenzy of the boats all firing, the Zippo commander gave the order "burn right!" The twin nozzles swung slowly toward the right bank. In the next instant, streams of raw, jelly-like napalm leaped toward the foliage. The only missing ingredient was flame! With nary a spark inside the rings, the only damage to the enemy was a severe "sliming" as experienced by the "Ghost busters." Nothing is more discouraging than the wet fart "fluutttt" sound of unlighted napalm!

Just as all seemed hopeless, a young VN sailor, much harangued by the Zippo commander, crawled forward amidst the chaos with a burning piece of rolled up newspaper! At the nozzles, he lay face down on the deck, one hand holding his helmet, the other extending the flaming torch toward the rings on the nozzles. Suddenly, a stream of napalm shot through the flame on the paper, ignited, and we were back in business! Enough burning napalm gas mix now remained in each ring, that subsequent shots carried the requisite fire. Continuing the somewhat unseemly fart analogy, I could only think of the friends in high school who bragged of lighting farts for distance.... I'm sure none of them reached 300 feet!

In a somewhat lower octave, I contacted our air cover: "Pony 05, if the bad guys are still around they are on the right at about boat # 3, the one spouting flame, over." Pony 05: "Roger, Remittance, me and my wingman are rolling in now; keep your heads down; out!" In the next few seconds I witnessed the greatest display of U.S. firepower ever! I watched as the two tiny planes rolled and circled until they were behind us on the right side, coming low and fast just above the jungle. I was on the command boat with Dai uy Tinh, just behind the Zippo, which had ceased firing. Just before reaching the command boat, the Ponies unloaded ... mini-guns and rockets! It was like they were clearing for a new highway; vegetation, including palm trees, flying everywhere! They pulled up, did a couple of spins, leveled out, and then over my radio, like sitting at home watching a ballgame with a beer in hand, came this perfectly calm voice: "Ahh, Remittance, Pony 05, how was that? Over." Then they heard the high-pitched voice of what must have sounded like a little girl who had just peed herself with excitement and awe, "PONY 5 ... HOLY SHIT!! .... JESUS CHRIST! ... THAT WAS AWESOME! OVER!" Pony 05: "Roger, Remittance, then we will just hang around for as long as fuel allows or until you reach your destination, out."

If I were judging, I'd score this contest nothing-to-nothing in casualties. However, if I were an accountant I'd have to put the VC ahead in minimizing expenditures—probably $50/$100 for the two B40 rounds; while the good guys must have expended thousands of dollars.

The obvious immediate "advice" from the advisers, after witnessing this type of encounter, was to bring the return fire up out of the water, down from the sky and the trees, and at least toward the side of the waterway from which the attack initiated. This entire scenario was neatly summarized generically in the November 1966 issue of *All Hands* magazine:

> American Navy men in Vietnam, whether serving in their own boats or as advisors aboard the vessels of the Vietnamese Navy, have a challenging assignment in helping this war-torn nation resist the Viet Cong.
>
> Their work is now bearing fruit, and the Viet Cong are feeling the pinch. "Charlie," as the unknown Viet Cong infiltrator has come to be called, still has the advantages that go with stealthy attack and rapid retreat. These advantages will, however, be of little use to him if he is denied the essentials he needs, most of which are now arriving in smaller and smaller quantities from the North—thanks in large part to aerial, coastal and river surveillance.[1]

I guess it was just a matter of perspective.

21

Establishing a Routine

I was pleasantly surprised that we were not attacked again as we proceeded northwest, deeper into the U Minh, and nearer the site of the new firebase. We could tell when we got within a few miles of the new base by the huge assortment of helicopters flying everywhere. Light observation helos buzzed around just over the treetops trying to draw enemy fire, while their partners, heavily armed Huey Cobra gunships, circled high above, daring some hapless VC to challenge their little friends. What seemed like hundreds of troop carrying helos ferried troops and laborers into the base and then raced out to pick up more. When they were inbound and loaded with troops, they zipped along at full speed just above the treetops in order to make them a tougher target from the ground. Huge heavy lift helos carried loads the size of small box cars, and later they brought in the howitzers. By the time we arrived and beached our boats at the edge of the new clearing, there was already a large sandbag bunker in the center, which I learned would house base command and all communications.

Dai uy asked me to join him and we made our way over to the area where the bunker had "grown." There he met an ARVN officer, who Dai uy told me was coordinating this initial phase. It was just after noon, and the plan was to have a perimeter established with multiple rows of barbed wire, and 105 howitzers in place by dark that night! They were determined to have no repeat of the French disaster.

The perimeter included a substantial length of canal front, which could not be protected by howitzers because of boats tied there. So it fell to the boats to remain in place through the night, fully exposed to fire from the opposite bank, which had thick layers of jungle growth up to the water's edge. Boat crews would have to remain at full readiness all night. While the base could not be physically overrun from that point because of the canal's natural barrier, the VC could certainly wreak havoc from that position. I went to Dai uy Tinh with my first real advice in a while, and he agreed to go to the acting base commander during the construction phase and suggest *strongly* that he let us ferry a team of his landscapers to the opposite bank and have them cut back all growth for at least 100 yards. I could not have been happier; he agreed to send a team first thing next morning. Now all we had to do was pray that the element of surprise would keep the VC from organizing a sizable attack that first night.

It became obvious from the lack of a serious challenge that night that the VC had been caught unprepared for the invasion. There were probes of the defensive perimeter that were quickly quieted by the direct fire of the howitzers. At one point several B-40 rocket grenades were fired from the jungle across the canal opposite our boats. They appeared to be targeting the bunker in the center of the clearing and not our boats; they sailed over our heads and exploded harmlessly in the clearing. Perhaps there would have been more, but a majority of the gunners on the RID 40 boats appeared to have settled down and taken the advice of my guys; their fire, especially from the 50 cal. machine guns, tore into the jungle at the point the rockets had been fired.

In the morning there was a change of plans; there was no reason for our boats to stay at the base since it was too early in the operation for there to be troop inserts away from the base. So we were sent back to Ca Mau and the other boats there headed towards the base with a full load of supplies. By every measure it appeared that the operation had surprised the VC, and everyone seemed pleased that both firebases had been established and heavily defended. Perhaps President Thieu would spend Christmas in the U Minh.

Meanwhile, without knowing it, I had set my mom up for some unanticipated anguish. On my last trip into Saigon I had gotten through to her on a short phone call from one of the central call locations for U.S. troops. At that point I did not want to tell her any names of locations, etc.: LOOSE LIPS SINK SHIPS! But I had told her that we were moving aboard the boats, leaving Go Dau Ha, and proceeding elsewhere in support of the ARVN. However, knowing how slow the mail was, I dropped a letter to her in which I mentioned that we would be operating near a little city called Ca Mau, but she would never hear anything about it, given all of the larger, well known cities from the DMZ to the Delta. Since her only source of news about the war was the evening national news, there seemed no chance that she would hear anything to cause her more concern than already present.

However, on the day we left to head into the Forest, the VC had randomly, it seems, decided to fire a single B-40 rocket grenade into the small Navy compound that night. The rocket grenade was on target, headed directly at the building where the U.S. advisors slept. Remember, these are plywood, screen and tin, so the shrapnel from a single rocket could cause significant injury. In what could only be called fate, or some said the hand of God, the grenade struck the steel flagpole standing in the center of the compound, dead center. The grenade detonated against the pole, sending its shrapnel harmlessly in all directions. Miraculously, the only casualty was the flagpole.

Now something like that would have been a one-liner in a radio message from the base, making its way to Naval Advisory Group Headquarters, for consolidation into the day's events. Considering that major events were compiled daily by all services, and provided to the press for the evening news, there must have been a time warp with no other news that day for something similar to the following to make it into the national news broadcast to my poor mother, over dinner the evening after the rocket attack:

> Yesterday Viet Cong insurgents launched a rocket attack against the small Navy base just outside of the city of Ca Mau in the South Vietnam Delta. The base supports units of the South Vietnamese Navy river assault forces, known as the Mobile Riverine Force. There are US Navy advisors operating with those units. At this time we have no word on any US casualties.

That was bad enough, but since the story was so small, and since there were no casualties, there was no further interest, so not another word in the news. It hung there over my mom for days until she stopped expecting a knock on the door, and then finally received my next letter.

By the time we made our next run to the firebase, the perimeter had been expanded several hundred yards in all directions by the clearing crew, including the area on the opposite bank of the canal.

The next phase of the operation involved the insertion by helo of ARVN troops with U.S. Army advisors, systematically into various segments of the forest, and having them work their way toward the main canal for pick up by the supporting assault boats. Strangely enough, as those operations got underway, and generated increasing contact with larger groups of VC, there were no more attacks yet on the boats on the canals, either north or south.

In our second week we had picked up our first group of ARVN soldiers and their advisor, and we were transporting them back to the firebase. I had ridden the Tango boat with my advisor just to change things up. As we headed back, I noticed the U.S. Army advisor crouched low back against the superstructure at the rear of the helo deck. I walked back and struck up a conversation, and was shocked when he told me that he would not be an advisor on one of our boats for anything! This was a guy who had been inserted with a group of ARVNs into the U Minh Forest, a VC stronghold, to sludge through the jungle muck looking for VC, and he thought we were crazy to ride our boats. I laughed and told him there was no way I would do what he did. We both decided it must be all in what you are trained for and used to. I later proved that point after hitching a ride to Saigon with an Army helo pilot, and being diverted for an emergency troop extraction under fire. I soiled my britches, and told him I didn't know how they did it. He told me that he would much rather be doing that than riding one of those floating targets on the canals; go figure.

Once we started spending three or four days at a time at the firebase, two things began to suffer, our diet and hygiene. While we were all still eating whatever our boat crews ate, which meant rice three meals a day, at least while we were in Ca Mau we could still give the VNs money for protein. However, when we were at the firebase it was pretty much rice and whatever greens the VNs foraged from the canal banks. We were all pleasantly surprised after several weeks when we started seeing a small but meaty fish showing up with the rice meals. I mentioned it to the Dai uy and he said that the crew had noticed them recently schooling by the hundreds along the canal in front of the base. I didn't give it another thought, until the next morning when I went to relieve myself. The accommodations were quaint to say the least, consisting of a couple of rickety piers a few feet over the canal with rudimentary bench like seats with holes through which you could look down and see the canal. I don't mean to be graphic but there is no other way to describe what happened next. I sat down and did my "doody," when all of a sudden there was a thrashing frenzy in the water immediately under my position. I looked down, and to my horror witnessed hundreds of the same fish that had graced our rice meal the night before, fighting over the "seconds." It was all I could do to keep from throwing up! Needless to say that after I related that story to my advisors, nobody ordered the fish anymore!

I mentioned that basic hygiene's an issue because even at the crude base in Ca Mau there was nothing better than cold water showers from an overhead trough. At the firebase there was no answer, until the second month, after several occasions involving the howitzers being called to put in rounds along the canal banks just north of the base by the ARVNs. Several of the RID 40 boat crews noticed that after one of the almost daily downpours, some of the craters filled with clear rain water. So, on occasion the boats would head up in pairs, tie up to the banks, and take turns bathing in the craters while the others stood watch.

Perhaps worse than poor diet and poor hygiene was the never ending attack every evening by squadrons of mosquitos. As the sun started down, you could almost hear them first, and then, looking at the horizon, it must have been what the sailors at Pearl Harbor first thought as the distant sky filled with Japanese planes, i.e., what are all of those things and where are they coming from? These mosquitos came as if in formation, suddenly rolling in to dive bomb the helpless bodies below. Some were so big they had to ask politely, "Where do you want it, your arm or your ass?" We would try huddling under mosquito netting but they would bite right through it. We doused in bug spray but they seemed to ignore it. Finally, we would huddle under a poncho and almost suffocate, but that was better than the alternative. The heavy rains were a double whammy, in that they were drenching, but when they stopped the mosquitos went airborne. Fortunately they were not nearly as bad in Ca Mau; thank God for small favors.

22

Christmas in the U Minh

I'm sure that when President Thieu boasted he would spend Christmas 1970 in the U Minh, it could be interpreted several ways. Those optimistic about the future of South Vietnam as a self-sustaining democracy must have thought, or at least hoped, that by December 25, 1970, the ARVN forces, with the help of the Mobile Riverine Forces and U.S. air support would have swept the last remnants of Viet Cong and North Vietnamese from the U Minh, and opened up the main waterways to a bustling commercial traffic. Others might have simply hoped it meant that government forces had maintained an offensive sufficient enough for the President and his family to spend a leisurely few days in the Forest. But I doubt that few if any interpreted Thieu's promise as the reality that played out.

We were spectators with the best seats in the house for the entire production. Up until the 24th of December, the RIDs at Ca Mau had rotated their time at the firebase. However, on December 24 both units had every available boat lined up along the canal side perimeter. The jungle had by then been cut even further from the canal on the far side. By the 24th of December it was clear that there would be no Thieu family outing in the Forest. For several days before that the helicopter traffic in and out of the base had started to dramatically increase. Sandbag defensive positions had been built or reinforced around the perimeter everywhere between the howitzers. I had not counted before but I swore there were more of the 105s. Dai uy Tinh informed me that he and I were invited to a small reception in the command bunker at 6:00 p.m. on the 25th.

Starting on the morning of the 25th, a steady stream of helos ferried in ARVN troops, who were formed up, briefed and sent out beyond the perimeter of the base in all directions. I did not know the inventory of men and equipment in the South Vietnamese armed forces on

December 25, 1970, but I would be willing to bet that fully 90 percent of all assets were marshaled in and around the U Minh Forest that one day. By mid-afternoon, helos of every conceivable size and shape were flying in concentric circles as far out as we could see. The base commander came out to meet with Dai uy Tinh and his staff to stress the importance of vigilance. He advised that extra observation helos would be flying low over the jungle beyond the clearing on the far bank and that air strikes and 105 howitzer strikes could be called in at a moment's notice. All was ready.

Dai uy Tinh and I waited outside the command bunker at 5:30; for the first time since I left Saigon I was wearing my green fatigues and black beret. After all, I was about to meet the president of South Viet Nam. I was in bad need of a haircut. At about 5:45 the parade of helos began. As if the security around the perimeter and in the air were not enough, these next helos looked like the advance party for a U.S. presidential state visit. Huge guys, *in business suits,* scurried out and set up yet another, smaller perimeter. At precisely 6:00, a sleek executive helo glided in and landed on the pad adjacent to the command bunker. The excitement was short-lived, when it was discovered that was a decoy helo. Immediately behind came another identical helo, which landed as the decoy took off. This was the real deal.

Two even bigger guys in suits jumped out, followed by a Vietnamese general with more medals than a Russian on May Day, and then an admiral equally well adorned. I am embarrassed to tell you that I do not remember the senior U.S. military officer present that night, or if there was a senior American civilian. President Thieu got off of the helo and hurried past us into the command bunker; we followed. The evening was a blur; the entire affair was over very quickly. There were not even introductions all around. Everything spoken was in Vietnamese, leading up to some obviously boisterous words from Thieu, to much applause. Small glasses of what I think was champagne had been previously poured and were hastily passed out. There was a toast in Vietnamese, and, like that, the whole thing ran in reverse.... Thieu and party departed ... other security ... etc., etc., until it was like it never happened. But you'd better believe that the press was told that the promise was kept, and it was ... at what cost? Who knows? For my part, I still have my Christmas card from President Thieu from December 1970.

I discovered the most curious thing during the writing of this book. I had saved all of my original research from my false start, and I occasionally updated that research over the years because a lot has been written since that first attempt. With all of my old notes, references, relevant magazines, etc., and all of my searches of material developed in interim years, I was unable to find ANY reference to President Thieu's Christmas in the U Minh Forest. His Christmas Eve fulfillment of his promise, along with the entire U Minh operation, was the "signature" event of my year in Vietnam. As I wrote in my description of the events of that day and the days leading up to it, Thieu utilized a large majority of all of his available military assets to make that happen. In addition, his stated goal of clearing the VC and NVA out of the U Minh seemed hugely important at the time, and the campaign was ongoing when I departed. And yet, nothing! Historically, it is as if it all never happened. Wouldn't it be nice if it was only a bad dream?

23

Another Boat Down

Just after New Year's, during the first week of 1971, Dai uy asked me to join him once more for an event by the command bunker helo pad. Some members of the press were coming in for a special "show and tell"; Thieu's visit had been hyped enough so this had to be different. As we were walking to the pad, two helos arrived and offloaded a gaggle of press. They were gathered around a display of assorted weapons arranged in rows, spaced so the gawkers could walk between the rows. The base commander came out of the bunker, greeted the press and immediately jumped into an upbeat briefing on the status of the operation in the U Minh.

To sum up his very positive report: Things could not be going any better. Though contact VC units had been lighter than expected, the commander and his superiors all agreed that was because the initial surprise was such a success, followed by aggressive expansion from two locations, that the VC had not been able to reorganize and mount any kind of counterattack. They were apparently not ready to counter the presence of the heavy assault craft on the canals. The B-40 rocket grenade, used somewhat successfully elsewhere in the Delta against the fiberglass hulls of PBRs, had done little damage to the heavily armored craft of the MRF, and only served to draw swift support fire from the air or from the firebase artillery.

There had been as yet no sign of any North Vietnamese regular army troops.

He then moved to what I considered to be the most fascinating part of his briefing. The weapons displayed on tarps on the ground were indeed all captured from the VC, but the real story was their origin. This assortment of firepower had not come here from the North down the Ho Chi Minh Trail, like most arms and ammo used by the VC in the South. These weapons were all of French origin… French designed and

French built, and all brought into the U Minh Forest by French paratroopers in 1952. But by far the most telling detail was that every one of these weapons was in working condition, 18 years later! The ability of the VC to use and maintain those weapons for 18 years was fascinating. However, as we would soon learn, their adaptation of their enemies' weapons for their own use did not end with those French arms.

I wanted to try to get to Saigon for the senior advisors meeting at the end of January, but I couldn't just book a flight. So a couple of days before the meeting, I went over to the command bunker to see about catching a ride on any helo, even if it meant making connections somewhere. The U.S. Army advisor told me that there were always helos every day to and from Can Tho, which would get me halfway to Saigon. I knew that there were helo flights to and from Saigon from Can Tho. So the next day I went over to the bunker mid-morning and was told that they expected a U.S. Army Huey troop carrier in later that morning with miscellaneous cargo from Can Tho, and that I should have no trouble catching a ride back with them. When that flight arrived I introduced myself to the pilot and he had no problem giving me a lift. Even better, he asked if I would like to sit in the seat next to the door gunner and get a good view of things. I could also wear a crew helmet and listen to the routine crew communications. Awesome! I did not let on to the pilot or anybody else, but this was my first helicopter ride, and I had never trusted helos! When I was strapped in on the left side just to the left of the door gunner on that side, I was looking straight out, with the same view as the gunner. The rear fuselage leading back to the tail was inches from my left ear.

Rotors wound up, we lifted off and almost immediately tilted forward and increased air speed. In seconds we were zipping over the jungle, gaining speed and then suddenly we seemed to shoot straight up. I remembered my lesson on how the outbound helos in a war zone avoided small arms fire, and I had just sat through that maneuver. The pilot called me by my first name and asked me how I was doing. Swallowing to hold back the rising bile I told him that was awesome and what I had expected. I walked into that; his next question was, "Oh, you've done this before?" So my facade crumbled and I admitted to being a helo virgin. Any hopes I had for a routine flight the rest of the way were dashed within minutes. The pilot told the crew that they had just been called to join another Huey for an emergency extraction of some ARVN troops engaged in a firefight with the VC somewhere in the vast Delta between us and Can Tho. He told me that they were returning to the firebase to let me off. I asked if that was a regulation driven decision or not, and he said no. Thirty more seconds of back and forth and I was good to go!

The pilot described the scenario to his crew: we would rendezvous with another Huey troop carrier and a Huey Cobra gunship. The ARVN were pinned down behind a rice paddy dirt dike, being fired on by VC in a tree line several hundred yards away. The Cobra would fly overhead while the two troop carriers flew low along the dike parallel to the tree line left to right until they reached the ARVN troops. With the ARVNs jumping in the right door of the helo, the left door gunner (my seat mate) would be firing into the tree line. At the first sign of return fire the Cobra would be unleashed. My parents always told me that hitchhiking was dangerous, but this was ridiculous!

In about 15 minutes the second Huey troop carrier came up behind us; while I couldn't see it yet, the pilot was talking to the Cobra pilot. Five minutes later and our pilot said something like "Here we go!," and we were nose down and picking up speed. We maintained speed and leveled out too close to the paddy dike for my liking, and now I could see the tree line off to our left and high above that was the Cobra gunship. The pilot said, "OK, ARVN coming up on the right in about 30 seconds; I'll be pulling up sharp and settling close to touchdown; we need to pull in six guys! Watch for smoke from some grass hooches in the treelike; that's where reported VC fired from."

I wish I had this on video, and could watch it in slow motion; Oliver Stone, eat your heart out! To the best of my recollection this is what transpired, in less time, I think, than a NASCAR pit stop! Our helo suddenly went nose up and dropped as the pilot decreased airspeed, compensated for lost lift, for just the right drop to bring the skids to waist level on the ARVN. The door gunner on the right side started pulling these guys in as they lunged at the open door. Simultaneously, the door gunner next to me said, "Taking fire from the hooches; I'm on it!" He opened up with his M60 machine gun. While somehow maintaining his position, the pilot called the Cobra gunship and said that we were taking fire from the two hooches in the tree line. I was trying to watch the impact of the M60, while watching the gunship slow roll into a steep dive toward the tree line. In seconds, what I think was a combination of 20mm cannon and rockets literally took out the tree line entirely for several hundred feet, in the center of which had stood the two grass hooches. As the gunship pulled up, we were gaining speed and altitude, and the second troop pickup helo was hovering and recovering ARVNs. I won't even venture a guess as to my heart rate at that moment; what a rush!

We dropped the ARVN troops somewhere as requested and headed for Can Tho. When we landed the pilot got out and helped me with my helmet and seatbelt. As I hopped out on shaky legs, he asked what I thought, and we played the "I would never do what you do" game. I thanked him again for the ride and the show, and he said he wanted to show me one more thing before I left. He simply turned me around where I stood and stuck his finger in a hole in the metal fuselage about one foot behind where I had been sitting! It had not been there when we took off. He smiled and asked his door gunner what he thought, and the gunner said, "Russian AK-47, I'm guessing; good thing we had a breeze!" They laughed; I didn't.

I made it to my Saigon meeting, where I shared the details of my adventure, and the progress in the U Minh. My boss informed me that he had been told that RID 40 would be moving shortly from Ca Mau up to another small navy base at the town of Kien An, the northern jump-off into the U Minh, from which we would begin servicing the Northern firebase. He had no more details, nor any reason for the move. I avoided the President Hotel for my one night in Saigon; I was just too drained. Hitchhiking back to our boats in the U Minh was uneventful, but the next morning was not.

I was talking with my Assistant and Chief Creed on the canal bank by our boats when a couple of the 105s fired several salvos, making me jump involuntarily with each round. Within minutes Dai uy Tinh yelled to me from the Command Boat, "Deek, come quick!" All three of us rushed aboard the command boat and Dai uy Tinh was already below in the communications room. I climbed down into a busy, noisy scene. My advisor on radio watch yelled over two VNs, "Tango 11 was just sunk; our guy is shook but all right. The crew is accounted for except the boat captain; the VNs called in artillery on the banks along both sides; there has been no other hostile fire on any of the boats." Good, concise report. Dai uy turned to me and said, "We get on Tango 3 and we go with two other boats, now!" He obviously did not want to risk the command boat until we knew more about what sunk the Tango. The Chief and I would go with the Dai uy and my Assistant would remain with the command boat.

We had been running boats to and from the firebase about two months now, but had not sent boats more than a few thousand yards further into the U Minh until the past few days. An ARVN unit had been dropped several miles further in and was working its way out to the canal for pickup; we had sent four boats, an Alpha and three Tangos to rendezvous for pickup. Because the canal started to narrow at that point the boats had proceeded past the planned pickup point, and one-by-one had to make awkward back and forth turns to reverse course. All had completed the course reversal when the second boat, a Tango, was mined and sunk. As we headed to their location we had no more information than that.

As we neared the sunken boat and the canal narrowed a bit, we could see that the lead Alpha boat had tied up against the bank. Two Tangos remained on the far side of the sunken one, tied to the canal bank. The mined Tango was on its side with about one-third of one entire side showing above the surface. It appeared to have split in half, indicative of a powerful underwater explosion. Looking beyond those remains, we could see what looked to be some of the crew of the lost boat sitting huddled on the deck of the next Tango just staring at what an hour ago had been their very powerful heavy assault craft.

Rather than jam too many boats into the narrowing part of the canal, Dai uy Tinh had wisely ordered the two boats accompanying us to stop and tie up to opposite banks. We proceeded to tie up next to the Alpha. After discussions in Vietnamese with the boat captain of the Alpha and by radio with the captains of the two remaining Tangos in their group, it was decided that there was adequate width and depth to bring the Tango with the extra crew members past their sunken boat to tie up next to us. The last Tango (sounds like a Jimmy Buffett song) remained in place on the far side of the devastation.

With that movement accomplished and the afternoon wearing on, several important decisions had to be made about security. Dai uy Tinh quickly decided that he would not leave any boats at that location overnight as much as he would like to have secured the location. Two things eased that decision. First, and most importantly, the body of the boat captain had been recovered from the well deck of his boat by two of his crew, who had braved the wreckage to locate their comrade. Second, the ARVN firebase commander had agreed to place motion sensors on both banks at the sinking location. That would allow his fire team to place artillery rounds in the area in the event there was any attempt to intrude by the VC overnight. The fear was that their sappers could easily strip the boat of its weapons overnight. With those concerns settled, the last Tango came past the wreckage, the boats formed a column and we headed back to the firebase. Dai uy had gathered the lead petty officer from the sunken boat, and the boat captain from the Tango that had been immediately behind them. I asked Chief Creed and our advisor from both of those boats to join us. I'm sure I was not the only one wondering about the new threat. Neither of the two from the sunken boat could walk on their own; they had been in enormous pain in their legs before receiving pain relieving shots. Most of the crew from the downed boat suffered from severe concussion trauma to their legs and lower backs.

In the short time it took to return to the base, we heard a very disturbing series of eyewitness descriptions of the sinking, which clearly explained the leg and knee problems of the surviving crew members. The boat captain and my advisor both recalled standing on the flight deck, back against the superstructure. Both wore their flak jackets and helmets, even in the heat of the morning, thinking that was protection enough against any threat. Then came what seemed like a muffled explosion directly beneath them and simultaneously a sudden tremendous upward impact. Both were thrown into the air and landed back on the deck, unable to walk. The description from both witnesses from the trailing Tango was even more chilling. Both had heard a muffled explosion and felt a shudder in their own boat. Looking forward, they both watched in shock and awe what seemed to be in slow motion, a 60 ton Tango boat coming up out of the water far enough for them to see both screws (propellers); it split and folded in the middle, rolled over and sank—all within a matter of seconds.

Back at the firebase, plans were hastily made to return to the scene as soon as possible the next day. A Vietnamese salvage assessment dive team was being flown in with a U.S. advisor, in all probability to determine what weapons and communications gear would be stripped and if the boat should be abandoned in place. They would be accompanied by an explosives investigator who would hopefully give us some specifics on the type of explosives used. This was far larger and more sophisticated than the small package used to blast a hole in the side of our Alpha back at Go Dau Ha. Thinking ahead, if this was a mine, where in the world did the VC, in the middle of the U. Minh Forest, come up with it, learn to use it, and get it in place? Beyond that, how would we prevent it from happening again?

During the early hours of the night there were several triggers of the sensors in the attack area, but after each trigger brought a response from the base 105 howitzers, everything was still until morning. It was mid-morning when the experts arrived and one Alpha and two Tango boats headed back to the scene. I again asked Chief Creed and my advisor from the trailing Tango at the time of the explosion to join me, along with the regularly assigned advisors to the three boats making the trip. The Alpha led and the experts rode with us on the first Tango. It was a long day at the site, especially for the divers, including the U.S. advisor, without whom the necessary work would not have been completed. After one look from above and input from the first dive, the consensus was that the boat was not salvageable, and should be stripped and abandoned in place. So the divers and their advisor switched hats to become a weapons salvage team, and the investigative eyes of the explosives expert.

By late afternoon we received the opinion of the explosives guy as to the type of explosive used and the delivery method. It was not good news for us, or for anyone riding a heavy assault craft of the Mobile Riverine Force. He determined that in all likelihood the explosion had been that of a 750 pound bomb, originally dropped from the belly of an American B-52 over South Vietnam; that was jaw dropping! He went on to explain that U.S officials were aware that a certain small percentage (5 or 6 percent) of the thousands of bombs disgorged from the B52s were in fact duds. It was also a fact that it did not take a highly skilled bomb tech to disarm such a dud and remove the explosive warhead material weighing about 390 pounds and the fuse. It was an easy jump from there to imagine the Viet Cong developing the perfect weapon for use against the heavy, slow moving boats of the riverine forces: a simple wire detonated mine packing just under 400 pounds of explosives. Detonate that explosive in a shallow canal under the flat bottom of a slow moving heavy assault boat, and it's turn out the lights, the party's over!

There was one important fact that somebody smarter than me had to chase; the Alpha boat, remember, was the only MRF boat designed from the keel up. It was designed specifically to be hard, if not impossible, to mine, due to unique hull design. More importantly, it was designed to be rigged with a minesweeping capability, consisting of a chain dragged hook system. If true, then every column of MRF boats from here on out, anywhere in Vietnam, should require a lead Alpha with their anti-mine chain drag deployed. Turned out RID 40 Alphas had them but had never deployed them. Dai uy Tinh and I both told our folks to immediately determine the condition of the systems on our Alphas and what it would take to get them working. Chief Creed and I both put out feelers where we could to find any Americans in-country with experience with Alpha mine sweeping. If there had been no threat, we would likely find no experience. There was a new tension among the crews on every boat that transited any distance after that.

24

Moving North

As soon as we returned to Ca Mau, Dai uy Tinh informed me that we had two days to get ready to move north to Kien An, where we would support the new firebase in the Northwest U Minh. My injured advisor was in more pain in his knee and hips, so I had him picked up by a Medevac helicopter. He ended up at the evacuation hospital in Da Nang, where it was determined that he would require surgical repair of one knee for certain, and potentially the second. Fortunately they determined that his hips would heal on their own. In any case, the war was over for him. I was happy for him, and it worked out for me since we were short another boat, and therefore down one on our advisor requirements. I would have no trouble with an award write-up in this case.

The advisors had little to do to get ready to move except to be personally ready, including putting anything they did not want on the boats in the truck, which would make the roundabout trek of about 200 miles from Ca Mau to our new home in Kien An. It was actually only about 50 miles as the crow flies, but there were no east-west roads in the Delta south of Can Tho. Given the circuitous route, I decided to send a second man to ride shotgun in the truck with our driver. The trip for the boats was actually some 25 miles shorter, distance wise, but we were still looking at potentially a 30–36 hour transit, with a stopover in Can Tho, where I planned to find a hot shower!

The transit was pretty much like remembering directions in a NASCAR race, *Keep turning left*! We were familiar with the sights as we proceeded north up the 75 mile straight stretch of heavily trafficked narrow canal which we had terrorized on the trip south. Then it was a left turn heading northwest up the Bassac, with a layover in Can Tho to give everybody a night off. My assistant and I grabbed a hot shower, some dinner, and a beer and that was all the excitement we could stand. Next morning we headed for the coastal city of Rach Gia on the Gulf of Thailand. Known mostly for rice processing and exporting, it was still our last chance for a decent meal before the final 10 miles of the trip to the small VN Navy base at Kien An, the northern gateway to the U Minh. The trip from Ca Mau to Kien An was somewhat relaxed because we travelled canals with heavy commercial use, and we did not expect to encounter a mine in those waterways. We were quite sure that the VC would rather catch a heavy assault craft on one of the two canals being used to and from the new firebases and potentially block the canal to further traffic.

The next morning we were pleasantly surprised to see that, even though small, the base at Kien An had actual buildings, much like we had left in Go Dau Ha. There were floating docks for the boats, and, best of all, we could have all the sand and sandbags we wanted, to build our own sleeping bunker ... with bunks. Our relative joy was short-lived when an hour or so after our arrival, word came from the command bunker that one of the Tango boats from the other RID at Kien An had just been sunk, apparently by a mine.

I ran and reached the Command bunker just as Dai-uy Tinh came out; he was visibly shaken. "It bad...," he said, "very bad; some crew dead or still missing. American Dai uy, like you, ride that boat." I went inside and asked one of the senior petty officer advisors from the other unit what was known, and he broke down. His boss—the lieutenant, Senior Advisor to that RID—had been killed in the attack. He had been thrown from the deck of the boat all the way onto the canal bank, and apparently had died instantly.

Nothing you can say; nothing you can do; it just *sucked*! I told the petty officer I was sorry and I left the bunker; it was closing in on me. Again the little voice started deep in my head, "What the fuck are you doing here? What the fuck are we doing here?" And then the little voice went for the jugular, "That could have been you!" Shit! The little voice was right; there had been a 50–50 chance that could have been me. In the entire chain of events that led that 750-pound bomb (which it surely had been) from the belly of that B-52 to wherever it dropped and flopped, to its dissection, and its transport to the Northern U Minh, to its planting in that shallow canal ... through all of that, if there had been one small glitch, a missed milestone, anything to cause a couple of days delay ... that would have been me. Insult was added to injury when it was discovered that the lieutenant's ring and watch had been somehow stolen before his body was recovered. I went to find Chief Creed and then Dai uy Tinh; I didn't care how, but the minesweeper chain rigs on our Alpha boats better be working before we head back into the forest.

The timing on this next stunt, for lack of a better name, may at first seem very poor, but in hindsight it was perfect. Everybody was physically and emotionally drained, and RID 40 would not have boats heading for the firebase for at least two or three days. I had carried around an unopened bottle of scotch (and I hate scotch!) since we left Go Dau Ha, waiting for this moment. Late afternoon/early evening the next day, I found the Dai uy and told him he had to come with me, I had something he must see. We went into one of the makeshift buildings where me and my guys had rustled up a table and a bunch of unmatched chairs. The advisors sat all the way around the table, upon which sat my bottle of scotch and two glasses. Before another word was spoken, Dai uy Tinh slowly turned to me, recognition registering on his face, and he smiled and said, "I kill you!"

I'm sure I don't have to bore you with the details. I simply said, "Dai uy, we never had the time for my men to get to know you. So now that we have a couple of days to regroup" (Chief Creed had now opened the scotch and was pouring the first of two shots), "my Chief, he wants to have a drink with you..." ; the rest is history. Dai uy Tinh was knee walkin' when they were done, and after a slow recovery he admitted that he had been fairly had. He was painfully aware of the old Yankee saying, "Payback is a bitch!"

Meanwhile, the advisors of RID 40 got downright serious about their sandbag bunker. Tirelessly, breaking only for food and hydration, they filled and stacked bags. Within two days the RID 40 Advisors' Sandbag Hilton was the envy of the entire base. The walls were double-wide, and inside they had utilized some old metal frame Navy bunks left when the U.S. Navy had turned over the base to the VNs the previous December. The bunks were over and under with plenty of head room and an aisle down the middle. My electrician first class had run power from a nearby source and rigged basic lighting inside. I will never forget those two days with those incredible guys. I filled and stacked sandbags with them, ate with them, shared stories with them, and most of all laughed with them. The nice thing was that my once reluctant assistant was right in there with us. I thank God to this day that I did not lose a single one of those men to the senseless situation we shared.

The second afternoon at the Kien An base I witnessed something

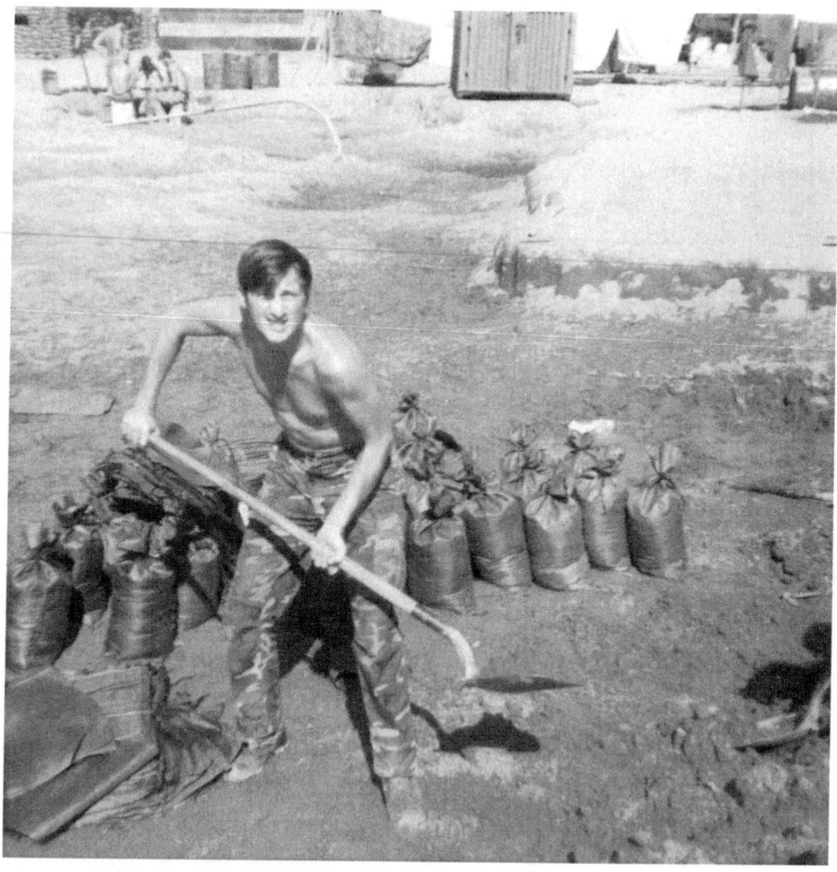

The author filling sandbags for construction of RID 40 advisors' bunker at support base in Kien An. The bunker was nicknamed "The Hilton."

that was so quick and so simple in the overall scheme of things, but it struck me right in the heart, and drove home the divide between me and the Vietnamese people we were there to help. I was walking from the "Hilton" to the boats when I first heard and then saw a group of VN sailors in a circle laughing and yelling loudly. As I moved closer, I saw the object of their raucous attention; they had a small puppy of indeterminate breed on a long rope, held by one of the sailors on one side of the circle. On the other side, a sailor held some sort of morsel of food that the puppy obviously wanted and was desperately trying to get. But each time he got close, the man with the rope yanked so hard that the puppy flew backwards and landed hard in the dirt. As they all laughed hysterically, the puppy shook itself off and ran back toward the treat, only to be jerked back again. Well, the Norman Rockwell in me boiled over; I yelled, "HEY!," so loud it startled them into silence. Before they could react, or I could think about the folly of my action, I walked into the circle, grabbed the rope from the assailant, picked up the puppy, and bulled my way back out of the circle. I turned back to the stunned group, and coldly said, "No more!"

I walked away. I wish I could tell you that this impulsive story had a happy "Rat"-like ending, but it doesn't. As I walked with the puppy and untied the rope, I started to realize that it (I had yet to lift it up to determine he or she) was ultimately doomed. So I went to find Dai uy Tinh. I found him in the Command bunker and asked if I could speak with him outside. I related to him what had transpired, and that I understood the difference in cultures, and even the probable final "disposition" of the dog. I asked him to please tell his men that I would respect them and their culture, if, in return, they would do the same for me. I asked only that they did not in the future mistreat their dogs in front of me and my advisors; it was that simple. I left the puppy in the arms of the startled Dai uy and never saw it again. But with about two months to go on my one year tour, for the first time I stole a few moments to make my own short-timer's calendar; I could not wait to go home.

We settled into a routine; the minesweeping chain rigs were in working order and were dragged by a lead Alpha boat on every transit to and from the base. The ARVN continued to have success with their quick strikes and pushes to the canals for pickup by the RIDs. We will never know whether it was the minesweeping of the Alphas, the successes of the ARVN, a change in tactics by the VC or all of those factors, but there were no more mining attempts during my final two months with RID 40.

25

The Flower Girl Is Dead

Two weeks before I left Vietnam, I had the worst day of my entire tour. As I get ready to write about it now, I prepare to cry, as I have so many times before when telling this story. To me it represents everything so completely senseless in that awful conflict. It was a point in time when the worst evil encountered the purest goodness, and slaughtered it without a thought. Worst of all, I was helpless to stop it.

The village of Kien An was right outside of the gate to the base. Like most places in the Delta, by day the rice paddies and the canals were open to the people who lived and worked there. However, all of the good guys, the non–VC, had to retreat into the confines of the villages and hamlets at night. It was a no-win situation for most of the residents outside of the major cities in South Vietnam. By day they were subservient to the government, and, because most of them did not live in "gated communities," by night they were at the mercy of the VC. On occasion the VC would pull off a brazen act of terror against the citizenry to show them that the government really had no control, and that they were really never out of reach of the VC. This was one of those days; one of those acts.

It was late afternoon/early evening and we could hear the sounds of a celebration beyond the gate in the village. Dai-uy informed me that the granddaughter of one of the village elders was getting married and what we were hearing now would be what we would call the reception. I relaxed on top of the "Hilton" writing a letter home, when suddenly the soft sounds of the celebration were interrupted by the quick burst of an automatic weapon ... then another; unmistakably Russian-made AK-47s. That was it, those two quick bursts, and then horrible screaming. I jumped down off of the bunker, threw my writing stuff inside, and bolted toward the gate, with no idea what I would do when I got there. I didn't have to think about that; the gates were open and a throng of people were being helped in. This was a stampede of terror-stricken people. Many of the civilians were covered in blood; some helped others along.

Then I saw ... a small Vietnamese woman in an all-white ao dai, the traditional full length dress for such events. Only hers was no longer all white; it was drenched in blood. Draped across her arms was the delicate body of a small girl, maybe six to eight, I don't know. She too was in a blood soaked ao dai. The woman, who I now assumed was the mother, was screaming hysterically, as she ran straight to me and placed the child in my arms, continuing to scream. Now I was caught up in the hysteria. I had the sense at least to yell at the nearest American to get help making sure the gate was secure; that this was not a way for the VC to gain access. Then I turned and joined the rush, which was being herded towards an area of outside picnic tables; the wounded were being seated at the tables or laid upon them as sheets and blankets were brought as soon as possible. I saw Chief Creed and yelled to him to come. All the while the poor mother was screaming at me.

As I laid the young girl on her back I noticed a hole in her upper stomach area, by now totally soaked in blood. Chief told me quickly that two VC had run into the celebration, sprayed the wedding party with AK's, and run out before anyone really realized what had happened. "Sorry pricks!" I thought. We didn't have a doctor or even a corpsman assigned, but we had one man from the other RID who was a trained paramedic. He was already everywhere with people needing attention, but I had a single focus. With Mom still screaming nonstop, I yelled several times for our "Doc" to come over. When he finally did, he took a quick look at the girl and yelled above the din, "She's gone!," and he turned to leave. I grabbed him and spun him around; I yelled, "She's not gone! Do something!"

And so in the same way you show a stubborn child who won't listen, he showed me; and I still see that picture in my mind today. He turned this amazingly beautiful young girl in the once sparkling white dress over onto her stomach, and pulled away the bloody fabric on her lower back. He didn't say another word; just turned to help those that he could. I took one look at the girl's back and turned away and retched. An AK-47 round is designed to cause maximum possible damage to human flesh and bone. Shortly after leaving the muzzle the bullet begins to tumble. As a result, it makes a small entry wound, but a devastating exit wound. This young girl's lower back had a gaping hole, and in that brief second I saw flesh, bone, organ, and blood, and I lost it. I looked at the poor mother who had gone strangely and mercifully catatonic, and through my own tears I just managed, "I'm so sorry."

I walked in a stupor back to the "Hilton," crawled back up onto the roof, put my head in my hands and sobbed until I had no tears left. From that night on I never lost track of the number of hours I had left in that awful place, and for the first time I found myself flinching at every sudden sharp noise as if it was the shot that would take me out.

The next two weeks crawled by, until my relief showed up! He was everything the RID needed—not just new blood, but someone who had been through the entire course of training, and had an introduction to the Vietnamese language. He had that light in his eyes of someone who is ready, and eager to get started. I tried not to let him see that my light had gone out. The main thing was that he seemed genuine, and that's all the group of RID 40 advisors asked.

There was one early bump in the road; on the second day in Kien An he asked if we could do a weapons inventory on all of the boats. Before I could stop myself, I laughed and said, "You're shitting me, right?" I explained to him that if we had been a U.S. "Brown Water Navy" unit, then a weapons inventory would certainly have been proper. But as far as I knew there wasn't even a baseline of what was on the boats when they were originally turned over to the VNs. All I could tell him was that, after we left Dong Tam, I was sure that we had a lot more weapons then would show up on any inventory list. And that was the end of that.

As much as I would like to have stayed off the boats during those last two weeks, I could not let that feeling show. So I made three more trips to the firebase, each lasting a couple of days, and each accompanied by my relief. Each trip to and from involved slowing down to pass the tangled wreckage of the sunken Tango, a point at which an eerie silence fell over the crews of every boat in the column. On my last return trip back to the base at Kien An I think I literally held my breath from the wreckage to the base.

My departure from Kien An was uneventful. Chief Creed and several of my top advisors had re-upped for another tour, so they had been there when I arrived in Go Dau Ha and they were in Kien An to say farewell. I know that real men don't cry, but I had formed such a strong bond with the Chief and a couple of the other senior guys that it would not have taken much. I loved and respected these guys like brothers. Dai uy Tinh was the same way; we had grown very close personally. He had shared much about his family and his career, as had I. He called his junior officers together for a small luncheon of sorts, where two amazing things happened. The Dai uy's number two man, his XO, the one I still think was VC or NVA, actually gave me a man hug as everyone else cheered. Second, although he would deny it I'm sure, Dai uy Tinh had a tear in his eye. I shared the emotion but for deeper reasons; not only would I miss our friendship, but I feared the future for him and his family.

And with that, I bid farewell to RID 40, and allowed myself a couple of days to "hitchhike" to Saigon, a night to freshen up (though it would take more than one night to make me presentable as an officer in the U.S. Navy), and be early for my check-in at Tan Son Nhut Airport. I stayed in one of the officer billets in Saigon and once again avoided the President Hotel. I did not want to have to explain not only why I was leaving, but why the U.S. guys were all leaving so fast. That was a "number 10" situation for which I had no explanation.

26

Tears on the Tarmac

I am going to try to capture here the entire gamut of emotions I experienced, and I think that I shared with those with me, from the moment I walked into the terminal at Tan Son Nhut Airport to catch my flight home, until I walked off of that plane at Travis Air Force Base, California. While the wedding slaughter in Kien An just two weeks before had been my worst day in Vietnam, the day I flew back to the United States was the best. It's funny, I can't remember a lot of the details about the waiting room at Tan Son Nhut, the charter plane (DC-8 or 707), whom I sat with, stewardesses, etc., but I do remember every emotion.

In the lounge, there was the buzz of anxious excitement. There was no segregation of services or rank; Army and Marine Corps made up the majority, and I assumed that those with the far-away stares or the nervous paranoia were the ones most recently in the field, perhaps under fire mere hours ago. There was nervous laughter in small groups and there were solitary tears. I think I was the only Navy officer on the flight. I had showered, changed into my green fatigues and jungle boots, and my black beret. I had gotten the best trim I could get back in Kien An from one of my advisors with a pair of shears, but I was not recruiting poster material. I sat alone, people watching, just like I still do at the mall, and praying for a safe flight home.

The next thing I remember is sitting on the plane waiting for the engines to run up. I remember it so vividly because when it happened, the lively nervous excitement of everyone on the plane turned instantly to silent trepidation. Not a word was spoken as we taxied out and then began our acceleration for takeoff. I know in my heart that every person on that plane was holding their breath and praying that there would not be one more VC or NVA rocket waiting at the end of the runway. Those of us in window seats watched, ready to yell, "INCOMING!" Everyone else had a white knuckle grip on the armrests and stared straight ahead or squeezed their eyes shut. We all had one thing in common, we were on day 365 of our one-year tour in Vietnam, the last page of our short timers' calendar. There was a one-year hole in our lives that we could never recover. We were all silently chanting inside, "Climb, baby, climb!" When the first person either needed to breathe or determined that we were out of range, he let out a cheer that was quickly echoed by everyone else. A large part of the weight on our backs had been lifted; the rest we would leave on the tarmac at Travis AFB, California.

Gradually things settled into more chatter, and then to exhausted sleep. I think we stopped in Hawaii before the last leg to Travis AFB. A few were still tired enough to sleep on that last leg, but for me and most of the others, there was the beginning of what would become a gut wrenching anticipation. I guarantee you that no one remained asleep after the word came that we were approaching the coast of California. I literally could not breathe; I prayed for a safe landing. I had the weirdest few minutes of realization that, regardless of my garbled feelings about Vietnam and the shitty politics of it all, I was still so incredibly lucky to be going back to the greatest country in the world. I was still a patriot; weird, huh? I realized my eyes were tearing up.

Then there it was, the coast of California! Everything went totally quiet again, and we held our breath, again. Over the end of the runway and still not a sound, but when the wheels touched down and we started our deceleration, the cheering started; we were home! The raucous cheering and laughter continued until we rolled to a stop. There were no boarding walkways in those days, so we waited for the rolling stairs to be put in place and the doors opened. This is the part I remember the most, and I cried then, I have cried every time I related it to my eighth graders, and I cry now as I write. As I stepped out and realized that I was home, my eyes were full, but what I saw next brought me to full tears; I saw men of all ages, from all walks of life, step off of the last step, get down on their knees, break into sobs and kiss the tarmac! Every time I see some ignorant, disgruntled ingrate burning or otherwise desecrating the American flag, I close my eyes and remember those incredible men on their knees, so grateful for this country that they were kissing its ground.

27

The Aftermath

I had left an America deeply divided over the war in Vietnam, and in the year I had been gone, things had gotten worse. Even though history would show that politicians lost the war in Vietnam, and those of us who fought there would eventually be thanked for our service, at the time, a large part of the population blamed the military. That feeling was not helped by a press that continuously accented the very worst of American behavior during the war; every bad act by a misguided individual became the norm. Therefore I was not greeted by a ticker tape parade with bands playing patriotic music and admiring children smiling and waving. Instead I was spit on in anger and heard cries of "baby killer!"

I wish I had a time-lapse video of my personal appearance from Kien An, Vietnam, to my first day of duty in Washington, D.C. It would be like watching an old Lon Chaney *Werewolf* movie scene of him changing into the werewolf, only watching it in reverse, me changing back into a Naval officer. In June 1971 I reported for duty at the Bureau of Naval Personnel, Washington, D.C., assigned to Enlisted Personnel Division, Special Projects, as Enlisted Vietnam Reassignment Coordinator ... translation, the receiving end of Nixon's Vietnamization of the war; the end of the ACTOV personnel flow out of Vietnam. My incredibly good mood about being home was dampened tremendously on my first day, when I was told not to wear my uniform to work because I wouldn't want anyone to know I was in the service. What the fuck? This is what we volunteered for? I clearly needed an attitude adjustment.

In a normal world, being in the personnel "assignment" business, or what we refer to as "detailing," is hard enough. In 1971 there were more than 600,000 people in the U.S. Navy, with a large number of them in motion, changing assignments. For each person leaving an assignment, there must be one qualified to fill that vacancy, and then one to fill that person's vacancy and so on. The formula is hugely complicated by the myriad of skill sets and training required. In addition, recruiting must be balanced with retirements and other losses.

When I assumed responsibility for the reassignment of enlisted personnel returning from Vietnam, the long-standing policy was that each person, in deference to their combat service, to the best of the detailer's ability, got assigned to one of their top three choices of duty, preferably their first choice. As you can imagine, even during the "normal" flow of people in and out of Vietnam, that was a challenge. However, Nixon's accelerated withdrawal was creating a flood of people requiring reassignment. Not only were there not a sufficient number of available openings, but certainly not of the type and in the locations requested, and *expected.* The straw that broke the camel's back in that reassignment game came in the name of Admiral Zumwalt. He quickly became the sailors' CNO, relaxing what he considered overly restrictive guidelines, rules and regulations. That was not my problem. At issue was his penchant for telling every enlisted man who caught his ear that it would happen.

In the early spring of 1971, COMNAVFORV briefed Adm Zumwalt that the VN Navy was struggling with operational readiness, logistics and maintenance due to the speed with which assets had been turned over and U.S. advisors withdrawn. Therefore, Zumwalt made a trip to personally assess the situation. While there, he of course mingled with the sailors whose number one request was "Can I be assigned to ________?" You can bet that in every case the blank was filled with some place exotic, or some place near their home town. And in every case, Adm Zumwalt had turned to his staff and told them to make it happen. Sure enough, within days of his return to the States, we got a list of "the Adm. would like to see these men get the indicated assignments." And when it couldn't happen, first I felt the wrath of the individual, and in many cases, the office of the CNO. It was a no win situation.

On an up note, one of my proudest accomplishments while assigned to BUPERS was not even directly related to my detailing duties. Prior to Adm. Zumwalt's assignment as Chief of Naval Operations, official Navy policy was implemented through formal documentation called OPNAV INSTRUCTION or NAVOP for short, issued under the signature of the CNO. A typical NAVOP would go through a bureaucratic maze of review and comment at multiple levels at numerous organizations before reaching the CNO's desk for his signature release. In order to expedite directives on matters he considered urgent, Adm Zumwalt cut through the red tape and began implementing policy through a series of personally authored directives called "Z-Grams." During his tenure as CNO, Zumwalt issued 121 sequentially numbered Z-Grams, all of which were immediately cancelled when he was relieved, because they were not official policy documents, though several were converted to formal NAVOPS.

Junior officers were rarely asked to comment on Z-Grams, but rather just expected to implement the policy directives contained therein. However, in October 1970 a Z-Gram concerning the authorization of a new uniform insignia for service in "the Brown Water Navy" in Vietnam ended up on my boss's desk.[1] My boss was a full commander, who worked for a captain who worked for Rear Admiral James Watkins, head of the entire Enlisted Personnel Division of BUPERS. James Watkins would grow up to be the CNO, and ultimately would become the first U.S. Secretary of the Department of Energy. Since I had just come out of Vietnam, my boss asked if I would read the Z-gram and brief him on its meaning, so he could brief his boss, who had to brief RADM Watkins; phew!

The document authorized a new "Small Craft Insignia for junior officers and senior petty officers who had served as officer in charge (OIC) of Riverine or Coastal Craft, under combat conditions in the Republic of Vietnam." It went on to expand the term OIC to include petty officer in charge, and established a six-month minimum time served in a qualifying role. I'm sure that my boss expected me to just explain the terminology and get on with it. However, after some thought, I wondered why U.S. Navy advisors who rode the same boats in combat, as advisors to Vietnamese Navy personnel in those same assignments, would not also be eligible. So, I sat down and naively prepared a proposed addendum to the document. My proposed addendum as written in 1971 follows:

> US Navy personnel who served as advisors to the Vietnamese Navy personnel in an "in-charge" position, and officers and enlisted whose units were turned over to the Vietnamese Navy before they had acquired the requisite 6 months eligibility as stated above, are authorized to wear the insignia provided the total operational time and advisory time on the craft equal 6 or more months.[2]

I attached it to the Z-gram and went back the next day to brief my boss; he was aghast! A new-to-the-Bureau, whippersnapper kid lieutenant could not possibly hope to add an addendum to a newly released CNO policy. I assured him that it made perfect sense if you understood the comparative roles of the riverine advisors and the U.S. "brown water" sailors. Now I had put a fly in the ointment. So he told me that I would have to help him shepherd it through his boss to RADM Watkins. I thought for sure that my effort would go down in flames at the desk of my bosses' boss.

My boss set up our meeting with his boss the next morning. I was as nervous as I had ever been in a chain of command situation; this was as high in the administrative chain I had ever been and it could end as a major embarrassment to me. The meeting went well, however, mainly because neither my boss nor his boss had any direct experience with the role of the Naval Advisory Group, so they could not muster an argument. Why not just let me go up and fall on my own sword? So the Captain initialed my proposal for forwarding to RADM Watkins, and I was to accompany him and my boss to present my case for the changes. Now I would be playing in the big leagues.

It took a couple of days to get on RADM Watkins's schedule and I sweated bullets the whole time. We were shown in to the RADM's office and he stood up from behind his huge desk, walked around it and motioned us to sit at a round table. I noticed that he carried the Z-gram with my proposed addendum with him; uh oh! He opened with some small talk; he was pleased with my department's efforts in keeping up with the ACTOV requirements, and I was surprised at the details he knew about the staffing levels. He was even aware that we had put in many hours on Saturdays since my arrival. He finally said, "Well, let me get right to the point with this Z-gram and your proposed addendum." Oh crap, I thought; here comes the hammer.

But to my amazement he said, "Sometimes it just takes a fresh set of eyes on these things. I can't believe we were about to cut out all of the brave junior officers and senior enlisted men in the Naval Advisory Group who rightfully deserve to wear this insignia. Good catch, Lieutenant; they all owe you a debt of gratitude." He continued, "However, a Z-Gram cannot have an addendum, so my recommendation to the CNO's office will be that this be rewritten to include your wording on those who served as advisors; it will be worth it. Why don't you take a stab at the changes and bring it back to me?" He stood; we stood, and I said, "Thank you, Sir!" He walked towards his desk as we headed for the door, but he turned, and with a wry smile, said, "By the way, Lieutenant, if I'm not mistaken, this will authorize you to wear this insignia now, won't it?" I smiled back and said, "Gosh, sir, I guess you're right; I never really thought about that."

So, with only a couple of months in DC under my belt, I authored a change to Navy uniform policy that was signed by the CNO. My original wording was not changed, and reads that way to this day in the Navy uniform regulation. As soon as it was published I went out and got my gold Small Craft Insignia. The biggest professional benefit for me out of that entire event, which was not immediately evident to me, was that RADM Watkins recognized from that interface that I was his best source of knowledge concerning anything Vietnam related, especially in the volatile personnel staffing business. From that time forward, though nothing was ever formally changed organizationally, it was clear that I reported directly to RADM Watkins for all things Vietnam in the enlisted personnel business. All internal red tape disappeared, and I found myself mentored from that time forward by the sharpest mind I had ever encountered anywhere.

During that same period of time, I was called up to the office of the Chief of Naval Personnel, RADM Watkins's boss, for an awards presentation, where I was presented with a Navy Commendation Medal. I had to secretly smile because my boss in Vietnam, Cdr. Van Westendorp, had told me just prior to his departure from Vietnam in March 1971 that he had recommended me for a Bronze Star. In April 1971, unbeknownst to Cdr. Van Westendorp or me, the awards board in Saigon had quietly downgraded my Bronze Star recommendation to a Navy Commendation Medal. I could only think back to my awards protest movement and wonder if what goes around comes around. It was really quite humorous for those paying attention at the awards ceremony. There was one other award, a Bronze Star presented to a Navy captain for his Vietnam service. First, the Admiral's aide read my citation, which included number of patrols in the U Minh, calling in air strikes while under fire, etc., and ended with the ADM pinning my Commendation Medal on my chest. Next the aide read the captain's citation; he had been an administrative staff officer in a Saigon office, and the write-up talked about paperwork processed, etc., except that the last sentence read, "...and all the while under the constant threat of enemy terrorist attack": Bronze Star Medal pinned on his chest. After the ceremony, the ADM asked me to stay back for a moment. When the others had gone he told me that he honestly thought that the two awards had been switched by mistake; he was personally embarrassed by the awards versus the write-ups. I asked if he had a minute, so I explained my rebellion against the "End of Tour Award" procedure, and he agreed that my good deed had come back to bite me in the ass.

One day in early summer 1972, out of the blue, I got a surprise visit from now-Captain Van Westendorp, on assignment to BUPERS in preparation for a choice assignment in London. I was impressed that he had sought me out, and we enjoyed a wonderful reunion. As we caught up, he glanced at my ribbons and asked, "Where is your Bronze Star?." Taking my explanation aboard, he mentioned as he left that he would right the wrong of an unjust decision. I thanked him, but thought that with a marriage in his near future and his London assignment, he would never revisit the medal award. However, I had greatly underestimated his resolve and perseverance. Steve, as I now referred to him, immediately sent a letter to the Commander Naval Forces VN, recommending reconsideration and award of the Bronze Star. Documentation shows that in August '72, COMNAVFORV recommended approval to the Commander-in-Chief U.S. Pacific Fleet. The documentation was then apparently lost in the administrative chaos of the war.

28

Heartbreak Revisited

One of the really interesting parts of my office's support to enlisted redeployment, rapid withdrawal, ACTOV, or whatever you want to call it, as the pace of the U.S withdrawal picked up, was to roll up all of our figures on weekly enlisted reassignments, totals to date, etc., and brief my bosses and Admiral Watkins on Fridays. Then we would meet with our officer detailer counterparts on Saturday mornings and roll their numbers in with ours, in preparation for a briefing to the Chief of Naval Personnel on Mondays. All of this information was then ultimately provided to the Secretary of the Navy, who then combined it with the figures from the other services for the Secretary of Defense to provide to the White House for President Nixon's weekly address to the nation on how well the troop withdrawal from Vietnam was progressing. I don't know whether to call it pride or not, but it was interesting to see the staffing level charts in Nixon's presentations, broken down by service organization, and realize that my office had direct input to that data.

As the size of the Navy's presence in Vietnam was reduced, and more and more personnel were pulled from field locations, and advisors pulled off boats, the reassignment coordination between the detailers in DC and the personnel office in Saigon became more and more intricate. So much so that in late summer 1972, my counterpart in officer detailing and I made a trip to Saigon for face-to-face planning of the last phases of the withdrawal. A year and a half after my "Freedom Flight" I was returning to Vietnam. What a rush!

My counterpart, a lieutenant commander, had never been to Vietnam, so he suffered a mix of excitement and trepidation. For me it was concern and anger about the course of events in the U.S., including the actions of protesters and politicians, and I was still seriously questioning the value-added by my year in Vietnam. While not wanting to dishonor those who lost their lives there, I was questioning more and more our whole involvement. In summary, my head was a mess about the whole Vietnam thing. So I was excited to have what I considered a rare opportunity for another look. When I left the last time I was bitter and confused, and I hadn't wanted to die in a lost cause. Maybe this time I could leave with my head up; but that wasn't going to happen.

Add the flight from Washington, D.C., to California and the California to Vietnam trip and we spent more than a day in the airplane. By the time we approached Tan Son Nhut, I had the LCDR convinced that at the airport and in Saigon itself we would probably see no signs of war, other than the huge numbers of soldiers and equipment. Much like Hillary, if he wanted to tell stories of running from the plane into bunkers while under enemy fire, he too would have to make them up.

The landing was without incident and we were met in the terminal by a rep from NAVFORV and a driver who took us to our quarters. We had decided that four days (three nights) would be sufficient time to settle the details of further withdrawal. As we weaved our way among the hundreds of vehicles of all shapes and sizes, my counterpart was enthralled. For me, it was like I never left; the sights and sounds were the same. In the year and a half I was gone I had heard no news about the U Minh Forest. It was as if, after Thieu's heralded Christmas visit, there was no further interest. I wondered as we drove through Saigon that day if I caught a helo to Kien An would I find any old friends there? Was there even a campaign being waged there anymore?

For the first two days we spent every waking minute on the details of the future withdrawals, translating the organizational forecasts from NAVFORV and the Naval Advisory Group (NAVADGRU) into projected manpower requirements, and from there projecting the reassignment numbers. On the third day, one of the junior officers in the personnel office offered to show us around the city. I agreed but only if part of the tour could be taken riding on the front of one of the motorbikes with the seat for a front bumper. If my traveling partner could not experience the terror of combat then he could at least experience the terror of playing front bumper of one of these strange motorized rickshaws in Saigon traffic! To add to the excitement, I offered the winning driver to each location a bonus! We had a great day of sightseeing, enjoying a Vietnamese meal and a Ba-Moi-Ba (33) Vietnamese beer. Late that afternoon we wrapped up the business end of things. My counterpart just wanted to grab a bite at the hotel restaurant and get to bed;

we had a long day of travel home the next day. I on the other hand had one more stop.

It was early evening when I caught a cab and asked the driver to take me to the President Hotel. Things looked the same as I paid the driver and walked into the lobby. It was no surprise that the desk clerk did not recognize me; I told him I was just going to the restaurant on the top floor. It was toward the end of the month so I knew that even in good times the Army was out of money, but I was taken aback somewhat as I stepped off of the elevator by the lack of patrons. Only a handful of Americans in the same nondescript attire either shot pool, or sat at a table or at the bar with a young lady at their side. There were several unaccompanied ladies on one side of the room but they were engaged in conversation and did not see me as I slipped past the bar to an outside restaurant table.

The waiter came over right away and I ordered a beer; the Cha gio, a crispy egg roll with extra Nuoc Mam fish sauce; and the garlic crab. The beer came and I sat there thinking how odd it was that it had been more than two years since I had said my goodbyes to this place, and in my wildest dreams never expected to see it again. As I daydreamed, a tiny, soft pair of hands from behind closed over my eyes. I took them down and turned to see the shocked smiling face of Frenchy. I stood, and for a moment, nothing was said. Then suddenly she hugged me, and then just as quickly stepped back and sat down; so I sat with my knees touching hers. She started to cry, and in her halting English she said, "Dai uy, I no understand. Your men always tell other girls someday they come back, but they never come back. You always tell me you never come back, but now you come back. I no understand!" And now she really cried. I was saved by the same hostess who apparently was still in charge. She approached, and was accompanied by several of the other girls. I stood and she gave me a kiss on each cheek, and said, "Welcome back, Dai uy; we miss you, but I surprised to see you. The girls want to know if you bring any of your men with you." I told her that I had not, and that if she would like to join us, I would explain.

She spoke to the girls in Vietnamese and they left despondently. The hostess and I both sat, so now it was the three of us … the American Lieutenant, the "Hostess," and the "Escort," at a restaurant on top of a French built, Vietnamese managed hotel, in the middle of Saigon, and I am about to explain to these ladies why the Americans, after all of these years of support, are pulling out and abandoning their friends and allies. You can't write a better script, and I could not come up with a Hollywood ending. So, I told them the "truth," but it was the fairy tale truth, as I knew it, but not as I believed it would play out. I told them that the American people were tired of sending their young men and women to Vietnam, some of whom never returned, with no end in sight. I went on to say that our president was confident that we could train the Vietnamese military to defend South Vietnam, but more importantly he was convinced that they would enter into a peace settlement that would guarantee the safety of South Vietnam ... blah, blah, blah! I listened to myself and almost believed what I was saying ... almost, but I knew better. There was no way that we were going to give the South Vietnamese military a bunch of weapons and a little advice and expect them to stand up against a seasoned Viet Cong and NVA who had defeated the Japanese and the French, and sustained the war long enough for the U.S to walk away. And nobody really believed anything being said during peace negotiations. Most people with a grain of sense and a little awareness of the situation in Vietnam knew that, regardless of political talks and promises, it was only a matter of time before the North somehow "acquired" the South. I was doing fine with my string of BS until Frenchy asked three straightforward questions, all three of which I answered unsatisfactorily. How long are you staying? Will you stay here tonight? What do you think will happen to us? My answers were "Tomorrow morning"; "No, I can't"; and "I really don't know." The fact that I could not make eye contact when I gave the last answer said more than the answer itself.

I didn't finish my beer and wished the hostess the best of luck. I walked slowly to the elevator and Frenchy held onto my arm. I turned to her and she asked one more time if I would stay with her that night. I would not be honest if I told you I was not tempted, but I managed to decline. She cried softly as I kissed her cheek, got on the elevator and left. I have tried desperately not to think of her fate at the hands of the North Vietnamese conquerors. I'm sure it was hard enough for the pure blood Vietnamese women who had "sold out" to the Americans, but for a young woman fathered by one former enemy and used by another? Again, I try not to imagine.

I was quiet and slept a troubled sleep most of the way home.

29

Career Change and the Fall

Under the terms of the Paris Peace Talks of 1973, all U.S. forces would be removed from the South and all military aid would cease. Sounded like a plan! My counterpart in officer reassignment and I saw things winding down, and we both finally had time to catch our breath and realize that we had been the ones holding the "light at the end of the tunnel" for so many Navy personnel, and helping to direct traffic. And then in March of 1973, in the midst of the hectic shutdown of the Headquarters of Naval Forces Vietnam and the Naval Advisory Group in Saigon, the commander of both of those organizations took the time to send a very complimentary formal Naval message to the Chief of Naval Personnel, with a copy to the Chief of Naval Operations and the Commander in Chief of the U.S. Pacific Fleet, thanking him for "assistance provided in achieving accelerated withdrawal."

My counterpart and I were called out by name, and, with our organizations, praised for our support. I have included a (poor) copy of that message as Appendix 2. I dwell on it and share it here because of its significance to me personally and professionally. On one hand it is a source of great pride that one of the highest ranking Naval officers at the time, in perhaps the most critical position in the Navy, at the most critical time, called me out by name for praise in a personal message to the four other senior Naval officers most concerned with the success of personnel reduction under the ACTOV program. On the other hand, the message is like a dagger forever lodged in my heart, because it clearly signifies my direct contribution to our accelerated abandonment of South Vietnam, and their ultimate defeat by the North.

With my job essentially ending at BUPERS and the Navy pushing for me to go back to sea and strive for command, I was on the fence. I loved the Navy, and I was proud that I had volunteered for Vietnam, even though the experience had left me with so many unanswered questions. On the other hand, if I stayed in, I should aspire to command at sea, and I already had the right tickets punched. But for that career path I would have to choose to give up a lot of what I now wanted. I was deeply involved in theater, spending every evening performing or auditioning; I even had an offer to buy a one-third interest in a dinner theater. In addition, eventually, I assumed I would grow tired of being a scalawag and want to settle down with a family; that would be far easier if not forever going from port to port. Once again, the wisdom of RADM Watkins put my head on straight; I could have it all.

He spent an entire morning with me, listening to my uncertainties, and then he said, "It's simple, become a supply officer!" I laughed, and said, "I can't; there's nothing wrong with my eyes or my knees!" I made reference to the common belief that only those physically unable to perform as shipboard officers became supply officers. He went on to explain that the Navy was changing, and that the Supply Corps was becoming the full business arm of the service, including the expanding role of contract management. With a career in the Supply Corps, I would probably see a maximum of two more shipboard tours, and with the rest of my assignments being ashore, I could pursue all of the theater I desired, and ultimately a family.

The final obstacle I mentioned was that each year, there were about 100+ shipboard officers applying for transition to the Supply Corps, and the competition was stiff with only one or two being accepted. He smiled and said, "You let me worry about that." The next day, I told him that his solution would be great if he could make it happen. He stood up, and said, "Come with me." We walked from his office to the elevators in another wing, rode up to the office of the Chief of the Navy Supply Corps, and walked in. He introduced me to the RADM and said, "This is Lieutenant Kirtley I was talking to you about and he has decided he wants to be a Supply Officer." I'm guessing that was the quickest and easiest transfer between specialties in Naval history.

From there it was a blur and there was no time for me to worry much about Vietnam. The Peace Accords had been signed, so we would see what happened, but I still firmly believed it was just a matter of time. Meanwhile, I received orders to the Naval Supply School in Athens, Georgia, for six months, and then reported aboard the USS *Tattnall*

(DDG-18), a guided missile destroyer stationed in Mayport, Florida. While we were deployed to the Mediterranean, and then participated in a historic two-ship exchange visit with the Soviet Union to Leningrad in 1975, things were falling apart rapidly in Vietnam. It was obvious that the U.S. could not, or would not, do anything to stop a North Vietnamese takeover of the South.

As the entire world watched on television in April 1975, North Vietnamese tanks rolled into Saigon after a frantic and embarrassing evacuation of the American embassy there. I drank that night and I cried. I cried for the tremendous loss of American lives, now all for nothing, and for the loss of Vietnamese lives, and I prayed for those that we had abandoned into the hands of the North Vietnamese and the Viet Cong. I fell into a drunken sleep with the vision of a laughing Dai uy Tinh the last thing I remember.

The war was over, and I could not have been happier with my new career. I certainly had no more thoughts about past awards. However, from his post in London, CDR Van Westendorp had yet again somehow breathed new life into his lost reclama concerning his recommendation for my Bronze Star, personally shepherding it through the Commander of the Pacific Fleet to the Secretary of the Navy, who then directed the CNO to cancel my 1971 Navy Commendation Medal, and award in its place the Bronze Star. On 16 December '75, as I excitedly prepared for my next assignment as Contracting Officer for the Naval Academy and Naval Station in Annapolis, Maryland, I received the following short note from Steve Van Westendorp: "Dear Dick, Well, as you can see from the attached, perseverance pays off, and we have carried the day, as it were! I thought I would send this off as a little Christmas present, and I extend my hearty congratulations both on receiving the well deserved Bronze Star, and for the super performance you gave in RVN which led to it." Talk about "*Shock & Awe*"!

Finally, in January '76, as I enjoyed every facet of my Academy assignment, I was called to the Office of the Superintendent, where RADM Kinnaird McKee presented my Bronze Star Medal. Now that was special! I sent a note of gratitude to Captain Van Westendorp, and after that, life and careers took over and we never spoke again. Steve's five year chase to secure my award against all odds taught me valuable lessons in leadership. First, if something is the right thing to do, then do it, regardless of personal ramifications. I still believe that my stance on "end of tour awards" in Vietnam was correct, though it possibly influenced the initial decision on my own award. More importantly, I learned from Steve Van Westendorp the value of courage, tenacity, perseverance, and a passion for those under your command. Serving under the Command of CDR Steve Van Westendorp was by far one of the best things to come out of my Vietnam assignment.

The author receiving the Bronze Star with Combat "V" from Rear Admiral Kinnaird McKee, the Naval Academy Superintendent, in January 1976, five years after the recommendation.

30

Reflection and Takeaways

I have had almost 50 years to reflect on the Vietnam War and my role in the exit charade called "Vietnamization," and, more specifically, the Navy's exit program called "ACTOV." Thankfully I've been helped by the myriad of books, essays, studies, reports, and documentaries over the years by all manner of experts, which gradually lifted the blame and stopped the unmerciful persecution of the military. Vietnam veterans were finally pulled from the shadows of shame and welcomed home, albeit years too late for many who died still being shamed and decried for valiantly and patriotically answering the call of service to country. Meanwhile, every year for fourteen years, starting in the mid–'90s, I was forced to reevaluate the war, and take a fresh look at my role in preparation for my annual presentations to another group of middle school kids, parents, and teachers, to whom Vietnam was becoming less and less relevant. For two hours each session I had to balance patriotism and pride in service, with an explanation of what went so very wrong, and why it mattered.

I still maintain that I have a unique perspective in that I was involved in the war in some way for the first six years of my career, and for three years of that I was a direct participant in ACTOV/Vietnamization, during my advisory role in-country Vietnam, and during my personnel reassignment role at BUPERS in Washington, D.C. Based on those experiences, and subsequent enlightenment, I think I can honestly assess the Navy's ACTOV program, and its overall place within the Vietnamization of the war as a U.S. exit strategy.

It was a given that my choice of the Naval Academy came with the expectation of future conflict. However, Vietnam, at the stage of the conflict by the time I arrived, was no longer normal or expected. It's bad enough that we lost over 50,000 of our youth in a war being sold as the noble defense of democracy, but by the time I arrived, the whole advisory effort was a facade, doomed to fail. I was convinced of that by the time I came back home.

I say it was a facade because it was missing a key element for success, i.e., *time*! In order for Vietnamization to have had any chance to work, *planning* and *progress* should have been the driving factors, not *personnel reduction* against *deadlines*. However, the American people were not willing to wait. Therefore, President Nixon's entire measure of the success of Vietnamization was in the numbers of troops withdrawn against his pledged numbers. Never mind that we were attempting to take a nation of rice farmers, historically dependent upon, even subservient to, larger nations, and hand them the means to defend themselves, but in no way were we actually making them capable of using those means effectively.

ACTOV was brilliantly conceived and initially well implemented, and then hurried, unsupported and left to wither and die on the vine. Prior to ACTOV, the U.S. Navy made one of the most miraculous military capability transitions in history when it went from the premier ocean-going fleet in the world, with *no* inland, "brown water" capability at all, to the largest, most effective brown water Navy in the world in less than five years. The combination of Swift Boats, PBRs, and heavy assault craft of the Mobile Riverine Force, with the leadership of junior officers and senior enlisted personnel, controlled the Mekong Delta at the start of Vietnamization/ACTOV. Given sufficient TIME and resources, experienced U.S. Navy advisors could have potentially given willing Vietnamese sailors the necessary skill sets for long term success, i.e., operations, repair, and maintenance. However, the program name itself, *Accelerated* Turnover to the Vietnamese (ACTOV), implies a hurried program. In fact, ACTOV and Vietnamization were totally incompatible.

Vice Admiral Zumwalt became Commander of Naval Forces in Vietnam (COMNAVFORV) in September 1968, and was cornered into making ACTOV support Nixon's Vietnamization plan. Keep in mind that the existing Vietnamese Navy at that time, consisting of approximately 20,000 men, was not made up of seasoned sailors with the same capabilities as their U.S. counterparts, whose expertise and experience covered years. Yet, Adm. Zumwalt directed the Advisory Group to get ready for a 40,000 man VN navy by the end of 1970. In a not so funny coincidence, it turns out that in order to meet those growth numbers,

VN recruit training, normally 12 weeks, was drastically cut, in favor of more on the job training.[1] That may explain why my training, and that of untold others, was cut short in order to fill vital advisor positions. Again, those staffing numbers were driven by time constraints for troop withdrawal, and not at all by a true and effective Vietnamization plan.

By 1970 and 1971, the Navy was turning over PBRs and heavy river assault craft at a pace that training and advice could not keep up with. That's why, in my opinion, in early firefights, American air support sometimes had to stand off to avoid the bubble of fire coming from the boats. Granted, fields of fire, effective targeting, etc., could be taught over time, but in many cases we just gave them an arsenal and said, "Go get 'em." We were trying to create an instant, stand-alone Navy which would be a mirror image of our own.

In addition, several very visible peripheral programs, intended to support ACTOV, also fell well short of objectives. Planned maintenance, for example, as discussed in detail earlier, was a victim of haste. It took the U.S. Navy years to change its culture from repair to maintenance, yet we tried to implement it in the VN Navy overnight with a pile of translated manuals. Not only did we not have the time to make planned maintenance a cultural change, but when American military aid was cut off in 1973, the logistical support necessary to sustain that maintenance dried up.

Another program with much promise, on paper I'm sure, when dreamed up and presented by some energetic but naive Saigon staffers, was the "Pigs and Chickens" program. The idea seemed to be developed around the Chinese proverb: "Give a man a fish, and you feed him for a day. Teach a man to fish, and you feed him for a lifetime." The plan was that at VN military bases like Go Dau Ha, the U.S. would help the VNs establish a self-sustaining food source, featuring pigs and chickens. So one day a small group of "pigs and chickens" people arrived at the base in Go Dau Ha to establish the program. Step one was to designate a dedicated area for initial stock, and build the facilities required, including pens with concrete floors for the pigs, and coops for the chickens.

Meanwhile, eerily similar to PMS, the Colonel Sanders team concurrently attempted to train a cadre of Go Dau Ha folks in long term farming/ranching, but it seemed clear to me that any pigs and chickens left with RID 40 would not see anything "long term." Once again, even perfectly executed, this program was doomed to failure as soon as we packed up and headed south. Undaunted, the team completed the pig pen and a makeshift chicken coop. Lastly, a pair of pigs and some hens and their male counterparts were introduced, and the box checked: "Successful Implementation of Pigs and Chickens Program at Go Dau Ha."

Perhaps the program would have thrived if RID 40 had remained long term in Go Dau Ha. However, once the word got out about our pending travel, the livestock disappeared, before the replacement boat group arrived. A new proverb was born: Give a desperate, starving Vietnamese enlisted man a pig (or chicken) and you feed him for a day. Give him two pigs and several chickens, and you feed him for several days. The pigs and chickens program, at least in Go Dau Ha, was soon "Number 10."

One program of particular interest to Admiral Zumwalt, while seemingly a no-brainer, also became a monetary sinkhole. The Navy's attempt to build better housing for Vietnamese enlisted sailors and their families failed because the VN families did not want to live in them for many reasons. The dependents felt like their location on or near the bases was inconvenient to family, shopping, jobs for second income, etc. Second, the families felt like living in the new housing made them easy targets for potential VC attack. Once again, failure to include the Vietnamese in the proposed solution doomed a program.[2]

Planned maintenance, "Pigs and Chickens," and enlisted housing are all programs that suffered from a combination of cultural misunderstanding and scheduling haste. There is no way to tell if time and continued investment would have turned those programs into successes. However, there is no question that hurried implementation and lack of long term commitment doomed those programs as sure as it doomed ACTOV and Vietnamization.

Another inhibitor to ACTOV that I personally experienced, and dwelled on herein, was the assignment of advisors not adequately prepared for their jobs. Remember the earlier discussion about many of the assigned duties of an advisor being "well outside the normal range of U.S. Navy experience." Let me be clear, I was not adequately prepared for my assignment as an Advisor to RID 40 in 1970. Unfortunately, I was unaware of my own shortcomings for the assignment when I was told during my training that I was a special case, and that I would get an abbreviated training course. In hindsight, again, basic to the skill set of an advisor to a foreign military organization is at least some level of conversational ability in the language of the subject country. Absent clear basic communications, there can be no successful advisory relationship. Second, an advisor needs a current assessment of the mission and capabilities of the organization he will support, both from the global perspective and from that of the specific unit to which assigned.

So I was handicapped going in. But I'm not sure that, even with perfect preparation, I could have had a major impact on the success or failure of RID 40. The bottom line is that I did my best with who I was and what I knew at the time. I am guessing that my peers, who were fully trained, or perhaps had different or more applicable experience, were able to feel like they were more of a contributor to the process. But in the end, they too were behind the power curve in the big picture. Without adequate *Time*, what happened was inevitable.

What do I think I did well given the circumstances? I watched out for my men and cared for their needs. I formed a bond with the RID commander, even though it was only possible because of his grasp of English. I won the hearts and minds of the many Vietnamese civilians I met, through formal and informal outreach programs. I was a good "supply" officer, before formally becoming a Supply Officer. I provided everything from food, ammo, and basic needs, to air strikes and medevacs. The only thing I couldn't provide was strategic or tactical military advice. Funny, isn't it—an advisor who can't provide advice! I'm talking about meaningful input to mission, strategy, and tactics to accomplish that mission. I was incapable, because I lacked relevant experience and requisite training. All I had was personal opinion. I thank God for the dedicated, skilled enlisted senior petty officers under my command; they were the primary reason for any success that RID 40 experienced, however success was measured; that success, however, was purely tactical.

If I was asked to make a hard, honest assessment of my personal performance against the strict written expectations of the Senior Advisor to the VN Commander of RID 40, in summary I would say that I offered no advice, either tactical or strategic, in regard to operations, and that I essentially made little or no difference in the overall outcome of events. In addition, under strict scrutiny, my Bronze Star Award, in all likelihood, benefited from reevaluation under the inflated criteria that I fought to eliminate from the award system. The original award of the Navy Commendation Medal was perhaps more appropriate.

I wasn't the only senior advisor who felt unable to live up to the job description, as witnessed by this excerpt from the 1968 end-of-tour report of another Navy lieutenant senior advisor:

> I do not feel my counterpart, or the other Vietnamese officers of their caliber and experience that I have had the occasion to work with, needed advisors. They did have many uses for liaison officers and it was in this capacity that I felt I functioned. I feel that my counterparts felt that the only real value they received from the US advisor was his ability to "cumshaw" material from the American units in the area, and that if he wouldn't do this for them he didn't add very much to their organization.[3]

As promised in my Preface, I want to provide some insight and comparison here from two individuals who had different, and perhaps more strategic, vantage points than me, but almost identical conclusions. I strongly recommend their books on the history and heroics of the Vietnam "brown water" Navy. As I wrote earlier, the Navy's rise in five years in the late '60s from nothing to having the preeminent brown water riverine fighting capability in the world was nothing short of incredible, and these two authors capture that story in breathtaking fashion. That brief period in Naval history is built around a myriad of true heroes, and their two works capture that rich and exciting history. Both of these authors also predicted and experienced the failures of Vietnamization and ACTOV, and included their thoughts and findings in their books. In every case, their global, systemic findings match my single unit findings. Several examples follow.

In his book *Brown Water, Black Berets,* LCDR Thomas Cutler describes a meeting on November 2, 1968, in which RADM Zumwalt briefed General Abrams, commander of all U.S. forces in Vietnam, that the Navy would turn over all operational responsibilities by 30 June 1970, not because good analysis told him that was possible, but because it was what the General wanted to hear; ACTOV was born. According to LCDR Cutler, Zumwalt also realized that the war had become a huge financial drain on the Navy, and that he had to find a way to stop bleeding dollars in Vietnam.[4]

I arrived in Go Dau Ha in April 1970, and Admiral Zumwalt left to assume his new position as Chief of Naval Operations (CNO) in May 1970. As described earlier herein, for me it was like jumping onto a moving train. And the train did not slow down with Zumwalt's departure. On the contrary, from his new seat of power, he exerted even more pressure on ACTOV, looking to impossibly balance accelerated personnel withdrawal while trying to provide the highest quality advisors, as more and more assets were turned over to the Vietnamese.

Of particular interest to me in Cutler's book was his review of an

April 1973 letter from COMNAVFORV (Admiral Zumwalt's relief), which had previously been classified Secret, on the subject of "Status of Vietnamization Upon Withdrawal of US Naval Forces." (This letter is dated one month after the pat-on-the-back letter from the same COMNAVFORV thanking me in part for my reassignment services.) It is obvious that this letter was very carefully wordsmithed, which is understandable since it was written just three years after Zumwalt left Vietnam, and it essentially was calling Zumwalt's baby ugly. Note the careful choice of words in the introductory sentence about the Vietnamese Navy: "In the case of the VNN, current capabilities are adequate but if current progress toward self-sufficiency is to be sustained, certain critical deficiencies must be remedied."[5] Eggshells!

The damage is found in the enclosure to the letter, listing those critical deficiencies, including: key officers not assuming responsibilities, poor performance of certain operational requirements, logistics, supply system, and (surprise) "There is insufficient command interest and monitoring of the unit's performance of the Planned Maintenance System."[6] Translation: All of those manuals you had laboriously translated into Vietnamese (except the technical words) have been used for toilet paper!

Four months later, none of that mattered because all U.S. funding support was cut off, and in November 1973 Nixon was restricted by Congress from sending American forces to assist if needed. With a detected touch of sadness shared by most former advisors, Cutler offers the following summary statement, which reads eerily like my own: "The accelerated pace of the turnover and the recognized shortcomings of the VNN at the time of withdrawal suggests that perhaps the process was too busy. Certainly the target dates were driven more by political pressures than by military assessments."[7] You think?

While wrestling with my own feelings about Vietnamization and ACTOV for so long, and trying to organize them into a presentable package, I was thrilled to discover the book *From the Rivers to the Sea: The US Navy in Vietnam*, by Commander R.L. Schreadley, USN (Ret). CDR Schreadley was assigned in 1969 to the staff of Adm Zumwalt, COMNAVFORV, and tasked with writing the history of the naval war in Vietnam up to that time. He was given carte blanche in conducting the necessary research. The results of his research were not published because they were considered too pessimistic. His book, however, was published in 1992, and it was worth the 22 year wait, especially for me, because he had accurately predicted from a more global perspective what I had personally experienced at the grass-roots, small-unit implementation level, and what I also accurately predicted after my departure. As I was putting together my final thoughts for this book, I kept going back to one paragraph on the second page of the Preface to Cdr. Schreadley's book. He writes:

> I took a special interest in the navy's "ACTOV" program—the accelerated turnover of US Navy assets to the Vietnamese. It was, I concluded, at the time, proceeding much too rapidly to have any meaningful chance of success. The United States was bailing out of the war, and the navy was leading the way. Disaster loomed for those we ostensibly were trying to help, and we were placing in extreme peril the advisors who would be among the last to leave.[8]

Again, these findings were the results of a study chartered by the Commander of Naval Forces Vietnam in the summer of 1969, and would apparently have been available for him and his staff to begin looking at corrective action several months before my arrival in Go Dau Ha. In other words, the guy in charge was told that his plan was flawed. Worse! The guy in charge, leaving to become the boss of the new guy in charge, was told by his own expert that his plan was flawed.

The last three chapters of CDR Schreadley's book are damning to leadership to say the least, but worse than that, they totally expose my naïveté at the time I volunteered. I was most taken aback by the following comment from CDR Schreadley, in regard to a pure systems analysis model of the situation in 1969: "the indisputable fact emerged that the Vietnamese Navy had not a snowball's chance in hell of picking up the burden of operations once the US navy was gone. Reports and statistics suggesting this, however, were ignored, buried, or explained away...."[9]

You can do this all day, i.e., go up one level of authority at a time, and play who knew what and why didn't they say anything? You'll reach one level of the game which pits Le Duc Tho from the Home Team against Henry Kissinger from the Visitors at the negotiating table in Paris. It doesn't matter how well you prepare or how well you think you play the game, you lose. Commander Schreadley sums it up neatly: "Never did US diplomacy achieve so little, at such great cost, and with such acclaim."[10] But at least Kissinger walked away with a Nobel Peace Prize! Le Duc Tho declined his; instead he walked off with South Vietnam. And me, at least I walked off with my ass intact—and, oh yes, eventually that Bronze Star. But 58,000 American servicemen and -women did not walk away; thousands of South Vietnamese people did not walk away; and thousands of Vietnam veterans who did make it home suffered mental and physical scars that they either carried to their graves or still carry today.

I am not saying that a successfully planned and executed Vietnamization of the war, resulting in a free Democratic Republic of South Vietnam, would have healed all of those wounds, but you can bet that the overall mental health and morale of our nation would have been better, sooner. No previous war had ever weighed on the conscience of the country so heavy and for so long. Why? Because Vietnam was different; we lost. The effect of that loss took such a toll on the country, especially the vets, that in 2012, the U.S. government not only felt the need to specially commemorate the 50th anniversary of the war, but they even established a Defense Department Program Office named the "Vietnam War Commemoration," and funded a *thirteen year* celebration honoring the participants.[11] It smacks a little of guilt to me. I don't go to any of those events; they are condescending. I am much better sustained by a sincere, "Thank you for your service," from a passerby, or a soft-spoken, cracked voice, "Welcome home, Brother!" from a grizzled ol' vet.

So, please don't look here now for some nice, slick, clever sentence neatly summing up my "personal assessment" of the advisory effort in Vietnam. It's complicated. We could not have asked any more of the brave junior-officer and enlisted U.S. Navy Advisors riding the rivers with their counterparts. Unfortunately they had all been duped into believing that there really was that proverbial light at the end of the tunnel, and that their sacrifice and risk would make a difference; but to quote an earlier reference, there was "not a snowball's chance in hell!"

As I wrote this last chapter, I did have one rather dramatic shift in my thinking about Vietnamization/ACTOV. I concluded that even had the process been given honest communication, time, funding and public support, it still would have failed. Actually, I don't think it would have failed; it just would never have succeeded. The more I read and then thought back through my year, the more I became convinced that the "advisory" phase would have been perpetual. I am convinced that the South Vietnamese were never going to assume total responsibility for their own defense. I actually believe that the evolution of the two Vietnams was so different, that the South could not ever adapt to stand alone, not just militarily, but culturally, politically, socially, etc. They were a country that had grown so used to being "co-owned," for lack of a better term, that I now believe they were culturally dependent on that co-ownership for survival. There is no better example than the fact that no technical words existed in the Vietnamese language for Planned Maintenance System procedure translation from English.

That doesn't let our senior leadership off the hook. Vietnamization/ACTOV was still a house of cards, doomed to failure from its inception for lack of time. And quite possibly, doomed to fail even if given an eternity. There is one thing for certain—there was no amount of training or experience or language fluency that would have allowed me to make a difference. Therefore, as awful as I feel, and will always feel, about our country's shameful abandonment of South Vietnam, I have stopped kicking myself personally about it.

Welcome home, Brothers!!!

The author, age 26, served a voluntary one year tour in Vietnam as Senior Advisor to Vietnamese River Interdiction Division (RID) 40, April '70–April '71. In his words: "It seemed like a good idea at the time."

Epilogue

I was doing my final review prior to submitting this manuscript, when I decided to check a small detail concerning Admiral Zumwalt's use of "Z-grams" for immediate policy implementation while he was Chief of Naval Operations (CNO). Zumwalt's passions were evident in the subjects of his Z-grams; that's why he insisted on personally authoring them, and cutting all red tape in their release and implementation. Using the Naval History and Heritage Command site as my source, I was reviewing the complete list of subjects of all 121 Z-grams when I suddenly had an epiphany! Until at least midway through his assignment as CNO, Admiral Zumwalt fully believed that ACTOV, and "Vietnamization," were still viable programs that could lead to a free, self-reliant Republic of Vietnam in the South. His Z-grams during 1970 and '71 clearly reflected that belief. Even with the damning unpublished review in 1969–70 by his personally chosen investigator/historian, Commander Schreadley, always hanging over him like a cloud, it is obvious that the Admiral never lost faith in the process, until it simply disappeared from his professional attention. This disappearance is supported by the absence of any Vietnam subjects in his policy directives/Z-grams after May 1972. In my opinion, he never saw ACTOV as a facade, but rather as a healthy, well planned program that died a political death beyond his control at some point in 1972. At that point, because in his mind he shared no blame, and could not influence the outcome, he simply turned his attention to more pressing matters for his Navy.

The subject of Zumwalt's Z-grams always clearly reflected his passions and priorities at the time of their release. From the time he took the CNO position in July 1970 until December 1970, Zumwalt issued a flurry of 64 Z-grams, at least 90 percent of which were on quality of life subjects for Navy personnel, like recreation services, civilian clothes, habitability, leave, liberty, etc.—i.e., things that he believed were irritants in the everyday lives of Navy service members. In October '70, he turned his attention back to his folks in Vietnam; he authorized the Small Craft Insignia. In December '70, he refocused on his "baby" in Z-gram #65: "The Vietnamization Challenge: Naval Advisors to the Job"[1] summarized the status of hardware turnover, and stated that "by all indications, the VNN personnel are doing well operating the assets we have turned over and are developing maintenance and support capabilities at a fast rate."

He followed that with the first of many statements in this and subsequent Z-grams indicating his sense that ACTOV and Vietnamization would continue for years to a successful conclusion. He stated the immediate need for Naval advisors to fill a large middle management gap in the Vietnamese Navy caused by their rapid growth. He went on to call for a "trend over the next few years" requiring higher numbers of language trained advisors. What followed was a paragraph unlike any I have ever seen in a military policy document. It was literally a personal plea, based on Zumwalt's own experience, for advisor volunteers, described as "the most heart warming and personally rewarding job you can perform," continuing with more lines of glowing description of the personal and professional gratification of advisory service. He went on to offer a list of never before seen incentives to volunteers.

Then in February 1971, Zumwalt issued Z-gram #73, "Enlisted Vietnam Volunteers."[2] He referenced the December Z-gram, and reiterated the need for U.S. advisors to supplement the VN Navy at all levels. However, this directive more than any other reflected Zumwalt's delusional belief that ACTOV and Vietnamization were succeeding and would continue as long as necessary to ensure success. In this lengthily detailed document, he laid out a three-tier training program, with incentives for each, including general duty for non-advisory roles. The next tier was what he called the "Present Advisor Program," in which volunteers would receive 7 to 11 weeks of specialized training, and "minimal language training." Volunteers for this program would receive a different and higher level of incentives, and would fill the advisory requirements until what Zumwalt called the "New Advisor Program" provided output. He envisioned this to be a one-year training program with participants arriving in-country conversant in Vietnamese, potentially for "two and three year assignments." The promised rewards for these volunteers were literally off the charts.

In June 1971, Z-gram #90, "Responsibility Pay for Senior Advisors in Vietnam,"[3] offered $50–$100 monthly pay incentives to officers in pay grades 03, 04, and some 05s.

It appears that perhaps Admiral Zumwalt began to finally distance himself from Vietnam when a year went by before there was any mention of Vietnam again in a CNO policy directive. In May 1972, Z-Gram #111, "Southeast Asia Buildup,"[4] simply commented to commands at all levels that the Navy's response to the NVA incursion into South Vietnam in March, including Naval air and surface ship shore bombardment had been exemplary but had caused inconveniences to sailors and their families due to longer deployments, etc., and asked that senior commanders be sensitive to family needs. There was no mention of in-country advisory roles, ACTOV, or Vietnamization.

For the two-year period May 1972 to June 1974—the last two years of Admiral Zumwalt's Naval career and his last two years as the Chief of Naval Operations—there were only 10 more Z-Grams issued, none of which mentioned Vietnam. After the signing of the Paris Peace Accords in January 1973, the cutoff of all U.S. funding, and Congress prohibiting the President in the future from sending any U.S. servicemen to the aid of South Vietnam, in March 1973 both Navy commands in Vietnam, NAVFORV and NAVADGRU, were disestablished. The U.S. Navy no longer had a presence in Vietnam; their storied history there was over.

Amazingly, the man who had just overseen the historical disestablishment of his own previous commands, the man who had "fathered" ACTOV and ridden its promises to become the youngest CNO in Naval history, made no reference to any of that in his change of command remarks, published as Z-Gram #121.[5] In fact, in what I took almost as a personal slight, he omitted any mention of the Naval Advisory Group. Consider this: After saying in his speech that he did not wish to dwell on his own accomplishments, he said, "What I prefer to do instead, is to draw your attention to the performance of our individual Navy men and women who, in times of peril during the past four years, rose to the occasion—giving selflessly of themselves, performing the impossible, and then coming back for more."

Here was the perfect opportunity for at least one line about the advisory effort since his departure from Vietnam and the disestablishment of the command. After all, the "past four years" he mentioned, July '70–July '74, included the last ten months of my own time in-country, July '70–April '71. Or what about the other 12,000 advisors still in-country when I left? Wasn't our time given selflessly? But his next words picked up with U.S. fleet and air support in 1972 and never looked back. Not a single word in that change of command speech for the men and women who lived and died for him in Vietnam early in those "past four years." It was as if Vietnam, the conflict that defined his career, had slipped his mind the day of that speech.

Perhaps he suddenly realized that his legacy would be tied to the humiliation of our failure in Vietnam. Maybe he found himself unable to affect the negative outcome by simply penning another Z-gram. Maybe by then it was old news? But none of that explains the seemingly sudden and complete abandonment of a whole community of Navy officer and enlisted men and women who were "all in" for him in their service in Vietnam, and to whom he had been so close for so long.

I don't mean to disparage the 32 year Naval career of Admiral Zumwalt, and the volumes written by those who believe he vastly improved the welfare of the Navy service member. Nor do I wish to taint his valiant post-retirement fight for the healthcare of veteran victims of Agent Orange exposure in Vietnam. But I believe that during that change of command speech he had a magnificent opportunity, with the perfect audience, to craft the perfect few words for the Naval Advisory Group; a brief epitaph; after all, the organization lived and died on his watch. I'm just sayin'.

Commander Kirtley's Service Career History

Commander Richard Kirtley graduated from the U.S. Naval Academy in 1967 with a B.S. in naval science. He earned a master's degree in acquisition and contracting management in 1979 from the Naval Postgraduate School in Monterey, California.

His first assignment after graduation from the Academy was First Lieutenant and Gunnery Officer on the USS *De Haven* (DD-727) based in Yokosuka, Japan, and operating in the Gulf of Tonkin. In 1969 he transferred to the Naval Air Test Center, Patuxent River, Maryland, as test pilot for an experimental drone helicopter, planned for gunfire support spotting in Vietnam. He volunteered for duty in Vietnam, and served in 1970 and '71 in the Naval Advisory Group as the Senior Advisor to Vietnamese River Interdiction Division 40. Following Vietnam, he was in charge of the Special Projects Office, Enlisted Personnel Division, Bureau of Naval Personnel in Washington, D.C., coordinating the rapid withdrawal and reassignment of enlisted personnel out of Vietnam, in support of President Nixon's "Vietnamization" program.

In 1973, Commander Kirtley changed his specialty designator to Supply Corps, and attended the Naval Supply Corps School, Athens, Georgia. After graduation he served as Supply Officer on USS *Tattnall* (DDG-19), completing a Mediterranean/North Atlantic deployment that included an historic formal visit to Leningrad, USSR, in 1975.

From 1976–1978, Commander Kirtley enjoyed an assignment as Purchasing/Contracting Officer for the Naval Academy, followed by attendance at the Naval Postgraduate School, Monterey, California, and receipt of his master's degree. From February 1980 to August 1982, he was Contracting Officer for the Portsmouth Naval Shipyard, New Hampshire, and then Commander of the Defense Contracts

Administration Office, Sanders Associates, Nashua, New Hampshire, until June 1985. From July 1985 to August 1986 Commander Kirtley was Supply Officer on the USS *Puget Sound* (AD-38), Because *Puget Sound* was also the Sixth Fleet Flagship, carrying the Commander of the U.S. Sixth Fleet and staff, he also served as Assistant Logistics Officer for the Sixth Fleet. In September 1986, he joined the Naval Air Systems Command as Business Financial Manager for a classified Joint Navy–Air Force Countermeasures Program. He retired on August 1, 1987.

Commander Kirtley is a qualified Surface Warfare Officer and Supply Officer, and he is qualified to wear the Small Craft Insignia. His decorations include the Bronze Star with Combat "V," Defense Meritorious Service Medal, Navy Commendation Medal, Combat Action Ribbon, Navy Unit Commendation, Vietnam Service Medal, Sea Service Deployment Ribbon, Republic of Vietnam Gallantry Cross and Palm Unit Citation, Republic of Vietnam Civil Action Unit Citation, and Republic of Vietnam Campaign Ribbon.

Commander Kirtley is a Certified Professional Contracts Manager (CPCM) by the National Contract Management Association.

Appendix 1

A LETTER FROM THE WALL

TO THE CLASS OF 1967 50TH REUNION

Written by the author but published without a byline in *Shipmate*, vol. 80, no. 8, 2017, p. 76.

Can you believe it's been 50 years since we tossed our caps? You guys look pretty good for 70+ years! We on the Wall look a lot better, but we stopped aging in our 20's ... a little Wall humor.

There are nine '67ers on the Wall, and we are with you this Homecoming weekend. You guys will be sharing stories from the last 50 years about service, family, achievements, etc., and we want to hear all of that. But first we thought we should all share some common memories. What brought 1,250 disparate guys from every walk of life together, and made us forever brothers?

We were born in the '40s and did what all kids do for their first decade ... played, fussed, and fought with our siblings, and we didn't pay any attention to world affairs. However, in 1954 the French were defeated, Vietnam was divided, and the U.S. started sending aid and advisors to help Saigon. There was some theory about dominoes, but we were caught up in Little League, Boy Scouts, and other things preteens enjoyed. Life was simple; life was good.

When we entered high school, the U.S. had 900 advisors in South Vietnam. However, we were busy with sports, clubs, theater, and, of course, GIRLS!

There were 1,250 different reasons why we each chose the Naval Academy in the summer of 1963. We forged a lifetime bond, built on the foundation of a grueling Plebe Year. The last real Plebe Year was '67, though Roger Staubach eased our pain! It was also a tumultuous year for the U.S. and South Vietnam. By then, 16,000 Americans were in-country, and both the U.S. and South Vietnam saw their presidents assassinated. Yet most of us never imagined that this war, so far away, would ever affect us. Our focus was on surviving Plebe Year. Remember the mad dash to Herndon?

The summer cruise in 1964 brought the TV commercial alive: "Join the Navy and See the World!" Some of us had never left home before entering the Academy, and there we were in Paris and London! Sailors in the Tonkin Gulf were not so lucky, as U.S. destroyers were attacked by North Vietnamese patrol boats. U.S. colleges saw protests against the war. Instead of pep rallies and cheers, their voices cried: "Hell no, we won't go!"

In June 1965, halfway through "Canoe U," we dispersed for summer training. At that time, 1,350 U.S. troops had been killed in Vietnam, a one-year tour rotation policy was in place, and "body count" was the new measure of success. The reality of the war became clearer as new names appeared on the KIA list in Memorial Hall.

Second Class year was a blur; we weren't in charge and running Plebes had lost its excitement. Finally it ended; we were "Firsties," as we split up for exotic cruises. We returned as leaders, Kings of the Hall, and we were in demand socially everywhere we went. Most of us look back on that year as one of the best of our lives, even with the pressures of grades, Brigade leadership, choice of duty, and the absolute realization that Vietnam would soon consume us all.

June Week '67 was amazing! Then with a strange mixture of excitement and emptiness, we shipped our cruise boxes, packed our cars, and put USNA in our rearview mirrors. The country was more divided than at any time since the Civil War. The U.S. had half a million troops in Vietnam, and over 11,000 had died. Now it was our turn, and regardless of our career choice, the war would define our service and our lives. In fact, within three years, for the nine of us on the Wall, our shared journey with the Class of '67 would be over.

Now, fifty years later, as you gather, we have a favor to ask. We know that we will be remembered at a somber memorial service on Sunday. However, we want to also be part of the revelry! So please, at some point, take a moment, not for a somber speech, but for a boisterous, raucous, rowdy toast, as if we and the other lost were standing there beside you!

We love you guys of '67, and we are proud to call you Brothers! BEAT ARMY!!!

Hal Cushman Castle
Barton Sheldon Creed
Richard Carl Deuter
Gary Earl Holtzclaw
Alan Arthur Kettner
Kenneth Dean Norton
Robert Ervin Tuttle
Thomas Joseph Weiss
Henry Arthur Wright

Appendix 2

On the following page is one of the final messages from the Commander of Naval Forces and the Naval Advisory Group in Vietnam as they closed all Naval operations there in March of 1973, thanking the personnel in the offices of the Chief of Naval Personnel for their support of the accelerated withdrawal of Navy personnel. The message specifically named the author and cited his efforts. The code "BZ" was written by Admiral Watkins on the document and is Navy signal code for "good job."

This document was given to the author by Admiral Watkins and is reproduced here by permission of the author.

Appendix 2

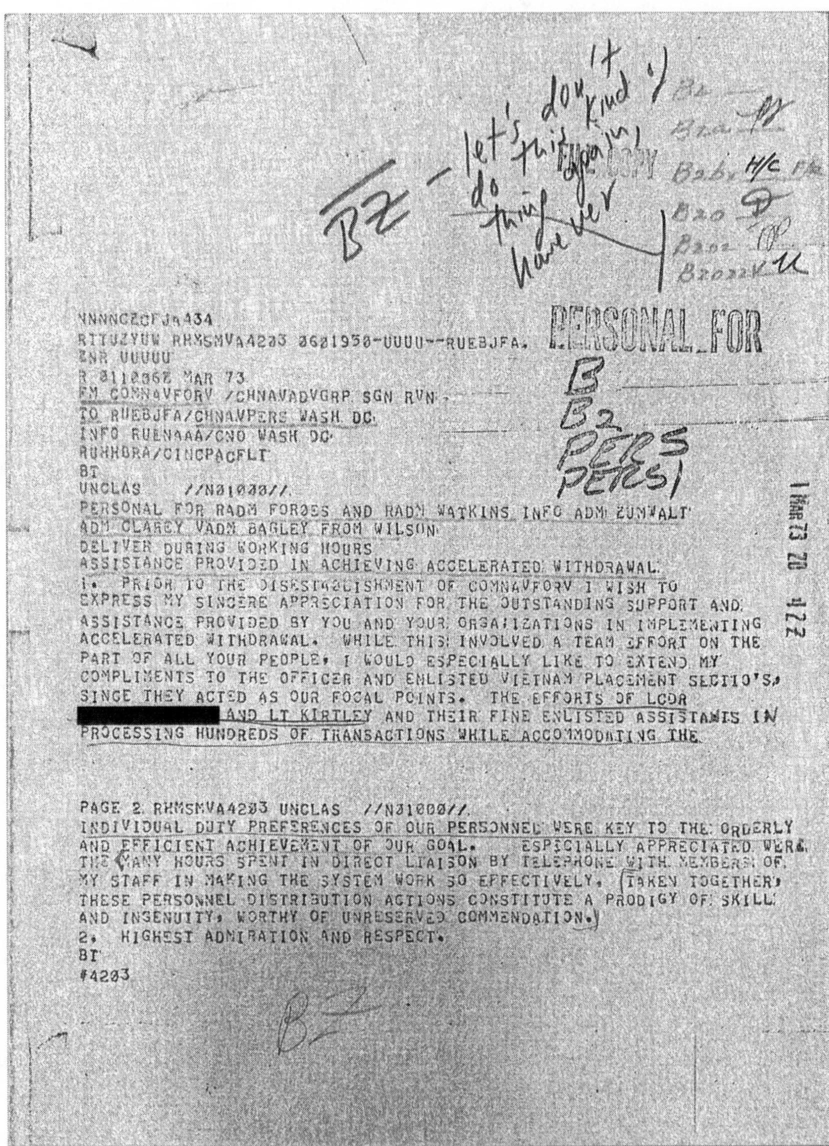

BZ - let's don't do this kind of thing again, however

PERSONAL FOR

NNNNCZCFJA434
RTTUZYUW RHMSMVA4203 0601950-UUUU--RUEBJFA.
ZNR UUUUU
R 011006Z MAR 73
FM COMNAVFORV /CHNAVADVGRP SGN RVN
TO RUEBJFA/CHNAVPERS WASH DC
INFO RUENAAA/CNO WASH DC
RUHHBRA/CINCPACFLT
BT
UNCLAS //N01000//
PERSONAL FOR RADM FORBES AND RADM WATKINS INFO ADM ZUMWALT
ADM CLAREY VADM BAGLEY FROM WILSON
DELIVER DURING WORKING HOURS
ASSISTANCE PROVIDED IN ACHIEVING ACCELERATED WITHDRAWAL.
1. PRIOR TO THE DISESTABLISHMENT OF COMNAVFORV I WISH TO
EXPRESS MY SINCERE APPRECIATION FOR THE OUTSTANDING SUPPORT AND
ASSISTANCE PROVIDED BY YOU AND YOUR ORGANIZATIONS IN IMPLEMENTING
ACCELERATED WITHDRAWAL. WHILE THIS INVOLVED A TEAM EFFORT ON THE
PART OF ALL YOUR PEOPLE, I WOULD ESPECIALLY LIKE TO EXTEND MY
COMPLIMENTS TO THE OFFICER AND ENLISTED VIETNAM PLACEMENT SECTIO'S,
SINCE THEY ACTED AS OUR FOCAL POINTS. THE EFFORTS OF LCDR
[redacted] AND LT KIRTLEY AND THEIR FINE ENLISTED ASSISTANTS IN
PROCESSING HUNDREDS OF TRANSACTIONS WHILE ACCOMMODATING THE

PAGE 2 RHMSMVA4203 UNCLAS //N01000//.
INDIVIDUAL DUTY PREFERENCES OF OUR PERSONNEL WERE KEY TO THE ORDERLY
AND EFFICIENT ACHIEVEMENT OF OUR GOAL. ESPECIALLY APPRECIATED WERE
THE MANY HOURS SPENT IN DIRECT LIAISON BY TELEPHONE WITH MEMBERS OF
MY STAFF IN MAKING THE SYSTEM WORK SO EFFECTIVELY. TAKEN TOGETHER,
THESE PERSONNEL DISTRIBUTION ACTIONS CONSTITUTE A PRODIGY OF SKILL
AND INGENUITY, WORTHY OF UNRESERVED COMMENDATION.
2. HIGHEST ADMIRATION AND RESPECT.
BT
#4203

Chapter Notes

Preface

1. Jennings, *The Politically Incorrect Guide to the Vietnam War*, p. 116.
2. *Ibid.*
3. Cutler, *Brown Water, Black Berets*, p. 303.
4. *The Navy in Vietnam*, Chief of Information publication, p. 33.

Chapter 1

1. Kamps, *The History of the Vietnam War*, p. 12.
2. *Ibid.*, p. 21.
3. *Ibid.*, p. 42.
4. *Ibid.*, p. 52.
5. *Ibid.*, pp. 71–72.

Chapter 3

1. Kamps, *The History of the Vietnam War*, pp. 121–122.

Chapter 4

1. *The Navy in Vietnam*, Chief of Information publication, pp. 14–15.

Chapter 6

1. Neil, "Sailing in the Midget Fleet," *All Hands*, November 1966, pp. 2–6.

Chapter 11

1. Jennings, *The Politically Incorrect Guide to the Vietnam War*, pp. 120–124.

Chapter 16

1. Pringle, "Meanwhile: Closing the Circle on Vietnam" (Opinion), *New York Times*, March 13, 2004.

Chapter 19

1. Marolda and Dunnavent, *Combat at Close Quarters*, p. 75.

Chapter 20

1. Neil, "Sailing in the Midget Fleet," p. 6.

Chapter 27

1. Z-Gram #51, "Small Craft Insignia," October 23, 1970.
2. Military Personnel Manual (MILPERSMAN), 1200–030, "Small Craft Insignia."

Chapter 30

1. Marolda and Dunnavent, *Combat at Close Quarters*, p. 73.
2. *Ibid.*, p. 74.
3. Schreadley, *From the Rivers to the Sea*, p. 176.
4. Cutler, *Brown Water, Black Berets*, pp. 303–304.
5. *Ibid.*, p. 314.
6. *Ibid.*,
7. *Ibid.*, p. 316
8. Schreadley, *From the Rivers to the Sea*, p. xiii.
9. *Ibid.*, p. 328.

10. *Ibid.*, p. 377

11. Obama, "Commemoration of the 50th Anniversary of the Vietnam War", May 28, 2012.

Epilogue

1. Z-Gram #65, "The Vietnamization Challenge: Naval Advisors to the Job," December 5, 1970.

2. Z-Gram #73, "Enlisted Vietnam Volunteers," February 18, 1971.

3. Z-Gram #90, "Responsibility Pay for Senior Naval Advisors in Vietnam," June 25, 1971.

4. Z-Gram #111, "Southeast Asia Buildup," May 4, 1972.

5. Z-Gram #121, "CNO Change of Command Remarks by Admiral E. R. Zumwalt, Jr.," June 29, 1974.

Bibliography

Books

Chief of Information. *The Navy in Vietnam*. Washington, DC: GPO, 1968.

Cutler, Thomas J., Lt Cdr., USN. *Brown Water, Black Berets*. Annapolis, MD: Naval Institute Press, 1988.

Forbes, John, and Robert Williams. *The Illustrated History of the Vietnam War, Riverine Force,* Volume 8. New York: Bantam Books, 1987.

Jennings, Phillip. *The Politically Incorrect Guide to the Vietnam War*. Washington, DC: Regnery, 2010.

Kamps, Charles T., Jr. *The History of the Vietnam War*. New York: Military Press, 1988.

Marolda, Edward J., and R. Blake Dunnavent. *Combat at Close Quarters: Warfare on the Rivers and Canals of Vietnam*. Washington, DC: Naval History and Heritage Command, 2015.

Percoco, Jams A. *Divided We Stand*. Portsmouth, NH: Heinemann, 2001.

Schreadley, R.L., Cdr., USN (Ret). *From the Rivers to the Sea: The US Navy in Vietnam*. Annapolis, MD: Naval Institute Press, 1992.

Articles

Anonymous [R.W. Kirtley]. "A Letter from the Wall to the Class of 1967 50th Reunion." *Shipmate*, vol. 80, no. 8, 2017, p. 76.

Hagel, David H. "A Memorial Like No Others." *American Legion Magazine*, November 2012, pp. 50–51.

Lind, Michael. "Why We Went to War in Vietnam." *American Legion Magazine*, January 2013, pp. 20–30.

Military Personnel Manual. MILPERSMAN 1200–030, *Small Craft Insignia*, February 2007, p. 530.

Neil, Bob. "Sailing in the Midget Fleet." *All Hands*, November 1966, pp. 2–6.

Obama, Barack. "Commemoration of the 50th Anniversary of the Vietnam War." Presidential Proclamation, May 28, 2012.

Pringle, James. "Meanwhile: Closing the Circle on Vietnam." *New York Times*, March 13, 2004, n.p.

Veith, George. "How to End a War." *American Legion Magazine*, November 2013, pp. 54–60.

Index

Index